Offensive Marketing

D0527846

Hugh Davidson graduated in Economics and Law at Cambridge and subsequently qualified as a barrister-at-law at Gray's Inn. After five years with Procter & Gamble, he moved to United Biscuits as Marketing Manager, McVities. This was followed by consultancy with Glendinning Associates International, first in the USA, then as Director of European Consulting. Hugh Davidson then joined International Playtex Inc. as President of Playtex Ltd. Canada. Over the next nine years he was European Vice-President responsible at various times for EEC, EFTA and New Business Development, and was also Managing Director UK. He was a member of the International Management Committee in New York. Hugh Davidson has contributed articles to many publications, including *Management Today*, the *Harvard Business Review* and the *Japanese Diamond Business Review*. He is a Fellow of the Institute of Marketing and a Fellow and past Chairman of the Marketing Society.

Currently, Hugh Davidson is Chairman of Oxford Corporate Consultants, a marketing-led management consulting firm, which specializes in corporate strategy and business development. Among clients for whom he has conducted projects over his consultancy career are H. J. Heinz, Volkswagen, Pedigree Petfoods, Monsanto, Shell, Unilever, British Rail, Rowntree and Hanson Trust.

Offensive Marketing

or *How To Make Your Competitors Followers*

Hugh Davidson

 PENGUIN BOOKS

PENGUIN BOOKS

Published by the Penguin Group
27 Wrights Lane, London W8 5TZ, England
Viking Penguin Inc., 40 West 23rd Street, New York, New York 10010, USA
Penguin Books Australia Ltd, Ringwood, Victoria, Australia
Penguin Books Canada Ltd, 2801 John Street, Markham, Ontario, Canada L3R 1B4
Penguin Books (NZ) Ltd, 182–190 Wairau Road, Auckland 10, New Zealand

Penguin Books Ltd, Registered Offices: Harmondsworth, Middlesex, England

First published by Cassell 1972
Published in Pelican Books 1975
10 9 8 7 6 5 4 3

Printed and bound in Great Britain by
Cox & Wyman Ltd, Reading
Typeset in Linotron Palatino by
Rowland Phototypesetting Ltd,
Bury St Edmunds, Suffolk

To My Parents

Contents

7

Contents

Part 5: Effectively Executed

Part 6: Offensive Marketing for the Future

Appendices

Foreword
by Dr Anthony J. F. O'Reilly

President and Chief Executive Officer,
H. J. Heinz Co., Inc.

Since Hugh Davidson and I collaborated in 1971, on the threshold of my US career with H. J. Heinz, much has happened to both of us. The original Foreword was written in the leisurely environment of the QE2. This revision has also been composed *en route*, showing that constant travel in international business is one thing that hasn't yet changed.

Hugh Davidson is an iconoclast. He is also an immensely readable writer, with a strong commercial sense. The strategy of his book underlines the belief that offensive marketing or, in his view, successful marketing, comprises certain attitudes and practices towards marketing, competition and planning which are, unfortunately, rare.

I examined the application of such principles to agricultural marketing in the course of my PhD at Bradford University. The specific objective was to analyse the impact of the Kerrygold brand on farm income in Ireland. The outcome of my thesis was neither what I expected nor hoped. Objectivity forced me to acknowledge that plundering the unsuspecting European tax-payer by accumulating large farm outputs was the quickest way to prosperity. Adding value at the farm gate through sound marketing was useful but less profitable.

I argued at the time that the Common Agricultural Policy could not continue to endure such plunder. Fortunately, that view has proved correct, since we now have quota controls on most

European farm products, especially milk. This has re-established a vital link between consumer and producer.

Hugh Davidson's book is dedicated to equitable linkage between consumer and producer. Once the shackles of bureaucracy embrace an industry, and the consumers' needs are bypassed, both consumer and producer suffer in the long run.

Good marketing practice is based on freedom of consumer choice, which is an essential element in a democracy. Supermarkets are a better model of the democratic process in action than Congress or the Houses of Parliament. Customers impose their will on the producer by exercising their right to make choices in a competitive market. Hugh Davidson's book highlights the process of cooperation between consumer and producer and illustrates how mutual responsiveness can benefit both.

His definitions are refreshing and simple. He believes that professional marketing involves a determination to achieve all the major innovations in a given market, a freedom from the shackles of industry tradition or interruptive bureaucracy, and a view of marketing as a profit-oriented approach to business that permeates not just the marketing department, but the entire business. Above all, he believes that offensive marketing requires a dedication to strategy and planning.

Hurrah! It has all been said before, but it has rarely been said so succinctly and so refreshingly. Not above employing popular gurus to bolster his case, he quotes Levitt tellingly: 'When it comes to the marketing concept today, a solid stone wall often seems to separate word from deed.' His answer is: 'Kill the bureaucratic plague; dis-establish the maintenance men; stop talking about offensive marketing and DO something about it.' He observes, in my view accurately, that good marketing is not so much a matter of intelligence and ability (as good and bad companies seem to have an abundance of both), but more a question of attitudes, organization and technique.

Mr Davidson has a certain elegance in his choice of mnemonics. He says that offensive marketing is a matter of POISE, that it should be Profitable, Offensive, Integrated, Strategic (embracing short- and long-term corporate plans) and Effectively executed. The book unashamedly assumes that the right attitudes and organization structures have a profound effect on corporate profit, and essays only one real definition of marketing (and a very good one it

10

is), that it 'is the process of balancing company needs for profit against the benefits required by consumers, so as to maximize long-term earnings per share'. In other words, he is saying that if you don't balance the short-term profit consumer benefit equation against your long-term ambitions, you won't have a business to realize those long-term ambitions against.

Successful marketing is quite simple to describe. A company's offerings must be so attractive to customers that they will want to buy and go on buying. The offerings must also be produced and marketed so efficiently that the company will make handsome profits. To succeed, both sides of the equation have to be matched. Good customer value or low-cost operation on their own are not enough in today's very competitive market-place.

The only way I know of achieving this simple formula is to have winning strategies, and strong well-motivated people to execute them. In Chapter 7 Mr Davidson explains how to develop winning strategies. He also warns that they wear out quickly unless they are updated to meet changing customer needs and new competitive moves. The world is full of lagging companies which used to have winning strategies. I am a strong believer in the importance of attitudes and was glad to see a whole chapter devoted to this. Qualities we encourage at Heinz are ingenuity, dedication, willingness to chance risk and ability to spot a problem and to pursue it doggedly. Talking about corporate culture is much easier than creating or sustaining it. From hard experience, I know that 'making it happen' requires example, emphasis and evangelism from all managers every day of the week.

One thing I missed in this book was a section on setting corporate objectives. This is a difficult area to get right. Medium-term objectives should always contain a 'stretch' element – without being so ambitious that longer-term aims must be trimmed to provide the jam that Wall Street wants today.

The author is at his best in describing marketing perverts. He instances five: *the consumer worshippers*, where the consumer is always right; *the New Luddites*, who view production men as an inferior form of human life; *the egotistical employees*, who pander to the company president, knowing that the latter believes that sales volume is more important than profits; *the milker*, who cuts everything, particularly above-the-line expenditure, and then runs for it;

and finally a superb title, *the galloping midget*, whose exploits are worth the purchase price of the book.

What Davidson wants is integrated marketing, believing that it is an approach to business rather than a specific discipline. He states that the main benefits which successful companies gain through offensive marketing are higher profits, a longer life cycle on existing products, and a better success rate with new products and acquisitions. Could we ask for more?

My own experience suggests general accord with these principles, and great difficulty in implementing them. In particular, it is extremely difficult to graft policies of innovation and imagination on to big, successful organizations. The entrepreneur, by definition, is almost a loner. Large businesses have a certain civil-service-like quality about them. Promotion in many instances is by non-mistake rather than by visible victory. Additionally, the gestation period required for new ideas to mature to profitability is often hampered by the internal accountancy disciplines of the organization. An idea, product concept or joint venture may take three to four years to mature to profitability. The normal reporting system of a business is the monthly account, followed by the quarterly report, the half-yearly review and the annual assessment. Unless such systems are intelligently interpreted, they can sound the death-knell for a slowly maturing but potentially profitable idea.

One answer is the venture management team, free from the shackles of the system. Quite simply, a multi-discipline venture team can bypass much bureaucracy and operate on a discrete timescale, free from monthly interruption and quarterly execution. This is not to write a blank cheque for the venture manager, but it is an attempt to position him in a manner which allows imaginative distillation of new ideas, without the interference of systems which are appropriate to successful ongoing business, rather than embryonic activity.

Additionally, new business development, which I define as any new product concept, initiative or liaison which can create a new and viable profit centre for the company, should be directly accountable to the Chief Executive. This does two things:

1. It involves the chief planning officer of the corporation, the Managing Director/President, in that area where planning is most important, i.e. the development of new business.

2. It elevates the whole concept of new product/new business development on the corporate totem pole, and gives a thrust and vigour to this aspect of the company's activities which it will not otherwise achieve.

From practical experience at Heinz, I can say that this structure has provided us with a rapid and apparently successful system of new business and new venture development. The drawbacks are that it is time-consuming, and for long periods of time sterile in terms of results achieved. Nevertheless, it remains among the most important responsibilities of any chief executive. The same is equally true of acquisitions, both in terms of defining the area of search, and in terms of participating in the negotiations for the acquisitions candidate.

Despite being an iconoclast, Mr Davidson is old-fashioned in some of his beliefs. He believes that consumers buy product benefits rather than advertising or promotions. He believes that the surest way to corporate growth is through product superiority. He believes that marketing is irrelevant unless supported by efficient low-cost operation. Additionally, he believes that all the other members of the marketing mix, such as advertising, promotions, pricing and packaging, respond most amiably to a superior product and will work hardest on its behalf. How many times have we all neglected this truism!

I found his book stimulating, provocative and original – or maybe it was that I was secretly flattered by his agreement with most of my pet prejudices.

Tony O'Reilly
Pittsburgh, USA, 1986

Author's Preface

This revised edition is more a new book than a new edition. While it retains the same basic principles as the original, the structure has been changed. Six of the first eight chapters are new; many others have been radically changed; all have been updated.

Offensive Marketing is aimed at practising business people who have direct or indirect involvement with marketing. It should also be of interest to students planning to go into business. It contains many practical examples. While these feature large- or medium-sized companies, the principles they illustrate usually apply to any size of business. I therefore hope that this book will also be useful to those running small businesses.

In both editions, my wife Sandra acted as editor-in-chief and secretary. She greatly improved the clarity and style of the book, pouncing on jargon and pompous phrases, and typed over 400,000 words – you are fortunate to be reading only 120,000 of them.

For the first edition Antony Carr, Peter Mitchell and Bruce Rowe made a number of excellent suggestions as well as providing case histories. Len Hardy and Ron Gray, respectively past and present Chairman of Lever Bros., were also most helpful. David Hill read the final draft of this new edition at least twice, fundamentally improved its structure, and made many valuable suggestions. Barry Clarke also went over the final draft in detail, and his comments have been incorporated in this new edition.

People who contributed much to specific chapters were Chris

14

Jones, Director of J. Walter Thompson ('Advertising'), Alan Wolfe, Marketing Director of Ogilvy & Mather ('Market Research'), Bill Ramsey, until recently Director of International Development at General Foods Corporation ('Developing Winning Strategies', and both chapters on 'New Products'), and Barry Clarke and John Hooper of Clarke Hooper ('Sales Promotion').

Many others helped in the preparation of this new edition by agreeing to be interviewed or by giving their views, including: Charles Auld, Managing Director, Nabisco Grocery Division; Godfrey Bland, Principal, Booz Allen & Hamilton; Gunnar Brock, Managing Director, Tetra-Pak, British Isles; Nick Butler, Principal BIB Design; Len Capp, Kodak Ltd; Christopher Clarke, Scrimgeour Kemp Gee; Gary Cooke, Product Manager, Duracell; Patrick Cullinan, Principal, Booz Allen & Hamilton; Ewan Davidson, Treasurer, J. Sainsbury plc; Peter Davis, Chief Executive, Reed International plc; John Downham, Manager of Market Research, Unilever; Kenneth Grange, Partner, Pentagram Design Ltd; Anthony Hapgood, Vice-President, Boston Consulting Group; Wesley Jordan, Managing Director, Hydrovane; Mike Penford, Account Director, A. C. Nielsen Ltd; Howard Phillips, Managing Director, Golden Wonder Ltd; the late Peter Rossi, Marketing Division, Unilever; John Whitaker, Managing Director, AGB Market Measurement, UK.

Andrew Franklin and Andrew Welham, both of Penguin, made an important contribution to this new edition.

I appreciated the extensive facilities of the Library at Templeton College, Oxford (formerly the Oxford Management Centre), and wish to thank the Librarian, Mrs Patience Hilton. Finally, I am grateful to my consulting clients from whom I have learnt so much (especially in South Humberside).

If this book does not meet its objectives after the involvement of so many able people, only one person is responsible – the author.

J. H. Davidson
Oxford, 1986

P.S. I would appreciate receiving any examples of offensive or inoffensive marketing from readers, with the next edition in view. They will be treated in confidence. Please send to Hugh Davidson, c/o Penguin Books Ltd, 27 Wrights Lane, London W8 5TZ.

Introduction:
Offensive Marketing

On 2 November 1978, four months after being fired as President of Ford, Lee Iacocca joined Chrysler as President. The same day, Chrysler posted its biggest-ever quarterly loss. Worse was to follow.

Chrysler was losing market share, quality was poor, and a year later Iacocca, previously an outspoken exponent of the free market system, was forced to negotiate a loan guarantee of $1·2 billion from the US government in order to keep afloat.

Nor was the external environment friendly. In the first half of 1979 the price of oil rocketed. Car sales dropped sharply and the market swung strongly towards small cars, where Chrysler was poorly positioned. To cap it all, interest rates shot up. By the end of 1979 only 13 per cent of Americans were prepared to *consider* buying a Chrysler, compared with 30 per cent a year earlier. Losses mounted from $1·1 billion in 1979 to $1·7 billion in 1980, and on 1 November 1981 Chrysler looked a terminal case. It was down to its last $1 million cash when spending was running at $50 million per day.

But three years later, in 1984, Chrysler made profits of $2·4 billion, more than it had earned in its previous fifty-eight years of history combined. How was it done?

Iacocca, the son of an Italian immigrant, and an engineer by training though a marketer by inclination, achieved this turn-around by:

1. Moving to a cost base where marketing could be effective. Production break-even point was reduced from 2·3 million cars in 1979 to 1·1 million in 1983.
2. Radically improving product quality. In 1980 rust warranty claims alone on one model cost $109 million.
3. Transforming the company from a financially driven organization into one which was marketing- and engineering-led, where people worked as a team, not as a collection of individual players.
4. Investing heavily in new products to develop a range with competitive appeal. A $6·5 billion Five-year Product Investment Plan was set up in 1980 and spending was sustained even in years when Chrysler looked destined for the mortuary.

In five long years, Iacocca and his team had brought Chrysler back from the dead, to resume its position as one of America's leading companies.

You have just read an example of offensive marketing. Iacocca realized that his first priority was to get production costs and quality into line, because otherwise marketing became academic. Then he had to change the whole outlook of Chrysler away from the factory towards the market-place.

With this solid framework he was able to successfully develop and launch the new K-Car range. Having got the company back on its feet, he began to innovate. In 1982, in a market where there had been no American-produced convertibles for five years, Chrysler introduced the LeBaron convertible. Two years later Chrysler created the American market for minivans – bigger than station wagons, smaller than vans, seating seven passengers. In each case Ford and General Motors followed.

Chrysler is now considered to be ahead of its American competitors in computer-aided design, in the use of corrosion-resistant body panels, and in speed of reaction. While it has undoubtedly been helped by the upturn in the American car market since 1982, Chrysler is now well placed to compete offensively in the next downturn, and in 1985 achieved profit margins double those of Ford or General Motors.[1]

This book is about offensive marketing, which combines the

age-old virtues of risk-taking with a modern approach to marketing. Offensive marketing is practised by only a handful of successful companies, and the phrase has been coined to differentiate the contents of this book from the sluggish and specialized concept that passes for marketing in many companies.

● **The Pursuit of Innovation**

Offensive marketing is not a neat concept capable of instant encapsulation in an elegant one-liner. On the contrary, because it describes particular attitudes and methods that cover the whole marketing spectrum, its boundaries are widely spread and ragged. In essence, it involves aiming to innovate every major new development in a market, from the humdrum accomplishment of being first in with a new larger size, to the heady success of breaking through with a totally new product or service. It obliges a company to lead rather than follow, and to respond to competitive moves by counterattack, not by imitation.

This may sound like the kind of thing every company should be doing, and indeed it is. But the fact remains that few companies do follow this approach, and while a statement of objectives is easy, putting it into practice needs more than wish-fulfilment. It requires a hard, disciplined plan, since the road to offensive marketing is not easy.

Offensive marketing is profitable, offensive, integrated, strategic and effectively executed. These five aspects can be summarized by the word P O I S E:

P for Profitable: proper balance between firm's needs for profit and consumer's need for value;

O for Offensive: must lead market and make competitors followers;

I for Integrated: marketing approach must permeate whole company;

S for Strategic: probing analysis leading to a winning strategy;

E for Effectively executed: strong and disciplined execution on a daily basis.

● **POISE Spelt Slowly**

Let us take a look at the individual ingredients of offensive marketing in broad terms.

Profitable: The object of marketing is not just to increase market share or to provide good value for consumers, but to increase profit. Offensive marketers will encounter conflicts between giving the consumer what he or she wants, and running the firm efficiently. One of their skills is to reach the right balance between these sometimes opposing elements.

Offensive: An offensive approach calls for an attitude of mind which decides independently what is best for a company, rather than waiting for competition to make the first move.

Integrated: Where marketing is integrated it permeates the whole company. It challenges all employees to relate their work to the needs of the market-place and to balance it against the firm's profit needs.

Strategic: Winning strategies are rarely developed without intensive analysis and careful consideration of alternatives. A business operated on a day-to-day basis, with no long-term marketing purpose, is more likely to be a follower than a leader.

Effectively executed: No amount of intelligent approach work is of any use without effective execution. Effective execution is not just a matter of good administration by marketing people. It is also vitally dependent on the relationship between marketing and other departments, and how far common strategies and objectives exist.

● **The Elusiveness of POISE**

Offensive Marketing was first written in 1971, ten years after 'marketing' began to take off in the UK. We are now a further sixteen years down the road and much has changed. The need for offensive marketing is greater than ever, but its achievement remains outside the grasp of the majority of companies.

Many of today's best offensive marketers were little known in the UK when this book was first written. These new marketers developed a clear strategy and pursued it with determination and flair, often flaunting conventional marketing wisdom. They include companies like Dixons, MFI and Laura Ashley among

19

retailers; Sony, Coloroll and Hazlewood in manufacturing; and McDonald's, Saatchi & Saatchi and AGB in services.

Some longer-established offensive marketers like 3M, Marks & Spencer, Smith & Nephew and Mars continue to lead the way. Other companies, like Oxford Instruments, Burtons, Jaguar and Fisons have become offensive marketers in the past few years.

But for most companies, offensive marketing remains an elusive concept, which has either not been striven for, or failed to take proper root. It remains the exception rather than the rule, and there is a wide and growing gap between the minority of companies which practise it and the majority which do not.

Conventional marketing has often become a victim of its own success. The acceptance of the marketing department as the hub of the wheel has multiplied its coordination role and created floods of paper. The pressure of housekeeping is so great that there is no time left to innovate. In many companies the marketing department, far from acting as the touchstone to innovation and enterprise, has itself become a bureaucracy, digesting and spawning numerous pieces of paper, acting as a passive coordinator.

The full-blooded application of offensive marketing requires strong qualities of persistence and character. Most companies know that marketing is a total approach to business, which must permeate every nook and cranny of the organization. But many continue to treat it as an amalgam of functional activities, like advertising, direct mail and promotions.

Theodore Levitt's comment of eighteen years ago is still disturbingly relevant:

> When it comes to the marketing concept today, a solid stone wall often seems to separate word and deed. In spite of the best intentions and energetic efforts of many highly able men, the effective implementation of the marketing concept has generally eluded them.[2]

Offensive marketing is less a matter of intelligence and ability – since most companies have plenty of both – than of attitudes, structure and strategy.

The O of POISE – offensive attitudes – is the keystone of the offensive marketing approach. It is a set of shared values, grounded in a commitment to superior customer benefits and low-cost operation. Once the O is strongly established, an integrated structure (I) and winning strategy (S) will have the chance to flow through. When the OIS has been achieved, profitability (P) usually follows, and effective execution (E) becomes a productive priority.

While O is the starting point, the whole package included in POISE has to be taken on board and persistently pursued with great determination. There are many fads in management which have come and gone. Offensive marketing is not one of them. It is a deadly serious approach to providing excellent value to the consumer and strong profit growth.

● Offensive Marketing in Action: J. Sainsbury plc

Few firms exemplify the offensive marketing approach better than Sainsbury. The business was started in a single shop in Drury Lane in 1869 by the great-grandfather of the present Chairman. The shop sold milk, butter, eggs and, later, cheese.

Today Sainsbury is the leading grocery multiple in the UK, and in 1984 received the US Food Marketing Institute Award for 'The Outstanding Supermarket Chain'.

The way in which this company operates the offensive marketing approach of POISE is traced below:

Profitable: Competing in the relatively undynamic grocery market, Sainsbury's pre-tax profits have grown at an annual rate of 18 per cent in the past ten years, and earnings per share from 3·9p to 14·6p at today's prices. At 5 per cent, the company's net margin before tax is high by the standards of its industry and almost double the level of its main competitor, Tesco.

A major factor in Sainsbury's profit performance is its high sales per square foot, which are double the average for grocery stores. Since about one third of operating costs are space-related, this gives Sainsbury a head start on cost ratios, enabling it to offer good value and make decent profits.

However, Sainsbury has always been aware that too high a sales rate can result in congestion and queueing, and in the 1970s it deliberately expanded space, knowing that volume would not keep pace, in order to get a better balance between profit margins and quality of customer service.

Sainsbury has become much more profit-oriented since becoming a public company. In the days when it was privately owned, profit was seen as the reward for customer service and the attitude tended to be: 'Don't add up the profits till the end of the year, and then you'll know how good a job you've done for your customers.'

Offensive: A strong belief in giving the customer superior value for money has permeated the business from generation to generation. Its exact expression has evolved over time, but the bedrock of high quality, competitive prices, no gimmicks, clean stores and clear labelling has remained unchanged.

Sainsbury policy on its own brand is to offer only products which are superior in quality to equivalent branded lines, or of comparable quality but cheaper. Buyers can expect to be cross-examined on whether their products are better or cheaper, and numerous blind tests, panel tests and technical analyses are done to check on quality. In recent years Sainsbury's prices have been typically 1 per cent below its main competitors' on a basket of branded items, 2 per cent lower on a mixed basket of branded and own-label lines.

Together with Marks & Spencer, Sainsbury saw the potential of private labelling well before others in the grocery trade, viewing it as an opportunity to give better value for money and to make Sainsbury stores distinctive. The company was a pioneer in raising the quality and image of private labelling. Sainsbury and Marks & Spencer have transformed own-brand groceries from lower-priced alternatives into strong brands in their own right.

Table 1 shows how, in long-term investment, Sainsbury has outgunned Marks & Spencer, spending an average of almost 7 per cent of sales mainly on new or refurbished stores, against around 4 per cent for its competitors:

Table 1. *Capital Investment, 1981–4*

Retailer	Spending (£ million)	Percentage (of sales)
Sainsbury	477	6·9
Tesco	300	4·4
M & S	302	4·0
ASDA	173	3·8

Integrated: Fifteen years ago Sainsbury was non-integrated, divided into separate trading and administration units. Today integration is one of its strengths. Having a single head office and an active chairman helps. So, surprisingly, does the network of committees which criss-cross levels and functions; there is a spirit at these meetings that allows questions to be asked because people do not feel they are in watertight departments.

Strategic: Sainsbury appears to have a winning strategy in grocery retailing. It consists of a broad range of fast-moving consumer products, offering superior value for money, in convenient and attractive stores. There have been occasional lapses, such as flirtations with slower-moving product categories, but these have been quickly corrected. The company still has scope for geographical expansion since only 60 per cent of the UK population is within easy access of a Sainsbury store.

Sainsbury's diversification strategy comprises three elements:[3]

1. Business should be broadened outside food in the longer term to spread risk and maintain real profit growth.
2. New opportunities should be related to the mainstream retailing business and exploit current strengths in management and trading.
3. Joint ventures should be used to cover areas where Sainsbury lacks expertise, and as a means of reducing the cost of diversification.

Results of this strategy have been the Savacentre Hypermarket venture with British Home Stores; the Homebase DIY chain, a joint venture with the Belgian DIY retailer GB-Inno; and the acquisition of a 21 per cent share of Shaws, a well-run grocery multiple in New England, USA, with a reputation for being a pioneer in check-out scanning and computer technology in stores.

Effective execution: Sainsbury is a centralized retailer. Day-to-day trading decisions are taken at a senior level, and implemented at branches with military rigour. The keys to execution at Sainsbury are people, training, speed of reaction, discipline and motivation.

Sainsbury attracts good-quality people and generally manages to hold them. Training is taken seriously. At any one time there are over 800 management trainees in the stores, and the task of training company people away from work is equivalent to running a school with over 600 pupils.

There is a weekly pricing meeting at senior level every Wednesday or Thursday, when prices for the weekend are decided. This is backed by a cascade telephone system, which operates a little like a chain letter, each person contacted calling another five people and so on. It was originally designed for product recall crises, but is now used for trading purposes and this enables the company to initiate a national price change within one hour.

Strong discipline is implicit, and facilitated by relentless financial monitoring and appraisal, areas in which Sainsbury has invested heavily over the years.

Performance is enhanced by the profit-sharing scheme, started ten years ago. This is dependent on profit margin. If margin is only 2·5 per cent, the average for the industry, payments are nil. They are geared above this level, and in 1984 average payout was 7·5 per cent of salary. Profit-sharing can be taken in cash or shares. In addition, the top 250–300 employees, down to the more senior store managers, qualify for share options.

Finally, board members regularly get out into the field. The Chairman personally visits half the stores every year and most of these visits are unannounced; a high proportion of employees have either seen or met him.

In describing successful companies, it is easy to exaggerate their skills and competence. Sainsbury is not perfect. There are still a number of smaller stores whose limited product range and lack of convenience do not meet the Group's overall standards. Queueing at the check-out can still be a problem; in food, the level of new product flair and innovation does not match Marks & Spencer; and the present Chairman's quality of leadership will be a hard act to follow in the 1990s.

Nevertheless, Sainsbury is an impressive British success story, and a fine example of offensive marketing in action.

● Checking a Company's Score for Offensive Marketing

If offensive marketing is as practical a concept as has been claimed, it should be possible to set up criteria by which the offensive marketing rating of a firm can be judged. Like any comparison between firms, the result will inevitably be biased

Table 2. *Criteria for Rating a Business on Offensive Marketing*

	Maximum score	Your score
Strong and differentiated customer proposition	15	
Ability to update and develop existing products/services	5	
Success in launching profitable new products/services which add incremental sales	7	
New markets successfully entered in past ten years	7	
Strong customer focus of total company, including operations, distribution and finance	10	
Strong profit focus of whole company, including marketing and sales	10	
Clear long-term strategy, refined where necessary, but strongly adhered to	8	
Commitment to constant improvement in quality and value for money	10	
More efficient/lower-cost operator than competitors	12	
Whether led or followed latest innovations in major markets	8	
Level of investment compared with competitors (facilities, advertising, Research & Development, people development)	8	
Total	100	

and subjective, due to differences in definition and in market situations. The battery of offensive marketing yardsticks which has been constructed will not escape these criticisms, but they contain sufficient objectivity to be useful.

● **Summary**

Offensive marketing differs radically from 'marketing' as traditionally practised. 'Marketing' has been widely misunderstood or misapplied. In the majority of companies, it is either an amalgam of marketing activities or a functional bureaucracy. Only a minority of companies apply offensive marketing.

Since this book was first written in 1971, the need for offensive marketing has greatly increased. In the past decade, flat markets, heightened competition and falling profit margins have made business more difficult. This environment has frequently produced the wrong response – short-term, negative, defensive thinking resulting in failure to compete effectively.

Offensive marketing is a dynamic approach to business. It is profitable, offensive, integrated, strategic and effectively executed.

The O of POISE, offensive attitudes, is the keystone of the offensive marketing approach. It is a set of shared values, grounded in a commitment to superior customer benefits and low-cost operation.

There is a wide and growing gap between the minority of companies which practise offensive marketing and the majority which do not. Offensive marketing involves some difficult options, but its benefits justify the hardness of the road that leads there.

1 | *Profitable*

1 | *Getting the Right Mix*

● Who Needs Marketing?

The practice of marketing is almost as old as civilization, and its validity has been proved over and over again. The oldest profession in the world used classic marketing techniques: it identified and satisfied a need; it created a market where buyer and seller could meet, in the form of the brothel; and it turned a handsome profit on the operation.

Buying a present for your spouse is also a marketing operation. You try to establish what would please him or her through knowledge of tastes, observation of needs and subtle questioning. Then you sift through this mass of data and select an item which you believe would be most liked and which you can afford.

The strength of marketing as an idea needs no justification. Its difficulties have arisen since it became known as 'marketing', and experienced the fashionable embrace of the large company.

● Profitable Marketing

'What do you do for a living?' is a question marketing people at social gatherings dread. Two minutes of superficial conversation are not enough to put it across. The absence of simple explanations may be one of the reasons why the marketing function is so widely misunderstood, and wrongly applied.

You could say what marketing is not. Marketing is not 'selling', though 'selling' is part of the marketing approach. To borrow a phrase, 'Selling is making people want what you've got, while marketing is selling people what they want.'[1] When people say, 'We must improve the marketing of our product', they are confusing marketing with selling.

Let us move on to some more sophisticated misconceptions. One of the most common definitions of marketing, often found in textbooks, goes something like this: 'The purpose of marketing is to meet consumer needs at a profit.' The trouble with this definition is that the conflict between meeting needs and making profit isn't recognized, nor is the role of marketing in finding the best balance between the two. It also ignores profit *levels*.

One sentence is the longest any businessman will tolerate on definitions, so here, briefly, is the only definition in this book:

> Marketing is the process of balancing the company needs for profit against the benefits required by consumers, so as to maximize long-term earnings per share.

Marketing is a philosophy and a method of achieving corporate financial objectives. It stands or falls according to how effectively it contributes to their accomplishment. In a Utopian world it does this by arriving at a perfect balance between company needs for profit and consumer needs for benefits.

The relevance of this balance is sometimes illustrated very dramatically in the travel industry:

> *The market for leisure travel by air is extremely price-sensitive, since there is limited product differentiation between airlines. Any airline with a sound reputation for safety, and low prices, will attract plenty of customers.*
>
> *However, costs and profits in this market are highly volume-sensitive. With an average load factor of 80 per cent a carrier could become rich, whereas only 70 per cent occupancy could result in bankruptcy.*
>
> *Therefore, any airline relying on a low-price approach has to carefully calculate both customer and competitive reaction,*

and get its occupancy forecasts right in order to achieve a profit.

In many companies, where particular products or customers may be unprofitable, lack of balance between customer and profit needs occurs less dramatically. A rigorous examination of the profit or loss generated by marginal products or accounts nearly always pays dividends.

The example below, from the car industry, strikes at the very essence of marketing, and shows that it goes well beyond the flaccid definition of marketing as merely satisfying consumer needs.

> *An automobile company can produce the cheapest possible car of the best quality by making just one model and running it off by the hundred thousand. But today car purchasers have widely differing requirements.*
>
> *A single model would not satisfy the diversity of needs of the total market, and a car tailored to the individual requirements of each consumer would be prohibitively expensive to make. So where does one go from there?*
>
> *Motor manufacturers have sought different solutions to this conflict between the cost efficiencies of mass production and the consumer's need for a tailored car.*
>
> *In the Eastern bloc, the answer is simple – go for economies of scale and limit consumer choice. In earlier days, the capitalist Henry Ford adopted a similar solution with his Model T Ford, available in black only. His solution led to the rise of General Motors.*
>
> *In today's European market, the larger manufacturers have between four and five different body shells, with many interchangeable parts. By offering a wide variety of engine types, styling and extras, they tailor cars to individual tastes without sacrificing all the cost benefits of mass production.*
>
> *For example, with five basic body shapes each, Ford markets 102 car models and Vauxhall 55. Both have a manufacturing strategy of large-scale flexible production, rather than mass production.*

Another battleground where profit and efficiency come into head-on conflict with consumer needs is the low-volume brand. A product's volume can decline to a point where it is no longer profitable to sell, even at a premium retail price. For a large company with high overheads, a brand with a turnover of £500,000 may be unprofitable.

True, on an artificial 'standard' costing, where its contribution to overheads is allocated in proportion to its share of company volume, such a product can be made to appear profitable. But usually it eats up a slice of selling, distribution, marketing and management time out of all proportion to its volume, so that a pro rata allocation of overheads is unrealistic.

If a brand of this kind is actually losing money on a proper costing, should it be withdrawn? After all, some consumers still want it and are continuing to buy, and isn't the purpose of marketing to satisfy the consumer? The answer is obvious: the brand should be withdrawn because it is unprofitable. An offensive marketer would be the first to press for such a decision. In a company applying offensive marketing, this conflict is being balanced in almost every decision.

Marketing always poses the question of what is best for the consumer. Offensive marketing asks two other questions as well:

1. What is most efficient for the company from the cost angle?
2. How do we balance consumer needs against company needs for low-cost operation?

Offensive marketers are as profit-oriented as the accountant, but do not share the latter's mainly inward focus on the business. They are looking for ways to increase revenue as well as to reduce costs.

● **Market-led and Asset-led Marketing**

To demonstrate how the offensive marketing approach enhances profitability, we need to look at market-led and asset-led marketing. But first a few more words about marketing in general.

Figure 1 illustrates the role of marketing. On the left-hand side are the assets of the firm – people, equipment, cash and, most notable of all, brand names. These generate cost. On the right-hand side is the market-place. This generates revenue.

The job of marketing is to achieve the best mix – by converting company assets into consumer value. In this process, two things happen at once. The market-place is being probed for opportunities. The company's assets are being refined, and exploited – and marketing is there to achieve an ideal fusion between assets and markets.

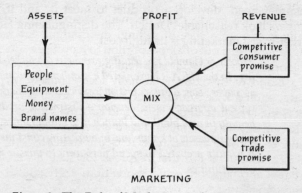

Figure 1. The Role of Marketing in the Firm

But what is the starting point in this process? Do we begin by searching the market-place for opportunities and then checking back to see if we can handle them? Or do we first put our key assets under the microscope, and then peer at the market-place for ways to exploit them? The answer is that both approaches should be pursued concurrently. Market-led and asset-led marketing are not conflicting ways of doing business. They merely view the marketing process from different windows, and are complementary. But it is important to recognize the difference between market-led and asset-led marketing and to get the most out of both (see Figure 2).

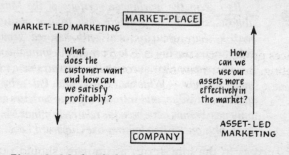

Figure 2. Market-led and Asset-led Marketing

Market-led marketing takes the market-place as its starting point and asks: 'What does the customer want and how can we satisfy the need profitably?' This is sometimes called 'classical' marketing, and is favoured by textbooks. The typical sequence is to find an unfilled consumer need, develop a product to meet it, and if the profit numbers look reasonable, launch. The distinguishing factor about market-based marketing is its high cost.

> *Procter & Gamble is a leading exponent of market-led marketing. In the USA it has entered a number of new markets, such as paper, soft drinks, pharmaceuticals and snack foods. Its typical approach is to develop a distinctive product, invest heavily in new plant and launch new brand names. While it is using its assets of know-how in marketing consumer products, it is quite prepared to spend massively to pursue new market opportunities.*

Asset-led marketing takes the company's assets as its starting point and asks the same question in reverse. It requires marketers to analyse and define assets as thoroughly as markets. This leads to thoughts like 'We've got these skills and resources – let's comb the market for needs which exploit them more fully.'

Asset-led marketing starts with what the company has, and what it does well, then works back to the market-place. Here is an example:

> *Pedigree Petfoods, part of the Mars organization, enjoys growing market shares and a high return on invested capital. It has pursued a mainly asset-led marketing approach during the past decade in the UK.*
>
> *Its role in the worldwide portfolio of the Mars Group is almost certainly to generate cash from a position of great market share security, and with assured growth from a category increasing by 6 to 8 per cent in annual volume.*
>
> *The company has successfully concentrated on building its major brands – Whiskas, Chum and Pal – by improving quality and value, and introducing new varieties and sizes. Its only new brands have been the relatively minor Mr Dog puppy food, plus one or two failures like Cupboard Love.*

For success in the long-term, a company should pursue both types of marketing. Asset-led marketing is quite different from 'milking' (see p. 42), because it usually strengthens consumer franchise as well as improving profits.

The table below illustrates the main differences of emphasis between the two approaches. It highlights the fact that if you are having a lean profit year, an asset-led marketing initiative might just help you hit budget, whereas a new marketing-led launch would turn a problem into a disaster (see Table 3).

The right approach for marketing people is to understand company assets as intimately as the market-place, and to achieve a continuum between the two, in order to maximize profits, as in Figure 3.

Table 3. *Market-led vs. Asset-led Marketing*

	Market-led marketing	Asset-led marketing
Starting point	The market	Company assets
Overall business approach	Marketing	Marketing
Risk	High	Low/medium
New investment	High	Low
New brand name	Yes	No
Effect on customer franchise	Broaden	Consolidate/ broaden
Project payback	3–5 years	1–2 years
Competitive response	Heavy	Low/medium

Figure 3. Assets/Exploitable Strengths vs. Market Opportunities

● Understanding Your Assets

To exploit their assets effectively in the market-place, marketing managers have to understand what they are. It is unfortunate that many marketing people fail this test, since an unexploited asset can be a profit gold-mine. Beecham has often demonstrated this with the brands it has acquired, from Maclean's and Lucozade in the past to Bovril and Horlicks more recently.

The first step is to build up a check-list of company assets. In preparing this, the marketing manager will need to talk to every department, especially operations and distribution, where the main costs usually lurk. Table 4 contains a check-list of things to look at. The second step is to pick out from this list 'key exploitable assets'. These are things which your company does best or uniquely well.

Table 4. *Check-list of Types of Asset*

People	Skills, experience, motivation, organization, direction, knowledge areas, communications, speed of reaction, outside contacts, training quality, philosophy, creativity
Working Capital	Amount, availability, utilization, location, credit lines
Operations	Relative modernity, exclusive elements, shop secrets, flexibility, economies of scale, efficiency in use, capacity utilization, added value, quality of service
Customer Franchises	Brand names, trade or buyer franchises, unique products/services, patents, superior service skills, access to third-party resources (joint ventures or agreements)
Sales/Distribution/ Service Network	Size, skill, coverage, capacity utilization, productivity, relations with external distributors
Scale Advantages	Market share, relative and absolute media weight, purchases/leverage, geographical/international coverage, sales/distribution/ service (above), specialist skills due to scale (e.g. market research)

● **Questions for
Leading Marketing Counsel to Ask**

As the person best qualified to relate assets to market-place, you then adjust your barrister's wig and ask the right questions, full of confidence that the answers will lead to higher profits. Among the most productive questions are:

Utilization of Facilities: What is the present level of utilization? Has the company got its price/utilization sums right? Can higher-value products be developed for use on existing plant? Can new services be launched using existing people? Are there any modified products or services that could be launched using existing facilities?

> *In the early 1980s Kellogg's had a problem. The percentage brand share of Kellogg's Cornflakes, while still in the low 20s, was declining over the long-term. The company had spare manufacturing capacity for cornflakes, but a firm policy of not producing for stores' private labels.*
>
> *Kellogg's solved this problem by launching Kellogg's Crunchy Nut Cornflakes priced at a heavy premium to the customer. It gained a 2–3 per cent market share, mainly incremental to other Kellogg's brands.*
>
> *Kellogg's exploited existing assets of brand name, flake technology, sales force, and plant, but with a separate advertising positioning which attracted new consumers at high margins.*

Product Range: How large is the product range? Has it just grown, or is it a properly thought-out system designed to cover the main sectors of the market? Can the number of products be reduced without harming sales? Answer to the latter question is almost always yes.

> *Playtex in the UK had a range of seventy-five lingerie products. It was noticed that the French company, with a higher market share, had only fifty products.*
>
> *A market test was therefore set up in the UK, reducing product range from seventy-five to fifty-three. Because this did a great deal for production efficiencies and inventory costs, profits could be held even if revenue fell by 8 per cent. In*

practice, in both the test and later national expansion, sales increased by 10 per cent, because the better-selling products were more visible in stores and got greater sales force attention. Profits rose by 25 per cent. The approach was extended to the USA.

Asset-led Market Expansion: Have we got any unique skills or assets that would enable us to successfully enter new markets?

By the mid-1970s Bic had built up a strong worldwide position in low-price ball-point pens, under the leadership of Baron Bich. One of its major assets was the ability to manufacture small plastic items, in very high volume, at low cost per unit, and to good quality standards.

Bic was keen to diversify into new consumer markets, where it could innovate by exploiting its skills in plastics technology. This investigation led it to the wet-shaver market, dominated by Gillette, which was trading up customers to increasingly elaborate and expensive products. Bic introduced the low-price disposable razor, sold in multi-packs, mainly through super-markets.

Gillette was predictably slow to react since it faced a painful choice. Successful entry with plastic disposables would trade down the value of the whole market. Inaction would result in share loss. Gillette did eventually introduce a successful plastic disposable product, but too late to prevent the establishment of Bic as a strong competitor in many countries.

Brand Name Stretching: Do we really know what our brand names mean to our consumers, and how far they can be stretched without losing vitality? When Beecham bought Bovril, it success-fully used the name to enter the stock cube market against Oxo. Hovis is an underexploited brand name, and could be effectively extended across a range of 'healthy eating' products.

Extension of Usage: Are there any new usages for our products?

Until the early 1970s Johnson & Johnson's Baby Shampoo was positioned exclusively for babies. Research indicated that it was also being used by mothers, 'because it was there'. A decision was made to market the brand on a dual strategy, with separate advertising, for babies, and for adults who wanted a gentle shampoo. Johnson's Baby Shampoo is now one of the largest shampoo brands in the world and the majority of its usage is by adults.

Quality: How good is our quality? Are the performance characteristics most important to our customers the ones to which quality control gives most attention? Fast food companies like McDonald's have strict specifications for speed of service and cleanliness as well as for product quality, since convenience and hygiene are important elements in their customer proposition.

Service/Delivery Specifications: Are they too high or too low in relation to customer needs? Are they related to customer profitability? There is no point in offering speedy service to low-margin customers who are quite prepared to accept slower delivery.

Sales Forecasting: How good is it? Poor forecasting can play havoc with purchasing and manufacturing efficiencies and with inventory levels. When he arrived at Chrysler, Lee Iacocca found that factory production bore little relation to dealer needs. The factory would produce for a 'sales pool', and salesmen would then try to flog off the contents of the 'pool' to dealers. Iacocca introduced the standard system of producing to a sales forecast, based on dealers' estimates of their own future requirements.

How Well is Marketing Working with Other Departments? We return to this in Part 3 under 'Integrated': the I of POISE.

Utilization of Customer Base: Are there any other products which we can sell to existing customers? Can our existing contacts lead us to new contacts in the same organization? Accounting firms, heavily committed to a mature product – the annual company audit – used this as an entry point for selling a widening range of consultancy services. They are now strongly positioned in the fast-expanding market of management consultancy, having retained their stable core business of auditing.

Marketing Value Analysis: What is the relative customer value of each part of every major product or service in relation to its cost?

Value analysis is an important marketing tool, but often a victim of lip-service; unless it is handled with the skill of a surgeon it becomes a high-flown excuse for reducing product quality. Witness the anguished cry of a marketing director whose brand-leader chocolate biscuit had just been 'value analysed': 'Why don't you just remove all the chocolate as well?'

● A Portrait of Five Marketing Perverts

To complete this chapter on profitability, we will examine a number of wrong attitudes towards the marketing approach, which prejudice both the understanding of its real nature and its effective application. These attitudes are most often held by marketing men, or their friends in the advertising agencies. Five have been picked out for demonstration purposes. They are all enemies of offensive marketing and have an adverse effect on long-term profitability.

The consumer worshippers

This group has already been referred to by implication above, but it is so influential that it deserves further treatment. The consumer worshippers believe that the consumer is always right and seem to be under the impression that they are working for *Which?* magazine rather than a commercial organization. *Which?* does a fine job and fulfils a key role, but is non-profit-making. Businesses have to make money for their shareholders, and the reckless pursuit of consumer benefit irrespective of profit results in bankruptcy.

Only profitable firms can serve the consumer effectively. And it is in fact quite possible to satisfy consumer needs superbly well while also returning above-average profits. The fact that companies are profit-oriented does not mean that they lack interest in the consumer. On the contrary, anyone who shops regularly at Marks & Spencer or John Lewis, or spends a few days talking to employees of companies like Heinz or United Biscuits, will recognize that they have a most genuine concern to provide the consumer with good value for money. The view that companies regard the consumer with Machiavellian cynicism is, I think, as outdated as that which objects to profit as an unmitigated evil.

The New Luddites

Once you have traced the traditional history of marketing, and acknowledged its emergence from an era of production orientation, where the machine's capacity rather than the consumer's need dictated the market, it is not too big a step to regard production as, in some undefined way, opposed to marketing.

This sets the stage for the New Luddites, who view production as an outdated and inferior form of activity. They refer to 'production-oriented' companies with a curl of the lip, and assume that the operations department must always behave as a docile servant of the marketing group to prevent a return to the dark ages of business.

This attitude is responsible for the bickering and lack of co-operation that is so often a feature of the relationship between operations and marketing departments. The posture of the New Luddite is, of course, totally unrealistic, because marketing depends on good operations for its effectiveness. Superb advertising, packaging and product planning will be of no avail if the product or service is of inferior or inconsistent quality. What is more, close cooperation between marketing and operations can turn up excellent profit improvements through reductions in cost.

The egotistical employees

A great deal has been written in the past few decades about the widening gap between ownership and control of companies. The shareholders own the capital, but the management exercises practical control and, unless things go seriously wrong, the only communication between the one and the other is in the pages of the financial press or, less likely, at the annual general meeting.

One little-noticed aspect of the increasing separation between ownership and control is the inclination of some employees to run businesses for their own delectation and pleasure, rather than for the benefit of shareholders. This is particularly inimical to the operation of the offensive marketing approach, the purpose of which is to increase long-term profit.

Employee egotism starts right from the top, with chief executives who are more interested in inflating their importance than in

41

accelerating profit. Since size usually equals power, they are quite likely to pursue growth as opposed to profit, and to follow an aggressive acquisition programme. Company presidents who state their corporate objectives as 'becoming a billion-dollar corporation' are often egotistical employees. Why don't they talk about 'becoming a hundred-million-dollar net-profit corporation'?

One type of egotist who regularly impedes the offensive marketing approach is the pseudo-professional. Now professionalism in the best sense, construed as job excellence, is clearly an admirable quality. But the pseudo-professional pursues irrelevant standards that do not relate to consumer needs, or which are calculated to be more rewarding to the employee than productive to the company.

Let us take a few examples that will be easily spotted by those with an observant eye:

1. Research & development (R & D) scientists are particularly prone to this disease. Being people of outstanding intellect, they naturally tend to be most interested in work that is technically challenging, irrespective of its likely commercial pay-off. To counter this, marketing men have to take the lead in directing R & D effort to projects with profit potential. These are more likely to involve putting blue speckles into washing powder than breakthroughs in biogenetics.

2. Copywriters at advertising agencies can also be difficult to motivate along offensive marketing lines. Some write advertisements to impress their peers or to draw attention to their skills, rather than to persuade the consumer. Such individuals care more about creative awards than sales graphs, although they usually pretend otherwise when talking to clients.

3. Internal bureaucrats who are more interested in following procedures than in meeting customer needs. These people can be damaging enough within the confines of a company, but when let loose on customers, as in a service business, they can be disastrous.

The milker

Milkers are just another instance of the egotistical employee. Because they are often marketing people, and at the same time can do a great disservice to the offensive marketing approach, they are treated separately.

Milkers are executives who think they will only spend a short time – perhaps a year or so – in their present job. They may be rolling general managers with an international company, or brand managers who move quickly from job to job. The technique is to cut every cost in sight, including advertising spending, so that a vastly improved profit can be piled up over a short period. The degree to which the milker has mortgaged the company's or the brand's longer-term prospects is not apparent at the time, and when revenue or profits turn down a year later, somebody else is in the hot seat to take the blame for yet another marketing failure.

The galloping midget

He is almost invariably male, twenty-five years old and with four years' experience in marketing. He defines marketing as the 'total business operation' (hardly acknowledging the existence of industrial relations or financial planning). Marketing is the only part of the business that matters and every department exists just to provide a service to it. Time is the only thing standing between the galloping midget and the managing directorship and it won't be long now. This arrogant and naive type does great harm to the offensive marketing approach.

● **Summary**

Marketing involves balancing the company's need for profit against the benefits required by consumers so as to maximize long-term earnings per share. There is a continuing tug of war between the firm's need for efficiency and the customer's need for unique benefits. Getting the balance right is not easy. It requires a thorough knowledge of a company's assets and an ability to relate these to profitable opportunities in the market-place.

To do this, the marketing manager must be an all-round businessman, with a good grasp of the basic principles of operations, finance, sales and distribution. This is a far cry from the still popular but inaccurate caricature of the marketing man as a dabbler in packaging, advertising, sales promotion and market research.

Getting the Right Mix

Marketing managers also need to lead the pace of their company's profit growth by ensuring that they achieve a balanced portfolio between high-cost/high-risk market-led initiatives, and low-risk/high-margin asset-led initiatives. This allows the company both to meet its short-term profit objectives and to strengthen its customer franchise in the longer-term.

2 | *Principles of Profitable Marketing in Action*

The previous chapter dealt in some detail with asset-led marketing. This one will illustrate the principles of marketing in action from the more traditional market-led angle. As has already been shown, this can be stated very simply: you merely identify a profitable consumer need, design a better product or service, and then make certain everyone knows about it. Offensive marketing also looks simple to execute when it is carried out successfully, but looks are deceptive. Consider the apparent simplicity of the Sydney suspension bridge or a Picasso painting.

● The Boomerang Sequence

Offensive marketing follows a boomerang sequence to transform consumer needs into profitable products or services. The three steps in the sequence apply to the marketing of any product – from pharmaceuticals to financial services. They are investigation, design and selling.

Investigation is necessary to discover what the consumer and the distributor want. Its object is to track down unsatisfied needs of the kind that the company in question is equipped to fulfil.

Design is the process of developing a product or service that meets the need which has been identified. It also includes the design of the financial plan, which ensures that the need can be met profitably.

Selling is the finishing touch by which the consumer (and the distributor) is sold the product or service developed during the investigation. Advertising, promotions, merchandising, sales force effort and packaging design are all part of the selling stage.

Figure 4 shows the boomerang in action.

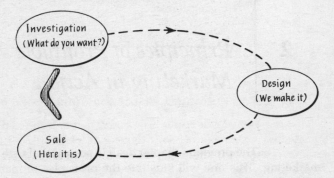

Figure 4. The Boomerang Sequence of Marketing

This boomerang sequence seems smooth and assured, but in practice its trajectory is usually distorted by all kinds of turbulence. Misinterpretation and wishful thinking are notable causes of this distortion, so that when the boomerang finally returns to the consumer it is often rejected.

Each of the three boomerang stages involves a number of departments and external agents besides marketing, and Table 5 traces their participation. It shows that virtually every department plays a part in design and sale, but that investigation is usually handled by marketing and R & D.

Of course, the boomerang sequence of marketing refers equally to existing products and services as to new ones. All reputable marketers will be continually searching for ways to make their current brands more acceptable to the consumer or more profitable.

Table 5. *Involvement in Boomerang Sequence*

Name of Dept	Investigation	Design	Sale
Marketing	●	●	●
R & D	●	●	
Operations		●	●
Finance		●	●
Purchasing		●	●
Distribution		●	●
Sales		●	●
Advertising agency		●	●
NPD/design agency	●	●	●
Sales Promo/PR agency	●	●	●

● Investigation – Inside the Consumer's Mind

You may wonder how you can ever hope to reveal the unsatisfied yearnings of, say, thousands of people all over the country, when you can't even choose the right kind of gift for your husband or wife.

The answer is that you have to listen to the consumer even more attentively than you listen to your spouse. Observe too; research is the eyes and ears of the commercial firm. It is both a listening post and an observation tower. As in the case of a computer, what comes out depends on the quality of the input. The marketing executive has to programme the questions and interpret the results. If you have a reasonably clear idea of what you are looking for, market research is a trusty aid in any investigation. But use it like a vacuum cleaner, to sweep over broad spaces, and the odds are that you will just pick up a load of rubbish.

Investigation of the market-place has two facets – finding out what consumers think (consumer research) and observing their actions in the market-place (market research).

Consumer research deals with attitudes and opinions towards existing products or hypothetical future ones. The techniques used vary, from simple structured interviews of large samples of consumers to lengthy discussions with groups, conducted by a qualified psychologist.

Market research is more factual because it is concerned with action rather than opinion. It observes happenings in the market-place, as reflected by trade or consumer purchases, and measures action based on money passing. This data is then projected into estimates of total market sizes and trends, brand shares, retail distribution, and pricing and stock levels.

Consumer and market research are complementary and act in unison. Consumer research is often used to check the reasons for purchase behaviour revealed by market research. Market research ultimately checks the market showing of products developed with the aid of consumer research. It is not difficult to identify the more obvious consumer needs if you think clearly and are not encumbered by the burden of tradition. Straightforward research on consumer habits, product usages, and attitudes to brands and markets will normally pinpoint obvious needs.

For instance, you do not have to be a particularly subtle investigator to conclude that improved picture quality for videotape, longer life for machine tools and greater speed or convenience for all products are desirable attributes.

Paradoxically, comprehensive research is usually worth undertaking in any markets that seriously attract your interest. Admittedly, the broad findings often merely confirm common sense, but at least they give a firm factual background, shorn of guesswork, from which to operate. There's also a sporting chance that they will reveal new opportunities.

To take a hypothetical example, a usage and attitude study involving 1,000 interviews about a particular food market might indicate that existing products were considered too thick or too sweet, that the level of usage among families with children was high enough to justify the introduction of a child-oriented product, or that most consumers added extra ingredients to existing commercial products, thereby making a more convenient 'all-in-one' brand a possibility.

Despite much clever talk in the marketing world about complicated and novel research techniques, it is apparent that most of the really successful new consumer products introduced in the past decade have fulfilled relatively obvious needs, which the simplest form of investigation would have revealed. The critical reason for their success was not shrewd investigation, but skilful design and selling. Most of the outstanding new products of the 1980s succeeded for these reasons, and Table 6 gives examples.

Table 6. *Outstanding New Products*

New Product	Product Category	Reason for Success
EastEnders	Long-life TV serials	Younger, issue-based development of *Coronation Street*
Wispa	Chocolate confectionery	Novel texture and high chocolate content in a filled count line
Canon PC-20	Copier for small businesses	Maintenance free, with replaceable cartridge

● Investigation – Don't Knock the Obvious

Following the obvious is very productive if you can find a unique way to execute it, as can be seen from the examples in Table 6.

EastEnders exploited an opportunity which had been obvious to the BBC for decades during which ITV's *Coronation Street* led the audience ratings. Compared with *Coronation Street, EastEnders* is targeted at a much younger audience and deals with topical personal or social issues in a dramatized serial format. Its style is further differentiated by a southern location, and at present it is the top-rating weekly TV programme in all areas except the north-west and the border counties.

Wispa related a new chocolate texture to an existing shape and price point. It competed mainly against count lines like Mars Bar, but also offered an alternative to block chocolate.

The Canon PC-20 office copier also used new technology to meet an obvious need. In entering the UK market, Canon did not wish to begin by attacking Rank Xerox in its prime territory of the large copier. It chose to target the small business with a low-price plain paper-copier, suitable for small-volume usage, and maintenance-free. The last was an obvious but important part of the strategy, since it was not economic to make direct service calls on small businesses. The solution was a sealed cartridge, which could be purchased from office equipment retailers, and needed replacement every 3,000 copies.

You may well ask why you should find the obvious when others have missed it during their own market investigations. The answer is that what is obvious to one person may be wrapped in a blanket of obscurity for another; much depends on the angle of vision.

Take the case of Archimedes, for instance.[1] He had the pressing problem of finding out whether the crown of Hieron II of Syracuse was made of solid gold. If only he could determine the volume of the crown, he could easily check on its density, since the unit weight of gold was known. But there was no existing technology for calculating the size of irregular cubic shapes. He was thinking about this problem as he got into his bath and watched the familiar sight of the water rising. It then occurred to him that, like the crown, his own body was also an irregular cubic shape, and that he could measure its volume by calculating the amount of water displaced when it was put in a receptacle.

For centuries before Archimedes mankind had possessed the same information, but had failed to make his simple deduction. There is a lot of data of the same kind lying around in files today, just waiting for an imaginative mind to light it up.

Dominant companies in existing markets often fail to see the obvious, when it does not fit in with established tradition. Or they see it, but hesitate to act because of the possibly prejudicial effect of new brands on their current franchise. Or they may be lethargic or complacent. The outsider can often see opportunities which the insider looks right through. In the American frozen-food market, for instance, four of the big new ideas of the past twenty years were originated by outsiders, not by General Foods' Birds Eye division, at the time the leading operator in the category, and the founder of frozen foods.[2]

The case history below is a good example of offensive marketing in action:

> The American frozen food market is divided into two major parts – commodity products like orange juice and vegetables, which are sold in a form fairly close to nature, and recipe products which involve a degree of processing by manufacturers.
>
> The commodity category has relatively flat volume, low margin and high-store-label penetration. The recipe side is the place to be, but Birds Eye missed the opportunity to build a strong position in it.
>
> That opportunity has been largely scooped by companies not

even in frozen foods in the days of Birds Eye dominance. They all had ideas which were at the time novel, though the needs they fulfilled were fairly obvious, and technology equally available to Birds Eye.

Kitchens of Sara Lee originally began distribution of high-quality cakes within a 300-mile radius of Chicago. It then decided to freeze its cakes so that it could ship them to the South. Eventually Sara Lee expanded this approach nationally. It has for many years led the cake sector of frozen foods.

Swanson innovated 'TV dinners', consisting of complete meals in foil trays, a sector it still leads, though it is now part of Campbell's.

Stouffers developed the high-priced luxury end of the complete meal market, with dishes like Lobster Newburg and Chicken à la King. It then capitalized on the trend towards healthy products by launching the successful 'Lean Cuisine' range, now worth over $400 million in sales. Stouffers is today part of Nestlés.

The frozen chip sector was developed and is now dominated by Ore-Ida, for many years part of Heinz.

All of these innovations stemmed from the consumer's need for extra convenience, and willingness to pay more for superior products.

In each case, outsiders saw the opportunities more clearly than Birds Eye, and exploited them successfully with less market knowledge and fewer resources.

To quote the words of Le Corbusier, the famous Swiss architect: 'Our epoch is fixing its own style day by day. It is there under our eyes. Eyes which do not see.'[3]

● Investigation – Beyond the Obvious

Before we move into the deeper realms of research, a word of warning is in order. Some companies proudly parade their use of the latest techniques of qualitative research as a sign of their 'sophistication'. But no one has yet proved any correlation between an organization's degree of sophistication and its level of profitability. Indeed, many of the top companies in *Management*

Today's growth and profitability leagues are more notable for their adherence to no-nonsense common-sense techniques than for the sophisticated methods used by their managements.

There is a danger that the pursuit of sophistication will be seen as an end in its own right, and obvious profit opportunities will be missed because the mass of information collected prevents a true understanding of basics. This is touched upon in the case above where, when Sara Lee innovated the frozen cake market, Birds Eye probably had more MBA graduates than Sara Lee had employees.

Effective use of advanced research tools is a proper weapon for offensive marketers, since these may uncover hidden opportunities and give them the chance to innovate. The emphasis, however, is on the word 'effective'. A lot of money is wasted on sophisticated research, not through any incompetence on the part of the researchers, but because the marketing executives commissioning it lack a definite purpose. Qualitative research is, after all, no more than a technique for striking into the unknown, and unless it is properly directed, it is unlikely to yield much useful information. One could compare it to drilling new land for oil – for every good strike of rich, new knowledge, there is a risk of finding a dry hole. So the simple message is that qualitative research should be used selectively and with finite objectives.

The most difficult innovations to research are those which either involve changes in usage habits or challenge long-held prejudices. For example, any research on the need for underarm deodorants or transistor radios thirty years ago would have shown the products had little potential. Today, research on liquids for cleaning clothes in cold water gets a cool response from some consumers, because the concept clashes with the traditional assumption that high temperature is essential.

By contrast, innovative solutions to well-established needs are much easier to research, because they do not require a basic change in habits or attitudes.

Market research is covered in more detail in Chapter 9.

● **The Flock Factor**

Offensive marketers carry out their own investigations, make up their corporate mind about what the information means, and create their own innovations. This book contrasts them favourably with maintenance marketers, who are satisfied with the status quo, absorbed with the routine of keeping things going and always trailing their competitors in a sadly out-of-breath condition. They are very inclined to copy successful moves by others and are responsible for what we may term the 'flock factor'.

The flock factor is a corollary of the well-known principle of economics that innovators who make super-normal profits will soon be joined by followers who will attempt to share in those profits. When an offensive marketer brings out a successful new idea, one can expect competitors to scurry behind like seagulls to a trawler's catch. Fortunately for justice and the free enterprise system, followers usually do less well than leaders. A study of fourteen pioneer products by A. C. Nielsen, a leading market research company,[4] showed that the first follower only achieved 47 per cent of the pioneer's volume three years later, and the second follower a mere 26 per cent. As Professor Porter observes from the USA:

> It is striking how many firms that were first movers have remained leaders for decades. In consumer goods, for example, such leading brands as Crisco, Ivory, Life Savers, Coca-Cola, Campbell's, Wrigley, Kodak, Lipton and Goodyear were leaders by the 1920s.[5]

The psychology of the flock factor is not very clear. One would guess that it stems partly from fear of being left out of a possible bonanza and partly from the paucity of really new ideas in circulation at any one time. While a board of directors will recognize that its organization cannot realistically innovate every new development in its markets (although this should be the constant aim), it will be wise to conduct a searching self-examination if it always finds itself among the followers.

Let us examine a couple of examples of the flock factor at work. They are worth looking at in detail because the flock factor is the complete opposite of offensive marketing and independent investigation. Fast-growing markets or sectors often lure followers into long-term unprofitability, as this example from the fruit-juice market demonstrates:

> *Until the later 1970s, pure fruit juice was a sleepy market in the UK, with low consumer and trade interest. Frozen concen-*

*trated juice never caught on as it did in the USA, and bottled
juice was relatively expensive, inconvenient to carry, and
synthetic in taste.*

*All this was changed by the introduction of the Tetra-Brik
packs, which made it possible to market a good-tasting product, with a three- to six-month shelf-life, at an attractive price.
This appealed to consumers, but the grocery trade liked Tetra-
Briks even more, since they could be stacked on pallets, were
unbreakable and, most importantly, did not require precious
chilled cabinet space. So the stage was set for massive expansion, and the value of fruit juice in brik packs grew from under
£10 million in 1976 to over £300 million today.*

*Del'Ora (Avana Group) entered the market quietly in 1975.
Adams' Just Juice was successfully launched in mid-1978, but
Del Monte went national in 1979 with heavy trade and
consumer spending, and replaced Just Juice as market leader
two years later. Mr Juicy (Unigate) and Five Alive (Coca-
Cola) were introduced in 1981. Over this period, grocery
multiples were busy bringing in private-label versions and by
the mid-1980s, massive increases in raw material prices put
paid to volume growth.*

*Now the dust has settled, it is doubtful whether any of the
pure fruit juice brands have made a cumulative profit in the
past five years. Fruit juice is hard to differentiate, all brik
packs look the same and the market is highly unpromising
for branding by manufacturers, though almost ideal for store
private labelling. (Private-label brands account for around 50
per cent of fruit juice value sales in grocery outlets.)*

*In the rush to participate in volume growth, the flock failed
to think through the profit implications.*

The same tendency to follow volume growth is a familiar sight in
'hi-tech' markets, especially ones where cost of entry is low:

*In 1981 Atari dominated the market for video games hardware
units and cartridges, with about two thirds of the business. At
this time only two other companies were making Atari-
compatible cartridges.*

*By 1982, there were eighteen companies in the field, includ-
ing big names like CBS, General Mills and Quaker Oats.[6]*

The excess industry capacity drove prices down, forced the major companies into heavy advertising of their cartridge products, and destroyed market profitability for all, including Atari.

Atari lost $540 million in 1983, and was divested by its parent company, Warner Communications, in the following year.

● **The Company Fitting Room**

Once the marketing executive has, through investigation, identified an unsatisfied consumer need, he then has to consider whether it is the kind of need his own company is well qualified to fulfil. Does the need exploit his company's skills, or do some of the companies already in the market possess strengths that it will be difficult to match? This question of 'fit' between company and market may not arise if the investigation concerns the improvement of existing products or concentrates on categories in which the firm is already represented. But even so close to home as this, the issue may come up.

For instance, an opportunity may have been unearthed in the higher-priced segment of a market when the company concerned only competes in the low-price sector. Is the company equipped to market higher-priced products successfully? This question should be considered very carefully before any decision is made to spend money on designing the new product.

Another issue which can arise at this stage is that of technology. The investigation may reveal a need which can only be fulfilled by technology new to the company. Again, the company should ponder whether the potential of the unfulfilled need seems great enough to justify an ultimate move into the new technology. The answer may be an immediate no or, if the project appears promising, a final decision may be postponed until some initial design work has been carried out.

The issue of company fit is most important when radically new markets are being considered. A company entering an entirely new category should not do so unless it has some definite point of superiority to counterbalance its lack of experience. However, in considering its suitability for new markets, it is best advised to take an offensive approach and not to underestimate its skills.

It is very easy to be intimidated by the apparent strength of the company in possession of the market, but, as the US frozen-food example showed (see p. 50), a determined competitor with a good idea usually has a sound chance of success even in unfamiliar markets. Objectivity is everything in these situations. A company should slightly, though only slightly, overestimate its strengths, while defining its weaknesses clearly – and honestly. Both strengths and weaknesses will obviously vary according to the market being considered. The subject of best fit between companies and markets is also reviewed in Parts 4 and 6 of this book, which cover strategy, new products and acquisitions.

Let us briefly look at two examples which illustrate degree of fit between companies and markets:

> *Procter & Gamble's skills lie in marketing fast-moving consumer goods, bought frequently by the consumer. Historically, it achieved its greatest success in product categories like detergents, anti-dandruff shampoo or toothpaste, where the quality of end-result performance could be objectively assessed.*
>
> *Procter & Gamble is most comfortable in markets where it can spend many years developing a demonstrably superior product, and, unlike viewers, likes nothing better than the side-by-side comparison of its own products versus a competitor on TV.*
>
> *In general, Procter & Gamble has succeeded in new markets that fit this profile. It has done well in the consumer paper market (toilet and facial tissues), in nappies with the successful though flagging Pampers brand, and in sanitary protection with the recently launched Always towel. In all these markets the criteria by which consumers judged product performance – softness, absorbency, absence of leakage – could be objectively assessed, just like the whiteness result of washing powders.*
>
> *When it has strayed outside this proven formula, Procter & Gamble has tended to struggle. Its performance in coffee and cake mixes has been unexciting, and efforts to enter the snack foods, soft drinks and biscuit markets have not so far succeeded. Food differs from cleaning and paper products in that it is harder to develop a clearly superior product, and even harder to avoid speedy copying by competitors.*

The other fit looked good at first, but became incompatible when the nature of the new market changed:

> *General Mills built its business as an excellent marketer of fast-moving consumer goods like cake mixes (Betty Crocker) and breakfast cereals. In the late 1960s it decided to move into toys, using its skills in marketing, especially to children. The fit seemed logical to many, since in those days the marketing approach had not penetrated the toy business, which also looked set for substantial growth.*
>
> *General Mills bought some well-established companies, with strong brand names like Parker Bros. (Monopoly) and Kenner. All went well for a number of years. General Mills became world leader in traditional toys, and was particularly strong in board games; sales and profits grew steadily.*
>
> *However, from the mid-1970s onwards, the character of the business began to change rapidly. First there were electronic games, where Parker Bros. made a successful though late entry in 1978. Then video games took over, and again General Mills scored well. But by 1985 they had fallen away, and it is estimated that Parker Bros.' sales halved between 1983 and 1985.*
>
> *Faced by mounting losses in electronics, General Mills tightened its grip over the Toy Division, installed new marketing recruits as product managers and became involved in the detail of product decisions. As one marketing manager recalled: 'We started to think we were in the presentation business rather than the toy business.' The mix between the steady market for consumer foods, and the volatile new combination of fashion and hi-tech in toys, no longer made sense. General Mills sold off its toy companies in late 1985.[7]*

Fit should also be considered in relation to distribution channels. Few things are more difficult for a company than launching brands into new or unfamiliar channels, whatever the strength of the product's customer appeal.

Many leading retailers and distributors have become effective marketers. Their requirements need to be considered as carefully as those of the ultimate consumer, using the same boomerang sequence of investigation, design, and sale. Having a product with high consumer appeal but low trade distribution is a frustrating and tantalizing experience, to which a growing band of marketing people are being introduced.

● So Where's the Profit?

To recap, thorough investigation of a business opportunity in the market involves answering three questions:

1. Is there a genuine need which is not properly satisfied at present?
2. Are we equipped as a company to fulfil it effectively?
3. Does it look profitable?

We have covered the first two questions and now comes the third. One is tempted to give the answer: 'Let's first design a product and then cost it.' In fact, this may be what one ultimately has to do in order to get a detailed picture of likely profitability. It should be possible, however, to draw broad conclusions about probable profit from the results of the investigation. The key point is that a proper investigation involves not only the location of an unsatisfied need, but also basic groundwork on likely profit. The sources may be rough but they are usually serviceable.

If you find that you will have to charge twice the normal price for something only marginally better than existing offerings, you should drop the project there and then and look for something more promising. Such an exercise will not pinpoint your likely profit with any accuracy, but it will safeguard you against sending the R & D department on a fool's errand that could not in any circumstances be commercially viable.

Do not be deceived into thinking that marketing is a science. It never will be, because it deals with consumers who are unpredictable, and with fragile ideas about the future which are hard to evaluate.

● Designing Benefits

We have completed our investigation and found an unfulfilled need which is profitable, fits well with company capabilities and seems likely to excite the customer. All we have to do now is to design a product or service to meet this identified need, and sell it!

The need pinpointed during investigation will resemble a police identikit picture rather than a finished portrait. The profile of the need is pieced together from a range of differing consumer opinions, interwoven with clues as to their wants, based on existing purchase behaviour in the market-place.

The role of design is to translate the identikit into a product personality, which consumers will ultimately recognize as the thing they envisaged initially when they expressed a need. Investigation translates a bundle of information into a need, and design turns it into a commercially viable benefit. The working of this process in the improvement of existing products and the development of new ones is illustrated in Table 7.

Table 7. *Needs and Benefits*

Consumer Need	Consumer Benefit Designed
Portable personal audio unit	Sony Walkman
Drip-free painting	Dulux Solid Emulsion Paint
Superior road-holding for drivers	Four-wheel drive (Audi Quattro)
More convenient payment for Marks & Spencer customers	Marks & Spencer Charge Card

The marketing department is responsible for defining relevant consumer needs, and for drawing up a brief to guide the R & D or design departments in their work; the tightness of this brief will depend on the extent of the technical challenge. If the consumer need is very specific, and the technical task a simple one – as in developing a cigarette to compete in a new pricing segment – the marketing brief for R & D or design would closely define the nature, quality and target cost of the product in detail. But if the research task is to achieve a major new invention, the marketing brief should leave the means for achieving the objective very open, and allow great latitude in time and expense.

In designing benefits successfully, the marketing manager needs to have four batons in his knapsack: imagination, technology, product design and common sense. Just one of these may be sufficient, but in some cases all four will be brought into play.

These batons are related to the examples in Table 7. The Walkman required an imaginative leap in the first place, and this was enhanced by compact and handsome design; the product used existing technology in a new way. First marketed in July 1979, the Sony Walkman has already exceeded 10 million sales units.

Its origin and development were far from conventional. Sony Chairman Akio Morita used to be a frequent flyer to the USA, his main market. He observed that the quality of stereo on planes was poor and the Sony Walkman technology was originally developed to provide better personal stereo for global businessmen. Once the technology was available, Sony had the vision to spot the application to the younger, pop, culture.

Dulux Solid Emulsion Paint solved an obvious consumer problem, which had been well known for decades. New technology made the solution possible, and good design highlighted the product's convenience in use.

Four-wheel drive for passenger cars, pioneered by Audi, and now being applied to less expensive cars, involved an upgrading of existing technology. This was allied to design features, like the aggressively flared arches on the Quattro, which fitted the high-performance image of the cars.

The Marks & Spencer Charge Card has been highly successful, but was pure common sense. Neither imagination, new technology nor superior design were present.

Of the four batons, good design is the most neglected.[8] There is no excuse for this neglect in the UK, where the leading design firms are among the best in the world. Good design can improve convenience and function, and enhance visual appeal. Well-designed products are often cheaper to make than badly designed ones, simply because they have been well thought-out. As Kotler and Rath point out, designers are frequently brought in too late, when the product is already in development, whereas they should be introduced at the concept-testing stage.

The example below illustrates how imaginative investigation and good design can be used in creating product benefits:

Designing Benefits

Duracell is a division of Dart & Kraft and its main product is a premium-priced but long-lasting range of batteries. In the late 1970s Duracell UK was investigating how to expand its product range. It was interested in product categories which could use Duracell batteries, were under-marketed and would fit the company's existing distribution network.

Research identified an opportunity for a range of products from pocket-lights to general work-lights, with common benefits of directional light beams and ability to use while keeping the hands free. The products would be superior to and more expensive than competitive offerings, with retail price points from £3 for the pocket-light to £10 for the work-light.

Towards the end of 1979 an outside design company was selected and briefed. The words 'portable light sources', rather than 'torch', in the brief emphasized that Duracell was seeking a highly distinctive product range.

As a first stage, the design company developed hand-made concepts, in perspex, and painted in black and yellow. These were hall-tested among consumers (see p. 210), and the reaction was favourable.

Development was then concentrated on the pocket- and home-torches which would sell at £3 to £4. The design company refined the concept, made working prototypes for testing against competitive products, and remained heavily involved in translating prototypes into factory production. Manufacturing costs were estimated at this point, two years ahead of launch, and ultimately proved to be highly accurate. The numerous meetings to oversee the conversion into a production item were all chaired by the Marketing Director.

The range was launched under the Durabeam brand name between 1982 and 1985 in the UK, and introduced into the USA from 1983 onwards. All four products in the range – a Tough Torch was added later – had similar performance characteristics of directional beam, longevity, free standing, and modern design in black and yellow colours.

Before the launch, Duracell was concerned that it was overpricing the products, but the reverse proved to be the case. For example, the Year 1 volume estimate for the Work Torch retailing at £13 was 140,000 units, maximum production was 400,000, and actual orders were 600,000–800,000 units. A *pleasant surprise for Duracell was that the two least expensive models became widely purchased as gifts.*

As stressed previously, investigation and design can be equally fruitful in recasting an existing brand as in launching a new one. The following case history of Chum dog food, one of the most successfully marketed post-war consumer brands, illustrates a variety of things. It shows the importance of psychological benefits, and is a classic example of market segmentation. It also demonstrates the principle illustrated by Archimedes in his bath – that the value of information depends on eyes that see and ears that hear.

> *Chum dog food was introduced in the early 1960s by Petfoods Ltd to counter Spiller's Kennomeat, but was an undistinctive product. It achieved only moderate success and by 1963, when a new brand manager was appointed, the Chum share was declining.*
>
> *The new man, who had no prior experience of the pet-food market, picked up in conversation with one of the company vets that pedigree dogs had different nutritional requirements from other dogs. On checking available consumer research, he discovered that almost 50 per cent of owners claimed their dogs were pedigree and that this percentage was growing. Consequently, it was decided to reposition Chum as 'the food specially formulated for pedigree dogs'.*
>
> *The R & D department discovered that this claim could be legally validated by incorporating large doses of thiamin into the product, since pedigree dogs are more highly strung and sensitive than others. The product was improved in other ways – by stiffening up the consistency, putting in large pieces of liver and making it look more like a meat loaf. A quality package and new advertising were also developed to underline the new claim, and the brand's price was increased.*
>
> *Gradually Pedigree Chum's market share stopped falling and began to climb. It gained brand leadership in the mid-1960s, and now, in the mid-1980s, has sales in excess of £100 million a year.*
>
> *The strength of the Pedigree Chum approach was that it appealed to the owners of pedigree dogs, who saw it as a tailor-made product, but also to pet owners who regarded their dogs as of pedigree quality or wished to give their mongrels the*

> *'best' food there was. Its positioning enabled Pedigree Chum to establish itself as the quality product in the category. Eventually Petfoods Ltd followed psychological logic and changed its name to the present Pedigree Petfoods Ltd.*

Finally, benefits need to be designed for the retailer or distributor, based on a clear understanding of their requirements. They should take into account how the product fits in with the retailer's existing range, bulk-handling characteristics and utilization of space in the warehouse and selling area.

> *In the past Procter & Gamble has appeared to take the view that the retailer is a distributor linking manufacturer and consumer, rather than a customer with specific needs. Consequently, Procter & Gamble products tend to be designed solely with the ultimate consumer in mind. Procter & Gamble feels confident that retailers will be forced to stock their new products because they offer good value for money and are heavily advertised and promoted.*
>
> *As retailers have increasingly succeeded in developing their own brand identity, and, especially in the USA, found reliable ways to assess internal handling costs by product, Procter & Gamble's traditional approach has become less tenable.*
>
> *There are clear signs that Procter & Gamble is now changing its position and starting to redesign products with retailers' needs in mind. For instance, in 1984, Ivory Liquid in the USA was redesigned to take up less shelf space, and Tide was reformulated into a smaller box, allowing retailers to use their space more efficiently.*

● Is the Profit Still There?

We established that only a rough estimate of likely profit for a planned new project could be made at the investigation stage. No such excuses are available once the benefits have been designed; now we have an entity that can be accurately costed and the marketing plan can be drawn up in detail, to determine pricing, trade margins, and advertising and promotion spending, all of which affect the profit on the bottom line. The requirement for offensive marketers is to design a profit for their company, as well as a new benefit for consumers, and the two should proceed as far as possible in harness.

The rough preliminary marketing plan, drawn up at the investigation stage as the basis for determining the product and package cost target in the design brief, should be gradually refined as the design reaches completion. The unexciting but essential work of drawing up alternative marketing plans should be undertaken, working on the principle that the price of the brand and the marketing support needed to launch and sustain it must be determined by the realities of the market-place. Ignore this principle and you will have no choice but to price your brand on a 'cost-plus' basis – the cost of the product and package which R & D produces, plus whatever you need for marketing funds and profit. It would be a remarkable coincidence if the resulting retail price happened to be one that the market would bear.

Profits on new products or services have an unendearing habit of disappearing without notice. Marketing people need to watch them every step of the way and particularly closely during the initial R & D design stage, and when the transition is made from pilot plant to full-scale production. We saw how this was successfully handled in the Duracell example (see p. 61), and how the Marketing Director was heavily involved in the process.

● **Validate the Design or Cut Your Losses**

We mentioned earlier that the link-up between investigation and design was not usually particularly smooth and that misinterpretation of needs could occur. As soon as the product or package is completed, it should be checked back with the consumer through research. It is so much better to discover at this point that the design does not meet the consumer need than a year later, when capital equipment may have been irrevocably committed and heavy advertising investments made. If the product developed has no point of difference or superiority over existing brands, go back to square one and start again, or discontinue the project.

This leads us to the question of sunk cost. Companies are often reluctant to drop projects on which large amounts of money have already been spent, because the executives are unwilling to admit that the expenditures have been unproductive. There is also a misconception that, in some strange way, heavy investment on a project automatically endows it with superior consumer appeal, or an above-average chance of success.

However, it is best to be honest and kill the project. If there's no oil below, it doesn't matter how deep a hole you dig. Some wastage is inevitable in trying to innovate new or improved products – all the checks and balances can hope to achieve is early identification of dead projects, and speedy action to minimize losses on them.

● Selling – The Return of the Boomerang

When our boomerang completes its return journey to the consumer, the marketer always hopes it will receive a rapturous welcome, as indicated by that arbiter of careers, the market share chart. Selling, in the broader sense intended here, embraces everything that influences the trade or the consumer to buy the product or service. It includes trade margins and merchandising, trade and consumer promotions, packaging and advertising.

This is, of course, a slight oversimplification because, as already noted, packaging development and advertising can also be a major factor in designing consumer benefits (remember Chum and Durabeam). Advertising's role is to get across the product benefit, with the intention of creating favourable consumer attitudes towards it. Promotion and strong merchandising bring short-term purchase incentives to the consumer's attention, and are designed to convert favourable attitudes into cash. In addition, the product must have sufficient trade appeal to ensure its widespread availability at the point of purchase.

● Summary

Offensive marketing follows a boomerang sequence of investigation, design and sale to transform consumer and distributor needs into profitable products or services. If this sequence is to be effective, the five elements of offensive marketing as summarized in POISE should be constantly applied. But it begins and ends with *profit*.

Investigation is necessary to discover what the consumer wants and market research is the eyes and ears of the commercial firm. Investigation may turn up obvious needs which other companies have missed because they were blinded by the traditional thinking of their industry. Alternatively, sophisticated research techniques may be used. In either case, it is important for a company to create its own innovations through independent investigation, rather than resorting to the 'follow-my-leader' approach epitomized by the flock factor. Thorough investigation involves not only discovering an unsatisfied consumer need, but also checking that it can be profitable and that it fits the company's skills, because this is the key to success.

The role of design is to translate the need defined by the investigation into a product personality. The need may be for improved product performance or for psychological benefits, and the design may require years of basic R & D, or be very simple to accomplish. Offensive marketers design a profit for their company as well as a benefit for the consumer and distributor, and will constantly check back with the consumer that their design has correctly interpreted the need.

The return of the boomerang comes with selling, which includes everything that influences the trade or the consumer to buy the product.

2 | *Offensive*

3 | *Offensive Attitudes*

● **The Right Attitudes Must Start at the Top**

Some of the topics covered in this chapter are outside the normal scope of a book on marketing. But this book is not about marketing departments or marketing activities, it is about the marketing approach. Whether or not a company adopts offensive marketing is decided by the chairman and the board of directors, not by marketing people. Chairmen following the offensive approach have to make hard decisions about attitude to quality, investment, costs and the consumer. In difficult times, with the familiar pressures to cut back on advertising, R & D, product quality and capital investment, willpower and courage as well as toughness are needed. Marketing people should always aim to influence the board, and energetically lead the execution of the marketing approach.

Offensive attitudes are a set of shared values and approaches, grounded in a commitment to customer service and low-cost operation. They give companies cohesion and momentum, and employees pride and a sense of mission. These attitudes underpinning 'offensive marketing' are not to be confused with 'aggressive marketing'. One sometimes sees headlines in the marketing press announcing that Company X is launching an 'aggressive' marketing campaign. The article is usually decorated with a photograph of the perpetrator, who is quite likely to be a galloping midget.

The article will describe how money is being thrown at a problem by cutting prices, launching a huge promotion or trebling advertising spending. The informed reader can often recognize the desperate throw of an ill-prepared marketer following a leader too late, or attempting to disguise a product's lack of competitive edge by making a lot of noise. Offensive marketers may well be aggressive, but they are also thoughtful, imaginative and forward-thinking.

● The Seven Spokes of the Offensive Approach

While a bicycle wheel with seven spokes would be offensive only to the cyclist, the analogy is a useful way of communicating the seven attitudes which comprise the offensive approach, as it illustrates the links between all seven elements. Innovation depends on long-term outlook and investment; value depends on innovation; vision moves the wheel; and each of the elements connects with the centre, to build a core of offensive

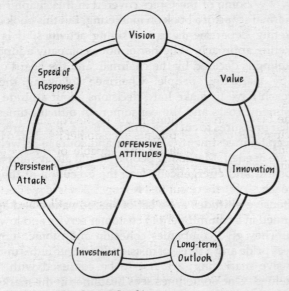

Figure 5. The Seven Spokes

attitudes (see Figure 5). The remainder of this chapter will cover these seven elements individually.

Spoke no. 1: vision and purpose

To succeed in the long-term, most businesses need a vision of how they will change and improve in the future. This vision gives the business vitality and motivates those who work in it. In reality, the word 'vision' is too large to describe many of the rather humdrum aspirations which have motivated many successful businesses. However, vision is used because, despite its abuse, it is the word that is generally understood in this context.

Visions are usually created by individuals and not committees, so it is not surprising that many company visions reflect the insight of one person with sufficient influence to impose his or her will on an organization. Such a person may be the founder of the business, like An Wang at Wang Laboratories. Or they may be part of a family dynasty, where successive generations have built on and developed the original vision, like Sir Marcus Sieff of Marks & Spencer, or Shoichiro Toyoda of Toyota; or a powerful chairman, who achieves influence by personality or performance, with little equity stake, like Roger Smith at General Motors or Sir John Harvey-Jones at I C I.

While visions are usually created by individuals, they can be continued and refined by successor groups or organizations. If General Johnson returned from the dead, he would be pleased at the way Johnson & Johnson has developed in the past twenty years.

The best business visions relate to the consumer and correctly anticipate future developments in customer needs. To be effective, visions have to be realistic and capable of motivating or even inspiring employees, like the Johnson & Johnson credo:

> We believe our first responsibility is to the doctors, nurses, patients and to the mothers and all others who use our products and services.
> In meeting their needs, everything we do must be of high quality. We must constantly strive to reduce our costs in order to maintain reasonable prices . . .[1]

A clear business vision will look into the future and allow a business to prepare for change ahead of its competitors. Many businesses develop competent forecasts of the future environment, but fail to confront the implications of it.

Anheuser-Busch, the leading American brewer, is aware of the growing concern about the abuse of alcohol. With mixed motives of genuine altruism and sound business sense, the company appears to see itself as 'The Largest and Most Responsible Brewer'.

> *In 1984 Anheuser-Busch sold 64 million barrels of beer for a 34·6 per cent share of the American beer market, well ahead of the 20 per cent held by Miller, the number two. Anheuser-Busch is increasing its share of the market, but also taking active steps to encourage responsible consumption of beer. These include:*
>
> *— financial support for organizations campaigning against drunk-driving.*
> *— funding of medical research on alcohol abuse.*
> *— Model Employee Assistance Programs for those troubled by drug or alcohol problems.*
> *— a nationwide consumer education programme 'Know when to say When.'*
>
> *Anheuser-Busch was the first American brewery to launch a low-alcohol beer, in late 1984. Although it is proving a small market sector to date, Anheuser-Busch dominates it, and is likely to continue to market a low-alcohol beer.*
>
> *Anheuser-Busch has a strong business momentum, and is well placed to respond to future changes in consumer attitudes or new legislative requirements.*

Weaker business visions may be unrealistic or irrelevant to customer needs. The Xerox corporate vision sounded good in the early 1970s, but has proved unrealistic. The company has plunged from being a superstar of the 1960s into a laggard of the 1980s.

> *Xerox was a spectacular growth company in the 1960s, and in 1970 the Chairman defined its purpose as 'to find the best means to bring order and discipline to information'. While in practice few security analysts knew what this elegantly crafted sentence meant, many heads nodded. Over the past fifteen years Xerox has made numerous unsuccessful diversification efforts, including educational publishing and computers, but has never been a leading player in word-processing.*

Visions must be relevant to the customer and capable of generating sufficient profit to sustain the continuation of the vision:

> *Control Data, a $5-billion computer and financial services company, was founded in the late 1950s by William Norris. His vision was: 'To address society's major unmet needs as profitable business opportunities.'*
>
> *In the past fifteen years Control Data has moved six plants to inner cities, created 100 small business centres, trained 5,000 disadvantaged people and offered computer-based education in twenty prisons.*[2]
>
> *Unfortunately, by the mid-1980s, Control Data's product range had become tired, and in 1985 the company's losses were $567 million.*

Spoke no. 2: value

It is not easy to deliver superior value to customers consistently over time, and strong commitment every day at all levels of management is necessary to achieve it. The case study on Sainsbury in the Introduction (see p. 21) illustrated this. Better value is achieved by offering customers a superior combination of product benefit and price. Any company which really cares about superior value will constantly check how it is doing, and stop at nothing to correct any backsliding.

Focus on value includes a relentless drive to improve quality:

> *Jaguar's success in radically raising factory quality is well known. Its stress on quality extends well beyond the factory gate. Recently, Jaguar instituted its franchise development fund in the UK. Dealer margin was reduced from 18·5 per cent to 15 per cent with 3·5 per cent held back. Every quarter all 150 dealers are assessed. The assessment includes letters from Jaguar drivers and a monthly consumer research survey of 200 Jaguar owners.*
>
> *Dealers considered to be responsible for inadequacies can be 'fined' part or all of the 3·5 per cent hold-back. Good dealers are not only paid the 3·5 per cent, but also qualify for an incentive payment which must be used to improve customer facilities.*
>
> *What Jaguar has done is to re-deploy part of the dealer*

> *margin into a quality improvement programme, at no cost to itself, but with considerable benefit to the customer.*[3]

The market regularly provides clues, hints, or even screaming headlines about each company's value offering. Here are some things to look at and questions to ask:

1. What is the sales trend of existing products in existing accounts? Sales figures are the mirror of a product's value.
2. What is the level and trend of market share? Again, look at existing products in existing accounts. Declining product value can be obscured by gains from new distribution or line extensions.
3. How do your products or services perform when *objectively* assessed by your customers against direct competitors?
4. Can your products sustain a price premium? If not, are they really better?

The gold standard in value is to provide a superior product and be a low-cost operator. This results in both satisfied customers and high profits. IBM has often met this standard:

> *Three of IBM's five key business goals relate to value. They are product leadership through superior technology, reliability and value; superior efficiency not just in manufacturing, but also in R & D, marketing and servicing; and superior quality. The achievement of these three value objectives are the basis for meeting IBM's other two goals – market share and profitability.*

Spoke no. 3: innovation

The offensive attitude to innovation is the determination to lead rather than follow. 'Innovation' is a word often used to describe high-profile breakthroughs – like the Apple II personal computer, or the Zantac anti-ulcer drug. In this book it is used more broadly, to embrace any improvement in customer value or in cost of operation, the two arms of offensive marketing. Therefore, while the Japanese were not particularly innovative in R & D terms in the

1970s, they were innovative in production and engineering techniques. This enabled them to market parity or better products at lower cost.

Innovation is most effective when viewed as a continuing process, applied to every area of the business. It is much easier to translate a bundle of individually minor developments into a major step forward than to seek and find the breakthrough innovation:

> *The UK Confectionery Division of Mars has not launched a successful new product since the late 1960s, when Twix was introduced. It has, however, pursued an innovative approach both to its existing business and in probing new markets.*
>
> *On the confectionery side, it has led its competitors in improving customer value, feeding back cost savings into lower prices or bigger bars. For instance, when cocoa prices fell sharply in the early 1980s, Mars moved to a 10 per cent larger bar with no price increase. The competition eventually followed and Mars increased bar size further and then came out with the '50th Anniversary Mars Biggest Bar Ever'. For the past decade Mars has also innovated in pack sizes, with multi-packs for home consumption, fun-size bags for children's parties, and a 100-gramme king-size bar.*
>
> *These value innovations 'up front' were fuelled by cost and efficiency innovations in manufacturing, selling and distribution on a continuous drip basis. This strengthened Mars's position as a low-cost operator.*
>
> *Mars's more ambitious innovations – an attempt to enter the snack-food market with a cheese wafer called Sprint, and a sortie into small chocolate cakes with Glee – failed. But its day-to-day trickle of minor innovations in confectionery helped the company gain market share and maintain impressive profit growth.*

As the Mars example highlights, it pays to pursue both the daily drip-feed innovation and to invest in the potential 'big bang', which can radically expand customer franchise if successful. The balance struck between the two depends on the kind of category a company is in. For instance, if Mars had been operating in a market with rapid shifts in technology like office equipment, its lack of major product innovation would have proved a serious weakness. So how does a company create an atmosphere where innovation thrives?

The daily drip-feed innovation is primarily a question of frame of mind, which depends on senior management example and emphasis. The 'big-bang' type is more difficult, because it involves risks both for individual employees and for businesses. To ensure that people will stick their necks out and champion new ideas, large companies need the right structure (see Chapter 4) and a supportive attitude to risk-takers.

To succeed as innovators, *businesses* should be driven by technology and fear, *individuals* by hope and excitement. Let us look first at technology and fear, strange bedfellows. At the end of 1984 *Fortune* magazine polled a large sample of American business school professors, consultants and security analysts, and developed a list of 'Eight Masters of Innovation'.[4] It then interviewed these companies to discover what made them successful innovators, and concluded that:

1. The driving forces were commitment to new technology and fear of being outpaced by competitors.
2. The most effective structure was lean, decentralized units, where engineers, marketers and finance experts were thrown together in tight groups.
3. Top management needs access to raw data rather than bowdlerized digests censored by middle management.
4. There has to be clear direction to channel and prioritize the flood of ideas.
5. It is better to start small with new innovations so as to control the risk. Put your toe into the water, check back with the consumer and then slide your ankle in. Don't jump in at the deep end with a large splash, because you may never reappear.

This is all good common sense, and worth more than the academic meanderings of professors of entrepreneurship, or the flashy 'intra-preneurship' programmes trumpeted by some large American companies.

The driving forces of technology and fear, however, have to be converted into profitable new developments by individuals. This is where the hope and excitement come in. Assuming that they have the right organizational structure, businesses wishing to be innovative have to encourage, recognize and reward risk-takers. How well a company does this can often be answered by asking three questions:

1. What are the major innovations we have achieved in the past ten years?
2. Who was mainly responsible?
3. What happened to those people and where are they now?

This exercise was recently conducted in a large multi-billion-pound organization with the following results:

> *This company made two major innovations in the past ten years. One was a new approach to market segmentation, picked up from observation of overseas practice. The other was new pricing positioning. In both cases, the critical skill was not generating the idea, but driving it through the organization and overcoming initial scepticism.*
>
> *Most people had no difficulty in identifying the three individuals most responsible for the two breakthrough approaches. Of these three, one retired in middle management, another has been passed over for promotion for the second time, and the third is now the equivalent of Ambassador to Outer Mongolia.*

The most difficult person I have ever had to manage was also the most innovative, and produced two breakthrough ideas. But many companies still hanker after that big new idea which has been thoroughly tested and involves no risk; and they still expect innovators to wear dark suits, have a wife and 2·3 children, drink orange juice and jog every morning.

One company which is famous for successful innovation, and was unsurprisingly in *Fortune*'s Eight Masters of Innovation, is 3M. In 1984 3M had sales of $7·7 billion and pre-tax profits of $1·3 billion (16·8 per cent). 3M offers some quite straightforward reasons for its success in innovation:

1. 3M regards itself not as an $8-billion company, but as over 100 individual profit centres around the world. Businesses are kept small and authority delegated.
2. R & D spending is kept at a minimum of 4·5 per cent of sales, year in year out, in good times and bad.

3. Researchers are allowed to spend 15 per cent of working time on projects of their own choosing.
4. 3M encourages risk-taking. 'Our people know if a new idea doesn't work out . . . they'll still be respected and have a job.'[5]
5. There is a continual sharing of information between individuals in business units and between different business units.

Finally, it is still true that necessity is the mother of invention and, if the right offensive attitudes are present, innovation can spring from disaster, as the following example shows:

In the early 1970s a new Managing Director took over at Playtex France. Playtex was one of three or four companies, all with market shares between 6 per cent and 9 per cent, vying for leadership of the lingerie market. In each of the previous three years there had been a different market leader.

Unfortunately, the Playtex work force then went on strike and the company rapidly ran out of product to sell. The Managing Director still had a large sales force and asked himself: 'How can I use this sales force effectively when there is no product to deliver?' His answer was to concentrate all sales-force effort on new accounts, promising delivery in six to eight weeks' time, when he thought the strike would be settled. He developed a quite sophisticated system of commando selling, in which each salesman worked on another man's territory, as part of a commando group consisting of four men under a manager, all staying in the same hotel. This system succeeded and, with refinements, was later used by Playtex all over the world.

The Managing Director then got to work on his American management and persuaded them to let him market beige-coloured bras, for which there was a large demand in France. Previously Playtex would sell any colour of bra anywhere in the world, as long as it was white.

In 1971, aided by two outstanding Sales Managers and a resourceful Production Director, he managed to move Playtex market share from 8 per cent to 15 per cent, and increased sales by 85 per cent. Playtex's market share is now in the 20s, and its leadership position in France has never been seriously challenged since.

Like many other offensive attitudes, successful innovation owes as much to willpower and persistence as to imagination.

Spoke no. 4: long-term outlook

Almost every company chairman in the Western world would like to take a longer-term outlook on his business, but few are given the opportunity. Short-term performance pressures have become intense, and a year is now a long time in the life of a company.

Recently, Marks & Spencer had a 'bad' half-year in which profits only grew modestly. Security analysts were almost unanimous in suggesting that Marks & Spencer had lost its touch and perhaps its way. Six months later Marks & Spencer produced half-yearly profits up by 22 per cent and the financial press was full of articles saying the company was back on track. But how much really changed over that half-year period in the life of a hundred-year-old company?

One year also seems to be the maximum time-span most pension funds and investment institutions will consider, because they themselves are subject to the pressures of short-term performance tables. A company chairman may well hold forth to his colleagues in the morning about the short-sightedness of the stock market, then go to an afternoon meeting of pension fund trustees and express dissatisfaction with their investment results over the past six months.

The effect of these short-term pressures is to:

1. Encourage milkers to silently bleed long-term assets for short-term profits. They can cut advertising, R & D and investment, and drive prices up unreasonably.
2. Force a focus on tactics rather than long-term strategy.
3. Shift priority from product-led innovations, using design and technology, to skilful use of 'marketing' tools to sustain products lacking any long-term competitive edge.[6]
4. Discourage investments which require a long-term view and can be justified only on this basis.

The problem is obvious and widely acknowledged. Patient capitalism and a long-term focus are often instanced as two of the main reasons for Japanese business success.[7] But the conditions which make this possible in Japan – different financing methods, life-time employment and greater patience – do not seem to be transplantable to the West. So we may as well accept that short-term pressures will remain strong and will probably intensify. Faced with this reality, how can a company foster a long-term outlook? Among the array of less-than-perfect answers, here are some of the better ones:

- remove the revolving door from the offices of managing directors, especially in subsidiary companies belonging to international groups. This would help to stop the operation being run solely to further the short-term career aspirations of the incumbent.
- fully exploit the possibilities of asset-led marketing (see Chapter 1).
- ensure that you are a low-cost operator, so as to survive or win a price war if one occurs.
- follow a highly conservative accounting policy. Over-reserve in the good years, so as to keep grain to bring out in the poor years. There is a great deal of judgement exercised in accounting and it can be used in your favour without cheating.
- accumulate a bank of fully tested ideas, so that you can draw a few more out at a time of crisis.
- be prepared to make a heavy investment if it is essential to your long-term health, even though it may result in temporary profit shortfalls.

'The foundation of Procter & Gamble's operating philosophy is to manage the business with long-term growth as the primary goal, rather than focusing on profit objectives in any single year.'[8]

Spoke no. 5: investment

The level of a company's investment is the best measure of its commitment to a long-term outlook. We are defining investment as the funds necessary to renew and improve all assets. The most important of these assets are:

1. Existing brands and customer franchises. For most companies, especially consumer product ones, these are the most important assets of all. It is quite common for companies to pay two to three times financial asset value (i.e. fixed capital, receivables less payables, etc.) in making acquisitions. The difference is 'goodwill' or marketing assets.

   Philip Morris paid $5·6 billion for General Foods, whose financial assets were valued at $2·8 billion. Its valuation of General Foods' brands and management skills was therefore also $2·8 billion.

   The investments necessary to keep brands and products in good shape include market research, information systems, R & D, advertising and sales promotion.
2. New products.
3. Plant renewal and improvement. This would include engineering R & D, a frequently neglected area.
4. Training and skill development.

Investment obviously needs to be directed to the right opportunities. For instance, Kodak has spent heavily and consistently on R & D, at about 5 per cent of sales for many years, but results have been disappointing.

Spoke no. 6: persistent attack

A great deal has been made of the analogies between marketing and military strategies in recent years. They are often described under the heading 'Marketing Warfare'. Some of these analogies are useful, and they are covered in Part 4. Clausewitz, the nineteenth-century German general, would be surprised to discover that his book, *On War*, has become one of the most quoted texts in marketing.

Because no war is ever won through persistent defence, an essential element of the offensive approach is persistent attack. This does not mean that a company should be attacking on all fronts all the time, since this would be impractical and unprofitable. At any moment, a company is likely to be attacking on some fronts, defending on others, and perhaps retreating or exiting on fronts where the prospects for success look dim. What is meant by 'persistent attack' is that the overall focus of a company's activity should be to attack and win. Any defensive effort is therefore part of a long-term plan which will culminate in a fresh attack, just as Montgomery always viewed defence as a temporary situation, part of an overall plan which would culminate in attack when the time and place were right.

There are several advantages for a company in encouraging an attacking frame of mind:

> – increased motivation; great satisfaction can be achieved by attacking and winning. Most people are prepared to hold a defensive position for some time, but to do so for years without any offensive sorties is discouraging.
>
>   Companies with the largest market shares, like IBM in computers, Kellogg's in breakfast cereals and Kodak in photography, have a great deal to defend, but follow an overall mode of attacking to gain more ground.
> – planned attack keeps competitors under pressure, forcing them to react and reducing their ability to frame sound long-term plans.
> – since no company likes to lose a battle, a tradition of attacking creates internal pressures to remain competitive in product performance and cost. Persistent attack makes most sense when allied to the other six spokes of the wheel, especially value and innovation.

Companies following the offensive approach respond to setbacks by counterattack, and have the will to fight back even from disaster:

> *Procter & Gamble decided to enter the tampon market in the late 1960s and by the mid-1970s successfully test-marketed a unique and superior tampon called Rely. As Rely moved to new areas in the USA in the late 1970s, it was still achieving percentage market shares in the low 20s, even though Playtex and Tampax had by then improved their products.*
>
> *Disaster struck in the early 1980s, when alleged cases of toxic shock began to appear, and Rely became the focus of product liability suits. Procter & Gamble withdrew Rely and took a $75-million write-off in 1981.*

Having exited from tampons, Procter & Gamble opened a new front in the feminine protection market by launching Always, a thin and more absorbent towel. Aiming for a 20 per cent share, Always has already achieved 17 per cent in Year 1, equivalent to sales of $125 million.

There are times when companies dedicated to persistent attack will withdraw from markets and concentrate their attack on more promising targets. Such issues are covered in Chapter 7, 'Developing Winning Strategies'.

Spoke no. 7: speed of response

Speed of response is a test of a company's fitness. An offensive marketer will respond quickly to changes in customer needs or in the business environment, and will counterattack competitive thrusts. Slow response usually indicates a problem in organizational structure or attitudes.

At one time it was fairly accurate to describe the big company as a supertanker, where the swing of the wheel only produced a slight reaction five miles later. The small business was characterized as the cruiser, manoeuvring quickly round the supertankers. Fifteen years ago this was probably true, and it certainly showed in profits. At that time *Management Today* annual league tables showed profit margins increasing as company size reduced. In the UK at least, this is now no longer so and the same leagues show that larger companies enjoy similar or better margins than smaller ones.

Many of the more effective large companies are seeking and gaining the advantages of bigness and smallness. For them, a more accurate analogy is a fleet of cruisers serviced by a battleship. We saw under 'Innovation' above how 3M achieved this, and Johnson & Johnson has a similar approach. BTR and Hanson Trust devolve autonomy to operating subsidiaries, which have clearly defined financial objectives. However, to combine the benefits of large and small, a business needs strong systems and financial controls. Otherwise the cruisers will be sailing in different directions or colliding with the battleship.

Even fairly centralized large companies can react surprisingly fast, especially in a crisis:

For decades Nabisco had ruled the roost in the US cookie and cracker market, with a share of over 40 per cent, well ahead of Keebler, a subsidiary of United Biscuits (UK).

In the early 1980s two very formidable new competitors entered this market, with distinctive ranges of cookies. PepsiCo's Frito-Lay Division, brand leader in snack foods, and backed by a 12,000-strong sales force, launched Grandma's Cookies, a high-moisture product well geared to Frito-Lay's skills in selling short-life merchandise. Then, shortly afterwards, Procter & Gamble introduced a similar type of cookie, crisp on the outside and chewy on the inside, with a long life, and supposedly protected by patent (supposedly, because the whole question of this patent is subject to legal proceedings in the USA).

Nabisco and Keebler both looked in deep trouble, but responded very quickly. Within six to nine months, both had introduced a soft cookie range, and Nabisco has now become the leader in this sector, though at considerable short-term cost.

However, for every 3M, Nabisco or Keebler, there are still many supertankers about – and the nimble small business should be capable of responding more quickly than even quite fit, larger competitors:

Sooner Foods, now owned by Rowntree-Mackintosh, started Riley's Potato Crisps as an outgrowth of a fish and chip business selling locally in the Scunthorpe area. In 1974 the present Chairman had just graduated from university and encountered the company. He saw potential and decided to join, to the puzzlement of his contemporaries who were starting with Unilever, IBM or Shell. At this time Sooner's sales were under £1 million a year, in a highly competitive market dominated by Imperial Group (Golden Wonder), United Biscuits (KP), and Associated Biscuits (Smiths).

Over the next ten years the market was placed under further pressure by the successful expansion of Walkers from its Midlands stronghold. But over the same period Sooner Foods increased sales to £35 million a year and gained a 6 per cent share of the snacks/crisps market against much larger and better-financed competitors. This result was achieved through

*a soundly targeted strategy, but Sooner's main strength was
its lean form and astonishing speed of response.*

Just as the criteria by which a firm's offensive marketing rating
can be judged (see Table 2, p. 25), so too can its rating on offensive
attitudes. Table 8 should enable you to measure your own
company's rating.

Table 8. *Criteria for Rating a Business on Offensive
Attitudes*

	Maximum score	Your score
Clear, realistic and motivating vision of the future, understood and accepted by most employees	15	
A strong commitment to providing superior value to customers, backed by low-cost operation	20	
Strong emphasis on innovation throughout the business, both daily trickle and 'big bang', in the right balance for the industry. Stress on technology, support, recognition, and reward for successful innovators. Structure where innovation can flourish	15	
Ability to achieve required short-term results, but strong focus on long-term objectives	10	
Commitment to continued investment in all assets, like brands, people, new products and equipment, even when faced by strong short-term pressures	15	
Overall focus on attacking competition, but at carefully chosen times and places	15	
Fast, good-quality response to new opportunities or competitive threats	10	
Total	100	

● **Summary**

It is well known that superior results may be drawn from average material, or that very able people can produce poor results. One of the keys to performance is attitude, and this in turn is moulded by the leadership, motivation and working environment provided by senior management.

Attitudes are, therefore, one of the keystones of the offensive marketing approach. The seven spokes of the wheel leading to offensive attitudes are vision, value, innovation, long-term outlook, investment, persistent attack and speed of response. Each of these spokes is connected, and together they summarize a set of offensive attitudes which should lead to dynamic performance.

The company **vision** should be realistic, relevant, easy to communicate and capable of motivating or even inspiring employees.

Value is an attitude which insists on giving customers a superior combination of product benefit and price. To do this usually requires not only strong marketing sense, but also a relentless drive to reduce costs and improve efficiencies.

Innovation needs to be pursued on two fronts – the daily trickle of ideas and improvements, and the ambitious projects. Success in innovation requires an attitude by senior management which encourages, recognizes and rewards innovative efforts, and a structure that supports this.

Long-term outlook is one of the most visible tests of senior management's resource and determination. Short-term expedients can weaken a company's vision and value, and reduce the confidence of employees in senior management's commitment to its stated goals. Several steps can, however, be taken to satisfy the pressure for short-term performance while still maintaining the integrity of long-term goals.

The offensive attitude to **investment** is that it is essential to renew and develop all assets, including people, brands and equipment, and to direct investment effectively.

Persistent attack involves an overall attacking mode and frame of mind, even though on certain fronts a company may be temporarily defending or retreating. A general attitude of attack motivates employees, places pressure on competition and creates internal drives for improved performance.

Speed of response is a test of a business's fitness. It is important to develop the capability to respond quickly to changes in the business environment or in consumer needs. Stress on this has enabled many larger companies to tone up their reflexes.

3 | *Integrated*

4 | *Integrating for the Offensive*

● The Principles of Integrated Marketing

'Integrated' means combining parts into a whole and may sound like just another meaningless buzz word, but it is not. When marketing is integrated the whole company participates, not just the marketing department. Every part of the business combines to satisfy consumer needs at maximum profit. Howard Morgens, past Chairman of Procter & Gamble, puts the case for integrated marketing succinctly:

> There is no such thing as marketing skill by itself. For a company to be good at marketing, it must be good at everything else from R & D to manufacturing, from quality controls to financial controls.[1]

Marketing is an approach to business rather than a specialist discipline. It is no more the exclusive responsibility of the marketing department than profitability is the sole charge of the finance department.

Unlike the more specialized roles of production, buying, selling and R & D, marketing is the function of every employee. The marketing approach challenges all members of a business, whatever their specialist function, to relate their work to the needs of the market-place and to balance it against the firm's own profit needs. For example, in a marketing-oriented company, the plant manager will ensure that quality-control standards evaluate those elements in the product which matter most to the consumer, while also aiming to meet the required product specification at minimum cost. The purchasing manager will check that materials purchased meet consumer requirements at the lowest possible cost. This will often involve moving away from materials whose cost is escalating, and substituting lower-cost constituents. But before authorizing such a change the buyer, jointly with the marketing group, will check any effect this substitution may have on consumer reaction. Within the company, the marketing department should lead and catalyse the application of the marketing approach.

However, it must be stressed that, to be effective, the marketing approach requires the full belief and support of top management – more about this later. The marketing department could no more apply an integrated marketing approach to a company on its own than a football club manager could win a match without a team.

Integrated marketing is the first, and the most difficult, step towards offensive marketing. Without it, marketing people operate in a vacuum and their efforts are ineffective.

Integrated marketing is one of the strengths of the Japanese. They have a reputation for being slow decision-makers and quick implementers, because by the time the decision is made everyone is behind it and moving in the same direction. As Kotler says of Japanese firms: 'Marketing decisions are the product or consequence of the inputs of not just "marketing" people but of other functional units as well.'[2]

Merchant bankers recommending acquisitions are very fond of saying that two plus two equals more than four. Where the marketing approach flows through the bloodstream of a company, the impact of the whole is much greater than the sum of the individual parts. Where marketing is bolted on to the body corporate like a wooden leg, the reverse is true.

● Barriers to Integrated Marketing

If integrated marketing is such a good idea, you would expect companies to be lining up to practise the art. It is strange that so few do it successfully. Here is an example of disintegration in one of the largest companies in the U S A:

> When Lee Iacocca joined Chrysler in the late 1970s, he soon concluded that 'all Chrysler's problems really boiled down to the same thing . . . there was no team, only a collection of independent players'.
>
> He discovered weaknesses in financial planning and projecting. 'Even the most rudimentary questions were impossible for them to answer.'
>
> Equally serious, the factories were producing to schedules not related to customer or dealer demand, with the result that there were massive inventories and monthly 'fire' sales, to reduce excess stocks.
>
> The system worked like this: 'At regular intervals the Manufacturing Division would tell the Sales Division how many and what types of vehicle they were going to produce. Then it would be up to Sales Division to sell them . . . to dealers . . . It had nothing to do with a customer ordering what he wanted on the car, or a dealer ordering what the customer was likely to ask for.'[3]

Iacocca soon put things right, but wondered how this could happen after thirty years of scientific management.

There are many reasons why companies do not follow the integrated marketing approach, and we shall look at four of the most common.

The first is also the most obvious. Businesses which are not close to the customer have not taken the first step on the road to offensive marketing, and are therefore in no position to apply an integrated approach. Take banks, for example:

> Few, if any, major U K banks are integrated marketers (but the American Express Banking Division is marketing-led, as is Citibank). They talk a great deal about 'marketing', but in most cases it is still a set of bolt-on activities like advertising, direct mail, new services and market research. In no sense could one say that banks are either customer-led or cost-driven.
>
> Compare banks with retailers. In grocery retailing there are many differentiated customer propositions to choose from. Sainsbury offers a broad range of branded and own-label

products of good quality at competitive prices. Kwik Save has a narrow range of brands at very low prices. Marks & Spencer markets a limited selection of high-quality foods at premium prices.

Outside grocery, creative market segmentation is spreading. Specialized chains like Next, the Body Shop, Tie Rack and Mothercare are concentrating on clearly defined areas, helped by flair in design and merchandising.

It is a shock to come back to banks. Each of the majors has about 3,000 outlets, clustered together on the same high streets, offering similar services at similar prices to the mass market, in bland surroundings.

Banks have been slow to move out of town. Business hours seem designed to minimize customer visits and they make access almost impossible for many blue-collar workers who cannot get away during lunch-hours. Saturday-morning opening was a grudging and patchy defensive response to building societies.

The major barrier to integrated marketing in banks is top management. They are not prepared to initiate the massive changes in organization and attitude necessary to make banks effective financial service marketers.

Instead, they fiddle at the fringes and are still basically technology- and operations-led rather than marketing-oriented. As Wendy Tansey points out, many UK banks are still 'opening accounts rather than providing an efficient and responsive banking service'.[4]

A second barrier to integrated marketing is top management's failure to implement their verbal commitment to improvements, as in this example:

The board was reasonably committed to the idea of improving product quality and some members, including the chairman, advocated this strongly to employees. At the same time the board was pushing hard on cost reduction, with impressive success. However, the pressure for short-term profits made it impossible to invest sufficiently in measures to improve quality. Indeed, some cost cuts affected quality, and those responsible for it became discouraged at the gap between top management's statements and actions.

A third barrier is a lack of consensus on important matters of strategy at board level. This can prove a decisive barrier to integration, since it spawns disruption and division. However, it may prove to be only a temporary barrier if the disagreements are resolved, as in this case:

> *The Marketing Director was keen to enter a new market sector, even though this would involve mastering new technology, heavy investment on capital equipment and a brand-new name. The minimum payback period would be four years, but the potential benefits of success would be high.*
>
> *The Financial and Production Directors presented a well-argued paper to the board resisting this move. They pointed out that while the company's products were well accepted by consumers and efficiently manufactured, there was considerable spare production capacity. Why could not the marketing department think more practically and develop exciting new products using existing capacity?*
>
> *The reader will recognize the conflict between market-led and asset-led marketing, and so did the Managing Director. He let things drift for a few months, perhaps deliberately, and then pushed the marketing department down the asset-led route, although allowing a test of the new brand. Subsequently, marketing succeeded in developing profitable new products using existing capacity.*

The fourth and final barrier we will mention is where a company has a clear marketing-led strategy, but integration is undermined by demarcation disputes or personal rivalries.

The following example, which demonstrates bad organization structure, will ring a bell with many who have worked in multinational companies:

> *The Managing Director of this UK subsidiary reported to the President of the International Division in the USA. The Manufacturing Director reported to the UK Managing Director on paper, but also had a strong link with the Vice-President, Worldwide Operations, located in the USA. Both American-based executives were of equal status, and pursued a strong but muted rivalry.*
>
> *The UK sales and marketing team had been strengthened*

and made some good moves. As a result, volume of orders improved by 35 per cent over a twelve-month period. Unfortunately, the factories could not meet this sales requirement, partly because sales forecasting was a bit weak, but mainly because manufacturing never seemed to be able to achieve planned production levels – 'a sustained record of failure', as the Sales Director acidly observed. Furthermore, management in the USA showed a marked reluctance to commit to any large increase in capacity, in case the UK business gains proved only temporary.

Short or late delivery to customers became the norm. Although the UK Managing Director spent three days a month personally chairing all production planning and sales forecasting meetings, he had little leverage over the Manufacturing Director, who was reporting back to his boss in the USA. Production blamed sales and marketing for poor sales forecasting. Marketing blamed production for failure to hit promised production schedules and inability to increase capacity.

The situation was exacerbated by the 'contribution' of staff groups and task forces flown over from the USA and in no time there were two companies – sales/marketing/finance on the one hand, production on the other. What should have been a volume and profit breakthrough by a highly capable group of individuals deteriorated into backbiting and customer dissatisfaction.

● Integrated Marketing in Action

Like most good business practices, the principle of integrated marketing is quite simple. It is just a matter of making certain that everyone working for a company moves together in the same marketing-led direction. The idea of moving towards a goal, and of the interdependence of individual players, is well understood by footballers. But its practice eludes many companies. It is of course more difficult for companies than for footballers because more players are involved, usually in different locations, and with less easily defined goals. However, the principle of combining diverse skills in pursuit of agreed offensive objectives is the same.

Integrated Marketing in Action

The Mars Group in the UK is an example of a well-integrated company:

> Mars has a number of clearly thought-out principles, many originating from strongly held personal convictions of Forrest Mars, Sr, the founder. They have changed little over the years and are well understood by most employees, although by no means perfectly executed. Here are ten of these principles:
>
> – offer superior value for money to customers, through distinctive and better products, mainly at similar or higher prices.
> – achieve a specified return on total assets (ROTA). The target return varies over time and by company within the Mars Group. Salary bands are related to sales growth and ROTA target achievement.
> – operate with fewer and better employees, paid at 30 per cent to 50 per cent above the average market rate.
> – remain non-unionized, where possible, but have a strong personnel function, and ensure all employees are kept informed on how the company is doing.
> – concentrate on building 'power' brands, which generate low unit manufacturing costs, allow for heavy advertising and promotion, and strengthen the company's bargaining position with retailers (three Mars Group brands – Mars Bar, Chum and Whiskas – achieve sales of over £100 million in the UK, and Twix is getting close).
> – adopt an attacking posture, innovate improvements and strive to gain market share.
> – advertise heavily, mainly on TV, with consistent campaigns. (The Chum 'dog-breeder testimonial', and the Mars 'Work, rest and play' campaigns have been running for fifteen to twenty years. They do not win creative awards.)
> – invest heavily in the latest and most efficient equipment, and run at high capacity (most Mars plants run at over 150 hours per week).
> – do not produce for stores' private labels, and where necessary market low-cost 'floor-price' brands to block the opportunity for private labelling (e.g. Katkins).
> – remain a private company, with a democratic atmosphere (few executives have offices, and all employees use the same eating and toilet facilities).

97

Not everyone would agree with all these principles. Some may appear unsophisticated. But the important thing is that the general thrust is understood and accepted by most Mars people at all levels. Regular presentations are made on how Mars is doing, and most factory staff know whether market share is rising or falling, how test markets or new sizes are going and what the competition is up to.

If everyone is rowing in the same general direction, the boat will move forward, and probably quite fast. The important thing both for employee motivation and for market results is a sense of moving forward. In the converse situation, where people are moving in different directions, everything stands still. Individuals may be working quite hard, but there is no feeling of momentum. This rapidly results in loss of motivation and poor market performance. For instance, a leading businessman recently described the National Health Service, which is a non-integrated organization, as a child's hanging mobile, responding to every breath of wind, giving the impression of continual movement, but in reality never moving from a fixed central point.[5]

 ### How to Achieve Strong Integration

Rather than provide a tedious check-list of things to do, we will illustrate integration with an example, in which *you* are the heroine.

You have just been appointed Marketing Director of a company which is a leader in DIY products. Sales volume this year will be £120 million and profit before tax is projected at £10·5 million. You head up a Marketing Department twenty-five strong, consisting of product management and marketing services, and you start work next Monday.

What you know about the company is based partly on the headhunter's analysis, and partly on your own findings from talking to retailers and reading a press cuttings file.

The interview with the Managing Director, who offered you the job, had not been very informative, but at least you had a chance to look around the main factory. You did not meet your predecessor because he has been shunted off to the Personnel Department at Group HQ.

The headhunter said that the company had good products but was losing market share. There was concern at the plateau in profits over the past few years.

The Managing Director, in his mid-fifties, came from a manufacturing background, was a good motivator, rather cautious, quite keen on the idea of marketing, but not totally sure about its scope. The most powerful person on the board was the Sales Director, who was close to his accounts, had trading sense, but operated through flair rather than numbers. Manufacturing was quite efficiently run, and the Finance Director, due to retire in two years' time, was quiet and somewhat old-fashioned. The Marketing Department contains a mix of long-serving employees from the sales force, and much younger imports from Gillette and Unilever.

You had asked the Managing Director what he expected of you. He said he wanted a more professional Marketing Department, and a resumption of profitable growth.

Three months later you take stock of the situation. It is not quite what you had been led to expect. The Managing Director is supportive and has the right instincts about investment and quality. The Sales Director is very shrewd but a short-term thinker and too close to the trade. The Marketing Department is spending most of its time on maintenance activity, much of it as a service to the Sales Department. There is also a culture clash between the old-timers, who are long on experience and short on skills, versus the newcomers, who are the reverse.

The real find is the number two in the Finance Department, who, before you arrived, was already developing a sophisticated system of net profit by individual product and major retail account. He started it on his own initiative, and had, with the cooperation of the Production and Sales Directors, managed to get work-study engineers out with salesmen and truck drivers. This gave him a basis for allocating selling and distribution costs by product and account, but no one had been too interested before your arrival. You are very interested indeed.

At this point, your main conclusions are:

> – you have a good relationship with the Managing Director. As an engineer, he likes facts, numbers and analysis, which suits you. You notice that he is uneasy with the Sales Director.

- the Marketing Department has too narrow a role and is divided against itself.
- the Sales Department is too dominant. It is writing the sales forecasts, which are of poor quality. Trade discounts are based on trade pressure. Extra services and deals are given to retailers to achieve more short-term volume.
- the R & D Department has good people, but is working on too many projects, and product briefs keep changing. A lot of the projects are housekeeping or minor cost savings.
- manufacturing is efficient, but the department feels that there are too many products, sizes and package types, and is worried by the poor sales forecasting.
- distribution is giving too high a level of service.
- product quality is variable and the Quality Control Department reports to the Production Director.
- the company's products do not justify their premium price and have not kept up with competitive improvements. This is confirmed by past research, but no one has faced up to the implications.

About this time, a new Five-year Plan needs to be written and sent to Group HQ. Previously this had been coordinated by the Finance Department. It was regarded as a chore, and consisted mainly of five-year sales and profit forecasts, with no strategies or commentaries.

The Financial Director is quite happy to let you put the plan together this year, working with his number two. Although there are some mutterings, especially from the Sales Director, along the lines of 'When is this woman going to do some marketing?' you don't feel too bad, because you started to plan two major consumer promotions soon after your arrival, through your newly appointed sales promotion agency, and also put in hand some short-term product improvements via the R & D Department. These will be coming on stream soon, and meanwhile you get to work on the new Five-year Plan, armed with the priceless new information on profit centres.

Your starting point is to arrange a series of meetings with other department heads, with the aim of producing *integrated* marketing strategies for every department. Your idea is to match the costs and operating efficiencies of each department against its obligations to the consumer, and to forge a median point between the two where profit will be maximized. You recognize that your task may involve not only modifying existing strategies but also helping to create new ones.

You get your new ally in the Finance Department to accompany you to all the meetings and your first stop is the Production Director.

This meeting goes well. You say that, based on the new product profitability analysis, there are a number of products which you wish to withdraw. Furthermore, your long-term plan is to cut the product range by one third and concentrate resources on five or six leading products which can be built up into 'power' brands.

He says that in that case he would like to change his manufacturing strategy, and reorganize the two factories so that one does high-volume inflexible runs on power brands and the other is more of a 'boutique' – highly flexible and capable of handling short runs efficiently. You agree to set up an informal meeting, with buffet supper, on the first Thursday of each month after work, between the top six people in production, R & D and marketing. The topic of the first meeting will be product quality, and your people will be presenting results of recent consumer blind tests between your main products and competitors.

The next meeting with the head of Distribution is also useful. He likes the idea of reducing the product range. You ask him why he delivers in forty-eight hours when competitors take between three and five days, and he says this is part of the superior service the company gives. He inquires whether anything can be done to smooth orders by day because he has big peaks on Thursdays and Fridays and lots of spare capacity earlier in the week.

The meeting with the Director of R & D goes according to plan. You agree to reduce the number of projects and concentrate your effort on a small number, some with short-term pay-offs, others involving technological challenges with large potential but higher risk.

The final meeting, with the Sales Director, has some surprises. He has already seen the major-account profitability analysis, and has decided to give each of his key account managers net contribution rather than revenue targets. What is more, he asks you for help in developing a revised discount structure, and starts to think about varying levels of account service related to account need and profitability.

Two years later, things are going quite well, even though the competition has made some effective changes which you had not anticipated. A profit of £15 million looks achievable (almost 50 per cent higher than when you arrived):

- quality has improved, and is evaluated objectively against competition on a regular basis.
- the Marketing Department has taken over responsibility for sales forecasting and this has greatly improved.
- the product range has been reduced and the Manufacturing Director has reorganized the two factories. Large savings have been made in manufacturing, distribution and inventory holdings.
- thanks to the focus on six lead lines, the Sales Director has broadened distribution and opened two major new accounts.
- you have reorganized the Marketing Department, brought in two people from the Production Department, one from Sales and two from outside, and redeployed twelve others elsewhere.
- the new National Account Profitability System is working well, and all major accounts are profitable.
- a number of product improvements have been made, and prospects in R & D for a new technology-based block-buster look good.
- you have, of course, radically improved the quality of advertising, sales promotion, marketing planning and packaging.

Finally, six months later, profits hit £17 million, the Managing Director retires and the Sales Director is promoted to take his place.

● **Test Your Business for Marketing Integration**

The 'factional' story above, depicting the Marketing Director as heroine, is too good to be true. In real life, she would have had less cooperation from other directors and needed more active support from the Managing Director than she received. But it illustrates the right approach and the tools available to the Marketing Director in achieving it – five-year plans, annual budgets, formal and informal meetings, lobbying for support, communication and evangelism, and new information. You can rate your own business for 'integrated marketing' in Table 9.

Table 9. *Criteria for Rating Your Business on Integrated Marketing*

	Maximum score	Your score
Do the Chairman and Chief Executive believe in and encourage the integrated marketing approach?	20	
Does the business have clear objectives and strategies which are regularly stressed to all employees?	15	
Does the Marketing Department have prime responsibility for writing up overall business strategy and long-term plans?	10	
Does the Marketing Director have periodical informal meetings with other department heads to integrate strategies?	15	
Do marketing and sales people make regular presentations to operations and distribution personnel about the state of the business?	10	
Do senior operations, finance and distribution people ever make customer visits or accompany salesmen in the field?	10	
Do the Marketing and Sales Departments work closely together?	10	
Do marketing people advocate and sell the integrated marketing approach within the company?	10	
Total	100	

● Summary

Where marketing is integrated, it permeates the whole company. It is no more the exclusive responsibility of the marketing department than profitability is the sole charge of the finance department.

Marketing cannot begin to be effective within a business unless it has the full support of general management and penetrates every nook and cranny of an organization. Marketing is the function of every employee. The integrated marketing approach challenges every member of a company, whatever their specialist function, to relate their work to the needs of the market-place and to balance it against the firm's own profit needs.

Few companies apply the integrated marketing approach in full. Among the barriers to integration are unclear or unbalanced strategies, lack of top-management commitment, poor team-work and bad organizational structures.

The Managing Director is primarily responsible for achieving an integrated marketing approach, but the marketing department should lead and catalyse its application.

The means for achieving this include taking responsibility for five-year-plan preparation, meetings with other departments to establish balanced strategies, close involvement with manufacturing and sales, regular discussion of market results with factory staff, job rotation, drawing marketing people from a wider range of disciplines and getting finance and production people to occasionally accompany salesmen.

Last, but not least, marketing people should constantly sell the merits of the offensive marketing approach within the company with the same skill and enthusiasm as they apply to marketing the company's products.

5 | *Organization for Integrated Marketing*

A quick glance at the organization chart and job specifications of a marketing department will usually reveal whether it is designed to stimulate an integrated marketing approach or to do a narrow specialist job.

It would of course be naive to pretend that organization alone can prevent complacency, defensive attitudes or a preoccupation with routine. Good organization, however, can create a climate where innovation, an independent approach and measured risk-taking will be recognized and rewarded. It will not in itself make offensive marketing suddenly take off in a business, but it will provide a framework in which, with qualified people and the right attitudes, an integrated marketing approach is most likely to flourish in the long run.

● Who Needs a Marketing Department Anyway?

Religions can flower without churches, or even, as the Quakers have shown, without priests. Equally, the offensive marketing approach can exist with or without a marketing department. Marks & Spencer, a strong exponent of superior customer value and high profit margins, has succeeded for over 100 years without a marketing department (although recently it has established a Marketing Services Department). Mercedes, with a distinctive and premium-priced product range, and good margins by car industry standards, employs over 9,000 engineers but has no marketing division. (There are people at Mercedes with 'marketing' in their job-title, but they are part of the sales division. The main board member has the title of Sales Director.) And, as Kotler points out,[1] few Japanese firms had 'marketing departments' until the mid-1970s, many years after the start of their successful global marketing strategies. Some still do not have marketing departments.

So is a marketing department an essential element of the offensive marketing approach? The answer is clearly no, especially where a business is run by an entrepreneur with a good feel for his markets and a nose for profit. This may equally apply to a large organization. General Motors' concept of its business and classic market-segmentation policies were worked out in the first years of the 1920s by a group of men without any specialized marketing training. Some of the strongest brand names today were developed at a time when the word 'marketing' didn't even exist – brands like Bovril, Oxo, Nescafé, Quality Street, Jaguar, Lux and Kodak.

A marketing department is not essential and is valuable only if it helps to catalyse the application of the offensive marketing approach. Bolted on to a company with inoffensive attitudes or a non-integrated structure, a marketing department merely adds cost and has little opportunity to contribute.

● **Day-to-day Operation of the Marketing Department**

There is no perfect analogy to illuminate the working of the marketing department. Opponents of the offensive marketing approach might suggest that the movement of the octopus – with eight suckered arms around a mouth – provides a close likeness. But probably the best analogy is the one which relates the marketing department to the orchestral conductor. This is flattering to marketing, because the conductor's leadership position on the rostrum may give a glamour and status out of all proportion to their authority or contribution.

What the marketing person and the conductor have in common is a programme whose execution depends on the combined efforts of a number of specialists. In the case of the conductor these are instrumentalists; for marketers they are copywriters, engineers, operations people, accountants, salesmen and researchers.

Neither the symphony orchestra nor the marketing plan will succeed unless each specialist clearly understands their own role and how it relates to others. Equally, the failure of one specialist to perform effectively, whether they are oboists who miss an entry or operations managers who miss an agreed deadline, can sabotage the whole programme. It follows that, like the conductor, marketers must know their overall objectives, and brief, motivate and coordinate their specialists in order to achieve these in an integrated way.

Marketing departments usually operate by briefing each department on its role in any marketing plan, by assessing the resulting proposal and by recommending it to company management for approval if it meets the brief. In any well-run company, marketing briefs will precede the initiation of significant work by a member of another department. The rationale for this is obvious. A designer who does not know the marketing objective behind the development of a new credit card stands an excellent chance of producing an irrelevant card design. A cost accountant can hardly be expected to make cost estimates for a new service if the marketing department is still guessing wildly about specification, or expected volume. Production managers cannot work out a sound manufacturing plan unless they are briefed on required quantities, timings, type of formulation and variety of packaging.

A good marketing brief will be clear and unambiguous, and will limit itself to a statement of objectives. It will not detail the technical means by which these are to be achieved, since that is the task of the department concerned. When the appropriate department has responded to the brief, by putting forward an operations plan, or a design, or a new product formulation, whatever the case may be, the marketing department will evaluate how far it meets the original brief.

And who do these marketing people think they are, daring to criticize the proposals of an operations manager or a designer?

Unless marketing people understand the answer to this question clearly, they are set fair for a ruinous relationship with functional specialists. The golden rule is that marketers should never question the technical competence of experts or attempt to tell them how to do their job. They should confine themselves to checking whether the proposal meets the marketing brief and stop there.

Let us suppose that you are marketing manager of a leading insurance company, and it has been agreed to modernize the company logo. The marketing brief is drawn up, setting out the objectives of the new logo. We shall keep it simple by saying that these are to provide an impression of greater modernity and higher quality than the existing logo design, while retaining a recognizable continuity with the past.

Five weeks later the designer presents four alternative rough designs. They are very exciting, but represent much too great a departure from the existing logo, and this is what you have to tell the designer. You are entitled to do this on the strength of your expert knowledge of the customers and your view that they would react adversely to a very radical change in design. But it would obviously be wrong to suggest exactly how the logo design should be altered to meet the brief, because you are not an artist and have no technical expertise in this area. If the designer is a professional, he will start again, having ascertained as far as possible where you draw the line between a design which is too radical and one which retains an acceptable continuity with the existing logo.

Once the marketing department is satisfied with the response to a brief, it will authorize action, unless the issue is so important that it needs to be cleared with general management or the board.

● **Carrying the Can and Calling the Shots**

A marketing department must do more than just handle the advertising and promotion functions. It should be responsible for setting overall marketing policies, allowing other departments to retain authority over much of the detailed implementation of plans.

Setting out the boundaries of the responsibilities and authority of the marketing department and its relationship with other departments is an essential step in achieving an integrated marketing approach.

First of all, a very clear distinction between strategy and planning on the one hand, and detailed implementation on the other, needs to be established.

Marketing strategy reflects a firm's best opinion as to how it can most profitably apply its skills and resources to the market-place. A strategy is inevitably broad in scope, but the plan which stems from it will spell out action and timings, and the detailed contribution expected from each department. This is the primary responsibility of the marketing department, with its knowledge of the customers and its bird's-eye view of the whole company, but needs to be fully discussed with other departments.

Detailed implementation of agreed plans is the responsibility of the functional departments concerned and they carry full line authority for this. The operations director is responsible for his people and equipment, and the sales director has control over the deployment of the sales force.

So where does this leave the marketing department? Must it just sit still and watch the implementation of its plans as a silent, but perhaps agonized, spectator? Fortunately, no. If the plans are implemented smoothly, there is no reason for the marketing department to intervene. But if they start to go badly, the department concerned is bound to let marketing know, and a way to handle the situation will have to be thrashed out.

Perhaps the marketing plan can be kept on schedule by some additional expenditure on overtime, or a reallocation of priorities, or it may have to be changed. If the consistently poor performance of a particular department is sabotaging the proper implementation of marketing plans, the marketing department should bring this problem to the attention of general management and lobby for the changes needed.

The distinction between strategy/planning and implementation is illustrated in Table 10, by a few examples from a manufacturer.

Although the ground rules of authority and responsibility should be roughly set out, if only to place the role of the marketing department in proper perspective, the effective operation of the integrated marketing approach really depends on the spirit of the organization. If there is an obsession with procedures and a neurotic preoccupation with demarcation lines or levels of seniority,

Table 10. *Strategy vs. Implementation*

Strategy/Planning (Marketing Department has major authority)	Implementation (Marketing Department has nil authority)
1. Operations schedule based on Marketing Department's sales forecast	1. Physical production of agreed schedules
2. R & D brief based on Marketing Department's assessment of market opportunities	2. Technical processes and lab work involved in carrying out agreed briefs
3. Agreement with Distribution Department that all deliveries should be completed three days after sales order placed.	3. Operation and routing of vehicles; siting of company warehouses necessary to fulfil agreed strategy.

little progress will be made. The best results are achieved in an atmosphere of cooperation, where the quality of an idea matters more than the seniority or background of its originator. To this end, an effective marketing department will operate by persuasion even when it has ultimate authority. It is in a very strong position to persuade others since it possesses all the facts about the market-place which underlie action plans, and has a clear picture of the total corporate operation.

● Carving Up Profit Responsibility

In a manufacturing company practising the offensive marketing approach, the director of operations has prime responsi-bility for meeting budgeted operations costs and standards. The sales and distribution directors are accountable for all costs gener-ated between factory gate and retailer/distributor shelf. This covers selling, distribution, trade discounts and promotions designed mainly to sell the product in. The finance director is responsible for administration and financing costs and for managing cash flow.

The marketing director has prime responsibility for all costs involved in getting a product off the shelf or out of a warehouse and into the hands of the consumer. This includes advertising, most sales promotion, packaging development and market-research costs.

In a company which adopts offensive marketing methods, marketing directors also have responsibility for profit before tax, administration and financing charges. This enables them to lead the application of integrated marketing and to achieve the best balance between customer needs and profit needs. While they do not have prime responsibility for operations and selling costs, they can have a strong influence on them. Figure 6 illustrates how the responsibility for profit carve-up on this basis would work in a company operating through retailers or distributors. The same basic principles would apply in a service business, with 'operations' but no factories.

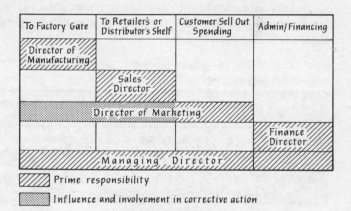

Figure 6. Carving Up Responsibility for Profit

● Structuring for the Offensive

This section will cover the four principles which contribute to an integrated marketing organization with an innovative outlook.

1. Marketing organization should reflect the structure of the market-place

Organization is the internal form you decide to adopt in order to meet customer needs and to generate maximum profit. It should obviously reflect your view and understanding of the market-place. If the structure of markets and the way in which they segment are misinterpreted, any organization based on this will also be wrong. As markets and customers change, so should internal organization.

In manufacturing companies offensive marketing organizations are usually built around external factors such as markets, customers and geographical areas, and an example is shown in Table 11. The marketing department will be divided into markets (marketing managers) and products (brand managers). Sales departments are typically split into national accounts and field sales, both reporting to the Sales Director. A simplified organizational structure is shown in Figure 7.

Table 11. *Marketing/Sales Organization in a Manufacturing Company*

External Factors	Internal Structure	Management Skills Required
Markets	Marketing	Marketing
Customers/Customer types	National accounts/ Trade marketing	Account handling
Geographical areas	Field sales	People-management skills

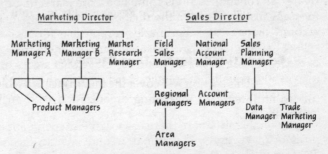

Figure 7. Marketing Structure in a Manufacturing Company

112

In retailing companies, organizational structure follows similar principles, but suppliers play a larger role in marketing since they supply finished goods. An example of this overall structure is shown in Table 12.

Table 12. *Organization in a Retailing Company*

External Factors	Internal Structure	Management Skills Required
Markets	Marketing and buying	Marketing
Suppliers	Buying	Purchasing
Geographical areas	Store operations	People-management

Financial service or travel companies would have a different organizational emphasis. The same principles, however, apply: that structure should be built around markets, customers, suppliers and geographical areas in a responsive way, since these are the external factors which contribute most cost and promise most revenue.

The worst type of structure is that based on production units which have no relevance to the customer.

2. Marketing and sales departments should be integrated

In many companies these functions overlap. The overlap should be a source of constructive team-work, not departmental rivalry. In consumer goods companies, the marketing department focuses most strongly on the final mass consumer, while national account managers are primarily responsible for marketing and selling to the retailer. The consumer cannot benefit from the efforts of the marketing department unless the retailer stocks the product in question. Equally, the retailer's decision on whether to stock it or not is influenced by his opinion of marketing's effect on the final consumer.

To cover this situation, there has to be close cooperation between product managers and national account managers, as Figure 8 illustrates. There is a similar need for close integration between buying and marketing departments in retail organizations.

113

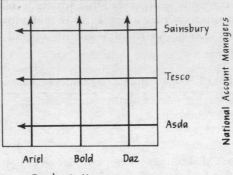

Figure 8. Sales and Marketing Integration in a Manufacturing Company

3. New products and new businesses should be handled by separate groups

The issue of the right organization for new products is covered in more detail in Chapter 16, and will be only briefly alluded to here.

There is a strong case for giving responsibility for new products to a group quite separate from that running existing products. The new products manager would have revenue and profit targets, and be highly influential. Whether reporting to the marketing director or the chief executive, he or she should spend a lot of time with the latter.

There are many advantages to this approach. New products or services get high priority and are not just something people do when they have time. Responsibility for new products can be pinned on one group, with clear targets to hit. The inevitable bugbears attending the development of new products receive the full attention of a senior person, with close access to the chief executive.

This approach also has pitfalls, but these can be overcome. Firstly, a new product group can get out of touch with the rest of the company and build its own ivory towers. This is unlikely to happen if the new products manager has well-rounded line-management experience.

114

Secondly, the point at which ideas should be handed over by the new products group to the marketing department needs to be carefully considered. It is usually best to let the new products group take a new product or service right through to the end of its first year of national expansion. The transition is facilitated if a product manager is seconded from the marketing department to the new products department, subsequently taking the new product back to the marketing department.

Some friction between the marketing department and the new products group is probably inevitable, but it is much better to have problems handling dramatic company growth than to face the much bigger headache of having a static business.[2]

The handling of new businesses is more fully discussed in Chapter 16.

4. Marketing men should be integrators not specialists

The final principle is that the marketing department should be a good 'mixer and fixer'. If marketers are to become as familiar with the assets of their business as they are with their customers, they will need to spend time really getting to know how other departments think, and what their main concerns are.

● **Pitfalls to Avoid**

There are four major pitfalls which marketers would do well to avoid:

1. The bingo effect
2. Wall-building
3. Marketing bureaucracy
4. The safety syndrome

First, the **bingo effect**. The most visible of the marketing department's activities are advertising and sales promotion. Marketing people often do not understand how easily their role can be misunderstood within the company. Sales promotions are only the tip of the marketing iceberg, but unless marketing people take the trouble to explain their full role, they will continue to be misunderstood, and their contribution may be trivialized.

The wall-building effect can be more serious. By establishing a group called the 'marketing department', you run the danger of erecting a sign which says: 'Keep out – all customer contact to be with marketing people only.'

Take the situation of the operations manager. Before 'marketing' was introduced, he would see customer letters, test new ideas among his operations people, and often talk with the sales manager. Since the marketing department was set up, none of these things happens, and all customer research is conducted by outside agencies. The operations manager used to work for a consumer he could see. Now he spends all his time meeting specifications, hitting production plans and controlling cost variances. The marketing department has built a wall between operations and the consumer. What will happen to product or service quality and industrial relations?

It is the job of marketing to destroy the wall and to link operations people with market problems and progress.

Marketing bureaucracy is a product of the success of marketing departments, but may end up drowning them. The stream of paper pouring around the marketing department becomes a flood. The reality of product managers – overburdened bureaucrats – is very different from their desired image. They often have little time to think, never mind innovate, and are always planning to spend that day in the field talking to customers, but rarely do.

The final pitfall is well known: the **safety syndrome**, which is related to the flock factor, examined in Chapter 2.

● **Everyone is a Marketer**

This chapter has emphasized how integrated marketing can be stimulated by the marketing department, but stresses that its ultimate success depends on the efforts of every employee. Table 13 illustrates what each department can do to improve value for the customer in a manufacturing company. Manufacturers often find integration more difficult than service companies, where operations people frequently have direct customer contact, either face to face or by phone. The table demonstrates that 'marketing' is done by everyone, not just by marketing people.

Table 13. *Marketing in a Manufacturing Company*

Function/Department	Major Activity	Impact on Consumer
Operations (Includes engineering & engineering R & D)	Product quantity/ Timing Cost per unit Quality control	Availability Price Quality
Finance	Control Management data Cash flow	Indirect Indirect Indirect
Sales	Availability in Stores Visibility Retail pricing	Availability Availability Price
Marketing	Matching products to needs Product innovation Trade pricing Packaging/promotion Advertising	Product appeal Product appeal Price Visibility and Image Visibility and Image
R & D	Product improvements New products Quality specifications Cost reduction	Product appeal Product appeal Product appeal Pricing
Personnel	Recruitment/Training Industrial relations	Indirect Indirect

● Summary

Organization on its own cannot prevent complacency and preoccupation with the status quo. But the right structure can create a climate where innovation, an independent approach and measured risk-taking will be recognized and rewarded.

The purpose of a marketing department is to catalyse and integrate the application of the offensive marketing approach. It represents the views of consumers to the company, and works out, with other departments, how to transform these into profitable products.

The marketing department has both authority and responsibility for determining marketing strategies and drawing up plans. Similarly, the marketing department is not responsible for the failure of plans due to poor implementation by other departments, although it is responsible for planning corrective action.

Marketing directors can best lead the application of an integrated approach if they have responsibility for profit before tax administration and financing charges.

Conflicts do occur between marketing and other departments. Constructive conflict is one of the hallmarks of offensive marketing, since it demonstrates the involvement of all departments and the desire to make a contribution. Four principles contribute to an integrated marketing organization:

1. Structure should reflect the market-place.
2. Marketing and sales should be integrated.
3. New products should be handled by a separate group.
4. Marketing men should be integrators, not specialists.

However, there are certain pitfalls which can weaken the integrated approach. They are the bingo effect, wall-building, marketing bureaucracy and the safety syndrome.

Finally, any company practising offensive marketing should ensure that it is organized along the right lines to encourage all employees, whether in sales or finance, personnel or production, to be marketers.

4 | *Strategic*

6 | *Grinding Out the Strategic Base*

● The Three Stages of Battle

Effective action is usually preceded by logical steps, which may be elaborately documented or followed intuitively. They are the objective, the strategy and the plan:

1. *Objectives* describe destinations (Where are we going?). They are usually stated in terms of revenue and profit.
2. *Strategies* set out the route which has been chosen, or the means for achieving the objective (How do we get there?). Often a number of alternative strategies are evaluated before a final one is chosen.
3. *Plans* constitute the vehicle for getting to the destination along the chosen route (What's the plan for getting there?).[1] They form the detailed execution of the strategy.

This threefold sequence provides a rational framework for decision-making directed towards a consistent end, and applies as much to chess and to warfare as to business: 'Chess is a . . . game in which drifting from move to move is sure to lead to disaster. It is vitally important to form a plan of campaign.'[2]

The process of making a journey provides a simple but useful analogy. Let us suppose that you have the good fortune to be travelling to Puerto Rico.

The *objective* of the journey is to get from your home to Puerto Rico. There are various alternative *strategies* for achieving this objective. You could fly there from Heathrow via Miami or New York. Or you could take a plane to Caracas and on to Puerto Rico. If you had plenty of time, it might be possible to sail by liner to New York and fly to Puerto Rico. Your preferred strategy will be selected from these alternatives based on criteria like time available, convenience of schedules, desire for stop-overs, cost, etc.

Having determined your strategy, the next step is the *plan*. This will include detailed arrangements for getting from your home to Heathrow, packing baggage, getting your ticket, method of payment and so on.

BMW's recovery effort in Germany provides a good example of the three stages of battle in a business context:

> *In 1960 BMW was on the verge of bankruptcy. It was producing motor cycles for a dwindling market, and making a poor return on its bubble cars and six-cylinder saloons. A takeover bid by Daimler-Benz, the makers of Mercedes, was narrowly avoided, and the group was rescued by a Bavarian investment group.*
>
> *Paul G. Hahnemann, Opel's top wholesale distributor, was appointed Chief Executive. His first objective was obviously to get BMW back on an even keel, where it was sufficiently profitable to survive in the long-term. Having got there, he would then move to a more ambitious objective of challenging Mercedes for leadership of the market for high-quality executive cars.*
>
> *He was convinced that there was an unexploited market for a sporty saloon car, which Mercedes was not tapping. As he pointed out, 'If you were a sporty driver and German, there was no car for you. The Mercedes is big, black and ponderous. It's for parking, not driving.'*
>
> *Consequently, he evolved a strategy for producing a range of high-quality cars with better performance and a more sporty image than any other saloon. This strategy has remained broadly unchanged since. But the plans for executing it have evolved and been refined.*

> *The successful rebirth of BMW is now a matter of history,*
> *although it has still not overtaken Mercedes. In 1984 BMW*
> *sold 434,000 cars and achieved net sales of $4·7 billion.*

This sequential approach sounds quite elementary. Yet it is surprising how often executives lapse into detailed discussions of plans and ideas before they have agreed objectives or strategies.

● Aren't Strategies Rather Academic?

Although few people question the necessity for objectives and plans for action, some people are sceptical about the value of strategies. Since the remainder of this chapter will appear irrelevant to anyone strongly entrenched in that camp, we shall briefly examine the case for using strategies.

The suggestion that strategies are too academic derives from the conviction that any discussion not related to immediate business action is theoretical and of no value. Strategies are academic in the sense that their development stems from a close analysis of all relevant facts and from the conclusions drawn from them. There was nothing academic about the results achieved by Zantac in anti-ulcer drugs or McDonald's in fast foods. Both succeeded through careful preparation of the strategies for market entry.

A good strategy will give clear direction as to general approach, but allow some variety in execution. For example, a company's product strategy may be to achieve and maintain performance and styling superiority over all brands in the same price bracket. The detailed ways in which this can be executed are infinite and offer great flexibility. But it should be emphasized that there would be no flexibility to market a parity performance product. In that sense the strategy does limit freedom of manoeuvre, but that is its objective, since in this case product performance is an issue on which no compromise is to be allowed.

The criticism that strategies are too time-consuming is based on the need for discussion with a large number of people in many departments. But such criticism is misplaced. Strategies are fundamental to integrated marketing. Wide-ranging discussion across departments is essential to achieve an integrated approach, since understanding needs debate. The very fact that strategies create controversy is a sound reason for giving them priority. It is much better to resolve disagreements early than to paper them over and risk slowing down action programmes. A marketing strategy discussed only within the marketing department is a pointless exercise.

A strategy serves as a basis of agreement for all parties on the goals towards which the company or product effort is to be directed, and helps ensure coordinated action. If there is no agreed strategy, the action taken may reflect varying assumptions as to how the objective is to be achieved, and pursue a zigzag course.

A strategy also forces management to be selective and ruthlessly to prune the less vital goals of the business. The clear identification of non-priorities can often be a troublesome process. Therefore, if a strategy has been painful to determine, it is likely to be a good one.

Those who still oppose strategy will, however, be encouraged by the fact that many of the world's greatest discoveries, such as penicillin and the law of gravity, were discovered by accident – so any budding Flemings or Newtons may safely ignore this section. They would be amused at the way the word 'strategic' has become a buzz word, applied as a prefix to almost any activity in the business vocabulary. So we have not only strategic planning, strategic management and strategic consultants, but also strategic merchandising, strategic purchasing and of course strategic marketing. If the wider use of the word connotes a broader acceptance that strategies should precede plans, it is to be welcomed.

● Native Grit and Native Wit

One of the best-known books for young barristers, on the art of cross-examination, points out that native grit is even more important than native wit. In other words, thorough preparation matters more than the occasional brilliant insight, and, in any case, the two usually go together.

The same applies to the development of strategy. This is the reason for the word 'grinding' in the chapter title. Strategy development is hard work and is most successful when preceded by rigorous business analysis, where every relevant fact and number is cross-examined in a disciplined sequence. Figure 9 summarizes the benefits of disciplined business analysis.

Effective analysis is comparable to a manufacturing process. It

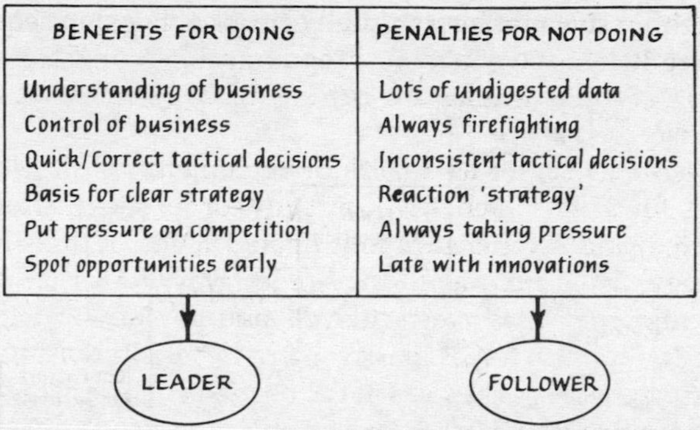

BENEFITS FOR DOING	PENALTIES FOR NOT DOING
Understanding of business	Lots of undigested data
Control of business	Always firefighting
Quick/Correct tactical decisions	Inconsistent tactical decisions
Basis for clear strategy	Reaction 'strategy'
Put pressure on competition	Always taking pressure
Spot opportunities early	Late with innovations

```
        ↓                          ↓
  ( LEADER )                ( FOLLOWER )
```

Figure 9. The Benefits of Disciplined Business Analysis

selects the relevant raw data, converts it into knowledge, and finally into understanding, which is the end product of analysis. As in the case of manufacturing, quality of raw materials and care in processing are essential for a good result.

We are living in the days of data glut. Marketers flounder beneath the torrent of paper which rolls in like the tide every morning. To turn the tide in your favour, you need to ensure that the routine paperwork – sales, profit by product and account, market analysis and so on – arrives on your desk in usable form, not as unsifted computer print-outs. The main producers of routine paper – finance, sales, administration and the marketing department itself – will tend to be production-oriented unless the recipients of this routine paper make exactly what they want as customers very clear.

Finally, effective analysis has only one purpose: action. Sometimes analysis becomes an end in itself, leading forever to further analysis. This is called 'analysis paralysis'. Or it can result in the DTs – delaying tactics – where the recipient of the analysis continually asks for further data, disguising his fear of risk and decision-taking.

● The Five-step Sequence for Strategic Analysis

In the context of this section the word 'strategic' is justified, because we are looking at the analysis needed to develop a marketing strategy. While there are many ways of approaching

125

this, offensive marketers usually adopt a five-step sequence, as in Figure 10.

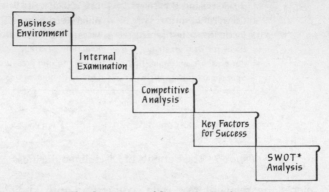

Figure 10. The Sequence of Strategic Analysis
* SWOT: Strengths, weaknesses, opportunities and threats.

The analysis of the **business environment** involves looking at the direct, indirect, and macro factors affecting your business now and in the future.

The **internal examination** is a medical check of your business, involving a great deal more probing than the typical executive check-up.

The **competitive analysis** defines your competitors, evaluates what they are doing well and badly now, and how they are likely to change in the future.

Key factors for success list the things that really matter in your markets, and identify the priority areas for building competitive advantages.

The **SWOT Analysis**, to use the awful abbreviation for which there appears to be no better substitute, pulls together the whole exercise, and involves a listing of your strengths and weaknesses, plus the opportunities and threats facing you.

We shall now briefly examine each of these five steps in turn.

Step 1: the three wheels of the business environment

Figure 11 divides the business environment into three wheels, representing the macro, indirect and direct factors affecting your business. Macro is on the outside, since the effect of macro factors is usually less immediate than direct ones like price changes or product improvements by your major competitor. The elements covered by the macro and direct wheels are straightforward, and Appendix 1 contains a selective check-list.

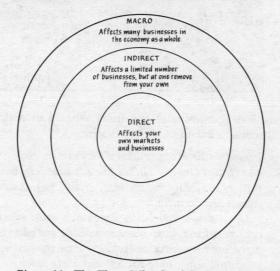

Figure 11. The Three Wheels of the Business Environment

The indirect wheel requires further explanation. It includes businesses which intrude on the edge of your territory though they are not direct competitors, just as Mars Bars are indirect competitors to Penguin Biscuits. It also covers related markets which are not competitive, but whose success greatly affects your own. For example, B R Rail Freight is heavily affected by the output of heavy industry, which accounts for the bulk of its loads. Equally, changing fashions in clothes influence the styles of lingerie women require.

Table 14 lists some 'indirect businesses'. The business on the left is 'related' to the one on the right.

Table 14. *Related Markets and their Effects*

Driving Factor		Beneficiary
Washing machines	→	Washing powders
Clothes	→	Lingerie
Home freezers	→	Frozen foods
Computer hardware	→	Computer software
Retail outlets	→	Manufacturers
Heavy industry	→	Rail freight
Cars	→	Petrol
Engineering	→	Machine tools
Farming	→	Farm equipment

Here are two examples of the three wheels in action. First, Penguin Biscuits, a brand of United Biscuits.

> *Penguin's direct competition is Kit Kat's six-pack, Twix, Club and United (another United Biscuits product). Indirect competitors are confectionery bars, crisps, bag snacks and ice-creams like Cornetto.*
>
> *On a day-to-day basis, Penguin is most affected by its relative pricing, in-store merchandising and advertising compared with its direct competitors. And the cost of chocolate substitute (since only Kit Kat and Twix among direct competitors still use real chocolate) is always an important factor.*
>
> *On a macro basis, most of the factors are longer-term. The continued trend towards more frequent and less formal eating occasions is positive for Penguin. The growing preoccupation with healthy eating is an unfavourable factor.*

This is shown more fully in Figure 12.

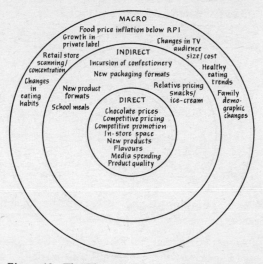

Figure 12. The Three Wheels of the Business Environment
– Penguin Biscuits

The British Airways example in Figure 13 illustrates the operation
of the three wheels in a rather different business environment:

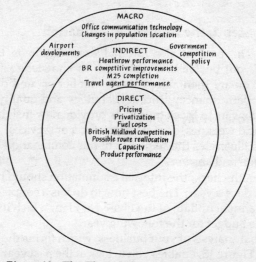

Figure 13. The Three Wheels of the Business Environment
– British Airways in the UK

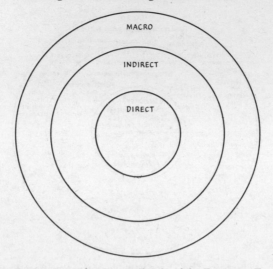

Figure 14. The Three Wheels of the Business Environment

Figure 14 gives you an opportunity to fill in how macro, indirect or direct factors affect your own business.

Step 2: the internal examination

The crux of the internal examination is the factual analysis of your business, which leads to knowledge and understanding. You are then able to ask a number of candid questions about past performance, attitudes, strategy and quality of execution. The answers to these questions provide new insights into the strengths and weaknesses of your products or services.

Figure 15 illustrates the sequence of this combination of analysis plus question and answer.

Like a health-check, the internal examination should be formally carried out once a year. The best time to do it is a couple of months before the annual update of the Five-year Plan, which itself should precede the budget for the following year.

The factual analysis of your business, which forms the top slice of the cake in Figure 15, enables you to look at the past year's events in perspective. It is also one of the strongest tools you have for ensuring that the marketing approach permeates the whole busi-

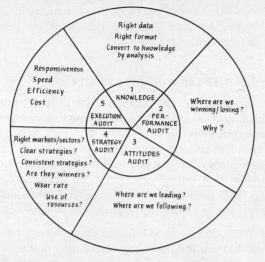

Figure 15. Model of Internal Examination

ness, since, as part of the internal examination, you will also be reviewing selling, operations and financial factors which affect your overall competitive position. In conducting the analysis, you are therefore assuming the mantle of overall business director, even though your title happens to be marketing director.

The framework for the factual analysis is outlined in Table 15 and given in detail in Appendix 2.

Table 15. *Framework for Factual Analysis*

Your Market(s)	Company or Product(s)
Overall Trends	Sales trends
Trends by segments	Market share trends
Factors driving market	Trade distribution trends
	Pricing
	Buyers/distributors/retailers
	Operations
	Product performance/value
	Marketing activities
	Innovation audit
	Allocation of resources audit
	Profit analysis

With this knowledge under your belt, you can then move round the model in Figure 15, and pose the questions on performance, attitudes, strategy and execution.

Step 3A: competitive analysis[3]

We have so far examined the outside environment, your markets, and your company or product/service performance within those markets. Now we add the vital element of competition. This has been divided into two sections. 'Competitive Analysis' identifies what you need to know about competitors and how to acquire that knowledge. 'Step 3B: Competitive Analysis Drill' (see p. 135) deals with how to use that knowledge. In this section, therefore, we will confine ourselves to three questions:

1. What do you need to know about your competitors?
2. What are the main sources of information about competitors?
3. How can you develop a good-quality system for analysing competitors?

Table 16 summarizes the main things you would like to know about your competitors, and the most difficult items of information to obtain are marked with an asterisk. The items on the left of the table will be known to most companies which conduct market research and remain alert. However, even where the data is known, it tends to be poorly organized and communicated.

A few companies know most or all of the items in both columns, even though information on competitive trade discounts and profit by market or brand may be fragmentary and based on enlightened guesswork. None of this requires industrial espionage or unethical conduct. It can be generated by hard, persistent and well-organized effort on a company-wide basis, led by the marketing department.

Now we come to the second question, that of sources of information. There are three types of competitive data – recorded, observable and opportunistic – and Table 17 (p. 134) gives some examples.

Let us take three examples at random. Competitive annual reports, especially for multinational companies, can be a gold-mine of information, since the amount of space given to your market or country usually indicates its importance to the group as a whole. Technical journals can be a valuable guide as to what the competi-

Table 16. *What You Need to Know About Competitors*

Most Companies Know	Most Companies Do Not Know
Sales by brand	Market segmentation
Share by brand	method
Distribution by brand	Trade discount structures*
Pricing by brand	Organization structure
Advertising expenditure	Sales per employee
by brand	Plant capacity utilization*
Sales promotion activity	Type of equipment used
Distribution system/	Labour rates
Depots	Raw material purchasing
Number of salesmen	methods
Number/Location of	Major suppliers
factories	Private-label volume
Identity of key executives	Future strategies*
Awareness/Attitude to	Company
brands	Philosophies/policies
Comparative product	New Product Plans*
performance	Motivation of key
Observable competitive	executives
strategies	Profit by market/product/
Total company profit	customer*
	Future investment plans

tion is interested in, as well as a source of ideas. After all, the Japanese firm Seiko picked up quartz-watch technology from perusal of Swiss technical journals, ignored by the local watch industry.[4] Planning applications in the localities of competitive operations can provide early warning of expansion or reorganization. However, few companies seek, organize and evaluate competitive data effectively. (See Chapter 7, the section on 'portfolio analysis'.)

Recorded data tends not to be analysed over time, and often fails to cross functional barriers. Observable data is typically recorded on a haphazard basis, with little evaluation. Opportunistic data is not always actively sought or disseminated. It is probably the most neglected of the three data sources and requires the most effort to organize.

The result of poor competitive analysis is a failure to spot competitive threats or to anticipate competitive moves. It brings

Table 17. *The Three Main Sources of Competitive Data*

Recorded Data	Observable Data	Opportunistic Data
Market or consumer research	Competitive Pricing	Equipment suppliers
Annual reports	Results of private-label or industrial contracts	Raw material suppliers
Credit reports	Promotions	Packaging suppliers
Trade press	Patent applications	
Employee journals	New product placement tests	
Stockbrokers' reports		
Technical journals	Test markets	
External analyses, e.g. Keynote, Mintel	Competitive advertising	
	Local planning applications	
Monopoly Commission reports		
Business press		
Media spending		

uncomfortable surprises and relegates a company to following rather than leading. In addition, there tends to be an emphasis on most recent events, and an absence of long-term perspective.

This situation provides marketers with a golden opportunity to take control of competitive analysis within the company and to upgrade it.

Here are some suggestions for how to achieve this:

- select key competitors to evaluate. Focus on three or four per market at most.
- select and brief data collectors in each department. This would include people in sales, purchasing, engineering, marketing, R & D and finance.
- apply the right resource levels to the task. It is usually worthwhile having at least a part-time competitive analyst, to chase, coordinate and evaluate competitive data.
- insist on regular returns from data collectors.
- publish regular tactical and strategic reports on competition. The tactical ones could be fortnightly and widely circulated. The strategic ones would be less frequent, perhaps quarterly, and go to senior management only.

Step 3B: competitive analysis drill

With a sound base of competitive knowledge, the next step is to put it to use. One of the best systems for doing this, which fits the offensive marketing approach, is the competitive analysis drill, used by General Electric in the USA.[5] This involves answering seven questions about competitors.

1. Who is the Competitor? Now? Five Years from Now?

Major competition consists of those products or services which the consumer regards as a viable alternative. It follows that the product may have different competitors in different segments of a market, as in the case of the British Rail passenger business:

> *BR's main competitor is the car, followed by express bus companies and airlines, these last, though more visible, being of much less importance. The exact nature of BR's competition varies according to purpose of travel, journey distance, time of week and type of customer.*
>
> *For example, the express bus is a significant competitor for leisure travel, but represents little challenge among commuters or business travellers. Airlines are in general competitors only for distances over 200 miles. And cars are strongest at weekends, when all members of the family are free to travel to the same destination, and the cost per person is thereby reduced.*

The identity of a company's or a brand's major competition should be reviewed regularly because the situation may change. Beware: don't just keep tabs on the usual competition, but watch out for newcomers emerging from unsuspected corners.

Factors which can cause changes in competitor identity include:
- acquisitions. General Motors recently entered the airborne defence sector by buying the Hughes Aircraft Company.
- deregulation. National Express buses became a significant competitor to BR only after deregulation in 1980.
- rapid growth in import penetration. Japanese examples are numerous. Italy and Sweden have also become strong in consumer durables throughout Europe via Indesit, Zanussi and Electrolux.

- changes in the relative importance of distribution channels.
- application of new technology to your markets. Quartz technology transformed the competitive line-up in watches.
- major changes in base raw materials.
- legislation.

All of these factors need to be watched closely. They may cause a shift in your allocation of resources or provide new marketing opportunities.

2. What are the Investment Priorities, Objectives and Goals of Your Major Competitors?

You know what your competitors have done in the past, and buried in there are many clues as to what they are likely to do in the future. As a marketing investigator, there are many pointers which will help you.

The attitudes and philosophies of your competitors deserve close study. With successful competitors, these attitudes tend to be deeply ingrained and change little, if at all. Any competitor of General Electric or Mars will know that their objective in any market is likely to be brand leadership, with little interest in being number two or number three for long. Many Japanese competitors are prepared to wait five or ten years before receiving a return on their investments when entering new markets.

However, attitudes do change, even among successful competitors. This may be due to new management, or to recognition that a particular long-established practice is not working, as in this example:

> For decades Procter & Gamble had a well-established practice of scientific test-marketing. The philosophy was to start by testing in a town or TV region, refine and develop the marketing plan in test, and, if successful, purchase plant for expansion on a broad scale and launch nationally.
>
> The effectiveness of this approach began to wear out in the 1970s, as competitors moved to distort Procter & Gamble's test markets. For example, when Procter & Gamble entered the tampon market with Rely in 1973, in a test in Rochester

136

> *(USA), Playtex increased its spending tenfold in this area.*
>
> *The Procter & Gamble Pampers test market in Sweden was invalidated by the local leader Molynlyke. And on a number of occasions Lever and Colgate surprised Procter & Gamble by their ability to read and act upon the results of Procter & Gamble test markets.*
>
> *By the mid-1980s Procter & Gamble had radically changed this philosophy, moving more quickly from test market to national distribution, and in some cases (e.g. Citrus Hill fruit juices) committing for national capital equipment before entering test areas. However, Unilever was very quick to spot this change in attitude and was 'allowing' for this as early as 1982.*

Another pointer to competitive priorities and goals is previous success or failure. It is quite normal to continue with a successful formula and to change one which is not working. If, as in this example, a competitor has been psychologically scarred by a particular product category or market, you ought to know:

> *A major international company had the capability to enter the French market in its prime product category. It had a superior product and know-how, and was faced with relatively unsophisticated local competition, following a strategy of low prices/mediocre quality.*
>
> *However, international management was not prepared even to consider entry to France. Seven or eight years earlier, this company had made a very ill-advised acquisition in France, and had to fold the acquired company after two years with heavy losses. It was possible to elicit the bare facts only in private conversation, since none of the present management team wished to talk about the experience. The fact that the market had changed, and that past mistakes could be avoided in future, carried little weight.*
>
> *It seems unlikely that this company will ever re-enter France.*

A third pointer to future competitive goals is direction of advertising and plant investment. Rational competitors advertise most heavily on products or markets which they believe have the most future potential. Knowledge of competitive plant investment, which can often be picked up from equipment suppliers or planning applications, is an invaluable guide to future competitive plans.

A final pointer is relative cost position. We are assuming that your company has mapped out its relative cost position by major market by competitors. Since your competitors may well have conducted a similar exercise, it is logical to expect them to give special priority to cost reduction in markets where they are at present high-cost operators. The message is that one should never be satisfied with a superior cost position, but always strive to improve it further.

3. How Important is Your Specific Market to Each Competitor and What is the Level of its Commitment?

The answer to this question tells you what effort each competitor is likely to make to defend or improve its position in your markets.

The factors influencing level of competitive commitment to a product or category are:

1. Percentage of company profits in this category in the UK and worldwide.
2. Whether the category is perceived as a growth area.
3. Management attitude, heritage, emotion.
4. Profit margins.

Anyone attacking IBM in mainframe computers, Kodak in colour film, or Xerox in office copiers can expect strong retaliation. But IBM would not react nearly so strongly in the typewriter market, nor Kodak in hospital equipment.

Table 18 shows relative importance and commitment by competitor in the UK cereal market. Importance is greater to Weetabix than

Table 18. *UK Breakfast Cereals: Commitment and Importance by Competitor*

Company	Importance	Commitment
Kellogg's	High	Very High
Weetabix	Very High	Very High
Nabisco	Low	Medium/Low
Quaker	Low	Limited

to Kellogg's, since for the latter the UK is not its largest market. The UK is important to Nabisco, but for biscuits and snacks rather than cereals. For Quaker, the UK is not a high-priority market.

4. What are the Competitors' Relative Strengths and Limitations?

This will become evident from your competitive analysis. When measuring your competitors it is important to use your own business as a yardstick. In what respects is each competitor better or worse than you are? Which of its strategies are working and which are not? Is it usually safe to assume that the former will be continued and the latter changed?

Some of the more important areas for evaluating competitors include:

- customer franchise.
- cost of operations.
- product quality and value.
- speed of response.
- persistence and determination.
- product development.
- financial position and attitudes.
- willingness to make long-term investments.

5. What Weaknesses Make the Competitors Vulnerable?

Knowing these gives you a trump card. You can then attack competitors with your strongest forces at their weakest points. A list of possible weaknesses that make competitors vulnerable follows:

- lack of cash.
- low margins.
- poor growth.
- high-cost operations or distribution.
- overdependence on one market.
- overdependence on one account.
- strength in falling sectors.
- short-term orientation.
- people problems.

139

- eye off the ball.
- predictability.
- product or service obsolescence/weakness.
- high market share.
- low market share.
- premium-price positioning.
- slow moving/bureaucratic.
- fiscal year fixation.

Most of these are obvious, and we shall examine only a few.

Lack of cash can always make a small competitor vulnerable to larger, better-financed companies. Del Monte entered the UK fruit juice market late, but, backed by the large pocket of R. J. Reynolds Industries Inc., soon spent its way into leadership against Adams' Just Juice, which lacked the resources to fight a long battle of attrition.

People problems can make a competitor vulnerable. If a competitor is experiencing high personnel turnover or frequent management changes, it becomes an attractive target for attack.

Low market share is a conspicuous weakness. But a competitor with a high market share can also be in peril, despite apparent dominance. It may have become complacent. Retailers or distributors may wish to topple it, or at least encourage stronger competition. And, most important of all, a company with a high market share may have a limited interest in launching new products because of the risk of cannibalizing existing products. It can also be open to a price war.

6. What Changes are Competitors Likely to Make in their Future Strategies?

This question will usually answer itself if the first five questions have been thoroughly analysed. However, it is worthwhile at this stage estimating where competitive divisions or brands stand on the portfolio analysis of the group to which they belong. (See Chapter 7 for a discussion of portfolio analysis.) Are they seen as strong investment candidates, or 'cash cows' (see p. 150) to finance developments elsewhere?

It is always more comfortable competing against a cash cow, on which profits are being maximized, than against a 'star' (see p.151), on which heavy investment is richly lavished.

7. So What? What Effects Will All Your Competitors' Strategies Have on the Industry, on the Market and on Your Strategy?

This is the question which pulls together the whole process of competitive analysis described above.

Step 4: Key Factors for Success

Having completed the first three steps – the three wheels of the business environment, the internal examination and the competitive analysis – we are now ready to grind on to Step 4, the key factor(s) for success (KFS).

Plotting the KFS in your markets enables you to identify how well equipped you are to enter or compete in them. You should not attempt to look at *all* factors for success, only the handful of most important ones – perhaps between four and six. Inability to meet all of them usually constitutes a barrier to entry to new markets or points to poor future prospects in existing markets.

The two main values of KFS are that they enable you to judge your fitness for existing or new markets and to identify priority areas for building competitive advantages. An edge over competitors in any of the KFS is likely to be important and exploitable.

The nature of KFS will vary widely by market. Useful questions to ask in determining KFS include:

1. What are the largest areas of cost in this business?

   In fast-food outlets they will be the cost of materials and labour, in cosmetics or perfumes they will probably be packaging and advertising, in railways the costs of track, signalling, and trains.

2. Looking at other companies in this business, what have been the main reasons for their success or failure?

   Product range may be a factor. In some businesses companies with the widest and narrowest product ranges are among the most successful, while those in between languish. In the defence business, relations and contacts with government are a key factor for success.

3. In which areas of this business is it possible to build a competitive advantage?

Looking at what has worked or not worked for competitors over the years will produce some answers. But there may be opportunities waiting there which have been overlooked by competitors.

Table 19 demonstrates the different KFS in the marketing of colour film (e.g. Kodak) and greetings cards (e.g. Fine Art Developments plc).

Table 19. *Key Factors for Success*

Colour Film	Greeting Cards
Good-quality product	Ability to read changing needs
Competitive price	Strong design capability
Wide retail distribution	Effective distribution strategy
Strong relationship with processors	In-store stock control/merchandising
Advertising support	Efficient production
	Efficient inventory control

The colour-film market is so dominated by Kodak, with a majority of the world market, that the KFS differ between Kodak and other competitors. The KFS in Table 19 are written from Kodak's viewpoint, and Kodak scores well on all five factors listed.

The product is good, though not superior to Fuji's. The price is higher than Fuji's, but not beyond the level justified by Kodak's reputation. The relationship with independent laboratory processors is so strong that Kodak was able to persuade them to invest heavily in new equipment at their own expense, prior to the introduction of the disc camera.

From the viewpoint of Fuji, or 3M, which does almost all store private-label film (e.g. Boots), the KFS would be different. Because of the entrenched position of Kodak, they would need to offer either a superior product or a lower price. This they do, Fuji's prices being 10 per cent below Kodak, and private label considerably cheaper. The other three KFS are broadly similar for Kodak or Fuji.

In the case of greetings cards, it is also clear that, to be effective, any competitor has to score well on all six factors. An effective distribution strategy is unusually important in this category, since the competing alternatives include mail order, franchised shops (e.g. Hallmark), supermarkets, stationers, variety stores, specialist card shops, newsagents and specialist wholesalers. In addition, because the product range is so wide, a sophisticated store merchandising system is essential, to ensure that space is related to sell-out to consumers, by individual card and by category.

Like everything else, KFS can change. Such a change can provide a threat to existing competitors and an opportunity to new ones. For example, to compete in the frozen-food market five years ago, it was necessary to have a large fleet of refrigerated vehicles. This gave an advantage to large manufacturers and was a barrier to entry for smaller ones. However, the move by many grocery retailers to central warehousing for frozen foods means that a small manufacturer can get to market if it owns only a few trunker vehicles. With the growth of independent frozen-food hauliers, even this is no longer necessary.

Equally, companies can change the nature of KFS by innovation, as Canon did in office copiers. Before Canon's entry into the market a KFS in copiers was a well-organized sales-service force to call regularly on offices. Canon's machines were largely self-maintaining, due to use of cartridges and replaceable parts, thereby reducing the importance of this KFS.

Step 5: SWOT analysis

This familiar technique is the final step in the strategic groundwork. It translates the four previous steps into a format which provides the basis for developing winning strategies.

The SWOT analysis (see Table 20) is a summary of your strengths and weaknesses, and of the opportunities and threats facing you. It can be applied to brands, markets, divisions or companies, and has three main functions: planning, offensive and defensive.

For example, let us look at International Thomson's decision to enter the package-holiday business in the mid-1960s, which illustrates the offensive use of the SWOT analysis:

> *At this time, International Thomson was a publishing and information technology company. In considering diversification it defined its main strengths as follows:*

143

Table 20. *Three Main Functions of SWOT Analysis*

Function	Result and Value
Planning	Connecting link between business analysis and strategy development
Offensive	Use your *strengths* to attack *competitive weaknesses*
	Identify and exploit best opportunities
Defensive	Highlights threats
	Basis for heading off most important threats or preparing counterattack

- *marketing-oriented with expertise in selling to the final consumer.*
- *well-trained and versatile management.*
- *ability to use the company's newspapers and magazines to advertise at low cost.*

   Among its weaknesses were:

- *limited financial resources.*
- *lopsided cash-flow cycle, stronger in the second half of the year, due to the newspaper business.*

   Based on this analysis, International Thomson therefore set up some criteria for new market selection, which included these requirements:

- *relatively low initial capital investment.*
- *growth potential.*
- *industries where Thomson's marketing skills would be relevant.*
- *reverse cash flow to newspapers, i.e. cash in the early part of the year.*
- *preference for service industries, though avoiding those with high technological requirements.*

   Applying these criteria, Thomson eventually chose the package-holiday business. As well as meeting Thomson's list of requirements, this industry was full of entrepreneurs with limited resources.

   Thomson bought three existing package tour companies and a small airline (Britannia Airways) in 1964. Throughout the 1970s it applied a consistent strategy of wide product range,

*competitive pricing and leadership in information technology
as a means to achieving superior customer service.*

*For many years, Thomson has been the clear market leader
in package holidays.*[6]

The quality of a SWOT analysis will obviously depend on the
thoroughness of the four steps preceding it, and its practical
usefulness can be enhanced by following a few simple rules:

1. Keep it brief, perhaps three to four pages at most.
2. Relate the statement of strengths and weaknesses pri-
    marily to the key factors for success identified in Step 4.
    This will ensure that you concentrate on the important
    strengths.
3. Strengths and weaknesses should, wherever possible,
    be stated in competitive terms. You are looking for
    exploitable strengths, areas in which you are stronger
    than the competition. It is reassuring to be 'good' at
    something, but it is more effective to be 'better'.

    Below are a wrong and a right positioning of a
    strength. The wrong positioning is a bland statement.
    The right one identifies a competitive advantage, and it
    formed the basis for Frito-Lay's entry into the US cookie
    market against Nabisco with a short-life product:

    Wrong: Frito-Lay has a large and well-disciplined sales
    force, 14,000 strong, selling crisps to a wide
    range of retail and catering accounts, with high
    frequency of call.

    Right: Frito-Lay has a *larger sales force than Nabisco*
    (14,000 v. 3,500), directly covers 40 per cent
    more accounts, at *three times Nabisco's call
    frequency*.

4. Statements should be specific and blandness should be
    avoided. Consider the wrong and right expressions of
    the Beecham strength below. The right one opens up
    the possibility of using striped-gel technology in mar-
    kets other than toothpaste – such as haircare – while the
    wrong one limits the exploitation of this technology to
    toothpaste only:

    Wrong: Beecham has a cost and quality edge over all

> *toothpaste* competitors in striped-gel manufacturing technology.
>
> **Right:** Beecham has a cost and quality edge over all competitors in striped-gel manufacturing technology.

5. The SWOT analysis should not just be confined to marketing issues, but should cover the whole company operation. For example, topics to cover would include technological opportunities and risks, the company's relative cost position v. competitors, attitudes to investment and risk, degree of marketing orientation and so on.

6. Be objective, both about your own company and about competitors. The SWOT analysis is an important strategic tool, not a device for making senior management feel good.

7. Objective analysis of competitors is also difficult. In general, companies tend to overrate the strengths of large competitors and underrate those of smaller ones.

Having completed the strategic grind, we are now at last ready to develop winning strategies.

● **Summary**

Objectives describe desired destination, strategies set out the routes chosen for achieving the objectives, and plans constitute the vehicle for getting to the destination along the chosen route.

Winning strategies are a necessity for any business which is to succeed in the long-term. They are rarely developed in a flash of inspiration, and more often evolve over time as a result of trial and error, plus rigorous business analysis.

The groundwork for strategy is prepared in five steps – the business environment, internal examination, competitor analysis, identification of key factors for success and SWOT analysis.

The three wheels of the **business environment (Step 1)** are direct, indirect and macro. Penguin Biscuits and BA were given as examples.

146

Summary

The internal examination (Step 2) is a model which enables you to ask candid questions about your own company or brand – its past performance, attitudes, strategy and quality of execution. Where are you leading or following? Where are you winning or losing? Are you in the right markets or sectors? Which strategies are working and which are not? Are any showing signs of wearing out?

Competitive analysis (Step 3A) covers what you need to know about your competitors, and how to acquire that knowledge. **Competitive analysis drill (Step 3B)** puts that knowledge to use. It involves answering seven questions about your competitors.

Key factors for success (Step 4) identify the performance areas in which you must match or beat competition in order to succeed. They enable you to judge your fitness in existing markets and chances in new ones and to pinpoint priority areas for building competitive advantages.

The SWOT analysis (Step 5) translates the four previous steps into a format which provides the basis for developing competitive advantages. It is the connecting link between business analysis and strategy development.

All this is hard work and requires as much native grit as native wit. It has only one purpose – action, in the form of strategy development. If it contributes to building a winning strategy, as indeed it should, the effort is worthwhile.

7 | *Developing Winning Strategies*

Supreme excellence consists in breaking the enemy's resistance without fighting. Thus the highest form of generalship is to baulk the enemy's plans. The next best is to prevent the junction of the enemy's forces. The next in order is to attack the enemy in the field. The worst policy of all is to besiege walled cities. [Sun Tsu]

Setting Offensive Corporate Objectives

While the setting of corporate objectives is the responsibility of the board of directors, the marketing department should always be asked for a viewpoint, because of its front-line involvement in the achievement of these objectives. Objectives are usually expressed in financial terms. At minimum, a company should aim for a rate of increase in earnings per share which will cover inflation, and give the shareholder sufficient growth beyond this to compensate for the investment risk.

The separation of objectives and strategies is a good intellectual discipline, but in practice there is considerable interaction between them. If the board of directors knows that the company has a fully worked-out strategy for entering a plump new market, it will be more inclined to set ambitious objectives. Equally, a board would be unwise to be unduly influenced by disappointing past results – this should make it even more determined to set and achieve tough objectives for the future.

There is an undoubted psychological element in setting targets, as athletes have often shown. After standing as the pinnacle of track accomplishment for many years, the record for the four-minute mile was eventually broken by Roger Bannister, but his feat was rapidly emulated by many others, suggesting that the four-minute barrier was as much psychological as physical. Lord Forte puts it well:

> It is amazing if one sets a target, how easily one hits that target. Unfortunately, I have learnt this at a very late age: I wish I had known it consciously before, instead of only subconsciously. If a manager says that this is the objective in two years' time, and we want to reach that turnover or make that profit, it is quite amazing how one does it – given the possibility, of course. You must not say, we are going to jump 8 feet, because that is out of the question. You'll break your neck. But what is the record – 6 feet 7 inches? Try and jump that. And when you've succeeded, put it up another ¼ inch. The art of reaching business targets is not to aim at the impossible, but to aim at the championship level – which you already know to be possible.[1]

Objective-setting is a good measure of a company's success in offensive marketing. Unless ambitious objectives are established, there is little incentive for executives to apply the offensive marketing approach.

● Offensive Strategy

As the Koran says: 'If you don't know where you're going, any road will take you there.' The most important question for marketing people is this: 'Why should customers buy our products or services rather than our competitor's, now and in the future?' Unless the answer is clear, convincing and backed by unambiguous evidence, you do not have a winning strategy.

The purpose of offensive marketing is to win. As business becomes more competitive, winning becomes more difficult.

Everyone would like to find a fast-growing market with high margins and little competition. But few are so fortunate, since most fast-growing markets prove profitable only to those with the strongest propositions and the most staying power.

Offensive strategy is all about setting priorities and avoiding bland, middle-of-the-road positions. It involves:

- selecting the most effective point at which to attack. The classic military offensive concentrates the attacker's strongest weapons on the enemy's weakest lines of defence. Marketing follows similar principles, and the most successful attacks are pinpointed on targeted segments, against selected competitors.
- concentrating business resources into the areas of best return. This usually calls for the movement of resources (operations, people, advertising, R & D) from areas of low return into areas of high return.[2]
- developing competitive advantages, so that your planned attack at a selected point is effective.

The strategic groundwork covered in Chapter 6 is essential for all three of these moves, and portfolio analysis, which is dealt with in the next section, is useful in clarifying the first two.

 Values and Limitations of Portfolio Analysis

Portfolio analysis is a useful graphic device for examining the competitive position of your products or businesses, and for conducting a similar exercise on your competitors. It is too crude to use in isolation, but can be helpful in focusing the more extensive analysis described in the previous chapter, or in triggering detailed strategic discussion. The structure of the portfolio also forces executives to set priorities and make choices. Portfolio analysis is most often used to determine resource allocation by product, or, in a diversified company, by type of business.

The most common forms are the Boston Consulting Group's (BCG) Share/Growth Matrix and the Competitive Position/Market Attractiveness Matrix, generally associated with McKinsey, General Electric and Shell. Both have the homely appearance of bingo cards, but greater utility. In its basic form, the BCG Matrix relates relative market share (RMS)* to market growth. A product with a high RMS in a growing market is a 'star', while a minor product in a falling market is a 'dog', as in Figure 16.

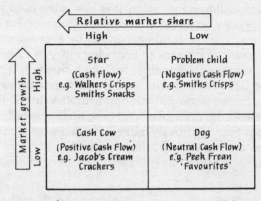

Figure 16. BCG Share/Growth Matrix (Nabisco UK)

The examples used relate to Nabisco Ltd in the UK. Walkers has many of the characteristics of the star. Its RMS is about 1·4 in crisps nationally against Golden Wonder, with high RMS in certain regions and trade sectors. Walkers Crisps is very profitable, even after heavy advertising and capital investment.

Smith's Crisps has a 0·4 RMS against Walkers (i.e. Smiths has a market share of about 10 per cent and Walkers has about 24 per cent) and probably also has a negative cash flow. It is a 'problem child'. The issue is whether to invest more heavily to make Smiths Crisps into a star, or whether to milk the brand and relegate it to dog status.

Jacob's Cream Crackers is a 'cash cow'. It is long-established, with a high share of the declining plain biscuit market. Cash cows are traditionally rather profitable, since they tend to benefit from scale economies and past marketing investment, while receiving limited resource in the present.

The Peek Frean range of budget biscuits is a dog. It has a

* e.g. if your share is 20 per cent, Competitor A's is 10 per cent and Competitor B's is 5 per cent, your relative market share (RMS) is 2 against Competitor A and 4 against Competitor B.

low RMS in the static 'bargain'-biscuit segment, and little future potential.

A classic application of the BCG Matrix is to use the cash cow as a means of building bigger stars and converting the more responsive problem children into stars. It is also often used as a tool in allocating priority between businesses or countries. For example, a company may use the funds generated by a strong position in a mature business as a means of financing entry to a new market.

Some international companies with high shares in static markets regard the UK as a cash cow, and use it to finance expansion to countries offering faster growth opportunities, in the Far East for instance. However, cash cows tend to be in short supply. They may have already been vigorously milked. Furthermore, one company's cash cow is another's opportunity for attack.

Booz Allen & Hamilton estimates that by traditional portfolio

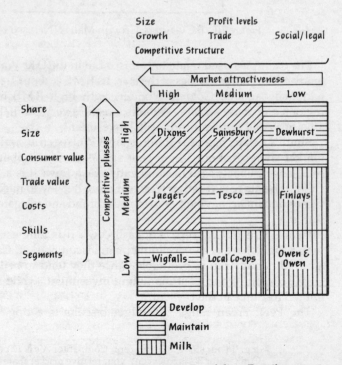

Figure 17. Investment Decision Portfolio – Retailers

analysis 72 per cent of business units in US industry are dogs, 15 per cent are cash cows, 10 per cent problem children and only 3 per cent stars, and we would not expect the proportions for either business units or products to be much different in the UK.[3]

The McKinsey/General Electric Matrix introduces more elements and is slightly more complex, but follows similar principles. The portfolio model shown in Figure 17 is a typical example, illustrating competitive pluses and market attractiveness for a range of retailers. For example, Dixons enjoys a strong position in a dynamic retail sector, while Owen & Owen occupies a rather modest position in the lacklustre department store segment.

This area of bingo, astrology and mixed metaphors is often taken too seriously. The examples given illustrate the subjective nature of the choices, and underline the need to use portfolio analysis with caution, always bearing in mind the dangers of simplistic application.

● **Types of Competitive Advantage**

Competitive advantage is achieved whenever you do something better than competitors. If that something is important to consumers, or if a number of small advantages can be combined, you have an *exploitable* competitive advantage. One or more competitive advantages are usually necessary in order to develop a winning strategy, and this in turn should enable your company to achieve above-average growth and profits in its industry.

This section will give a number of examples of types of competitive advantages. It is not exhaustive and a more detailed list is provided in Appendix 3.

Superior product benefit

Having a better product is one of the most powerful competitive advantages, especially if the nature of the advantage is important to the consumer. In cars, for example, superior styling and appearance are of considerable interest to buyers, whereas greater safety makes less impact on most consumers.

The rapid application of solid-state technology to TV sets gave Japanese brands product superiority over most American TV sets in the 1970s:

153

Motorola, a US firm, developed solid-state technology in 1966, but gave it less priority than the Japanese. Solid-state technology provided superior reliability, less servicing and lower energy consumption than vacuum-tube sets. It also made possible much greater automation in production.

Hitachi was the first company to convert its whole product range to solid state, in 1969, and by the following year all major Japanese competitors in the USA had converted.

At this time, Motorola was the only American firm with a 100 per cent solid-state set, and it was not until 1973–5 that most US firms converted. For three to five years Japanese firms enjoyed product superiority and by the mid-1970s they were strongly established in larger colour TV sets.[4]

However, a better product will only form the basis for a winning strategy if it is backed by correct pricing, distribution and marketing strategies.

Perceived advantage

The superior product benefit just covered can be physically proved by demonstration, by objective analysis or by blind product tests among consumers. *Perceived* advantage, by contrast, is in the mind of the consumer – a result of a product's imagery and personality.

Perceived advantages are usually built through advertising and packaging. They are seen most often in products associated with social occasions or visible consumption. Examples are clothes, cosmetics, soft drinks, alcoholic drinks, sporting goods or cigarettes. Marlboro , with its cowboy image, has powered its way to a 22 per cent share of the US market. The brand is well marketed, but there is no reason to believe Marlboro cigarettes are objectively superior in consumer acceptance.

Coca-Cola is an example of a brand whose image and heritage are sufficiently strong to overcome apparent product weaknesses:

For some years before the launch of New Coke, Pepsi-Cola was preferred in blind tests to market leader Coca-Cola by American consumers.

Then in April 1985 Coca-Cola introduced New Coke, which had been preferred to original Coke in scores of blind-taste tests. However, consumer reaction to New Coke was so mixed that the original formulation, renamed Coca-Cola Classic, was reintroduced as a sister brand six weeks later. Subsequently it heavily outsold New Coke. So we have the paradoxical situation of Coca-Cola Classic outselling the same product to which it lost on blind test. This confirms what was obvious to many – that the advantages of Coca-Cola lay in its image and history, not in the product.

Perceived advantage can also be developed by design or styling. The price commanded by Mercedes cars is above the level one would expect from an objective analysis of performance and reliability:

The price of a new Mercedes 280 S E is 56 per cent more than a new Ford Granada 2·8 Ghia. Size, maximum speed, acceleration and miles per gallon are similar. Perceived and actual reliability of the Mercedes is high. It is too early to assess the reliability of the new Granada, but the previous model was slightly above average and scored well on absence of rust.

Comparative price and performance figures are shown in Table 21.

Table 21. *Granada vs. Mercedes**

Model	Price (£)	Maximum Speed	Acceleration 0–60 (seconds)	MPG at 56mph	Length (inches)
Granada 2·8 Ghia	13,164	129	9·0	38	184
Mercedes 280 SE	20,600	121	9·5	35	185

* What Car?, December 1985. Price includes comparable equipment, such as ABS braking and sunroof.

Low-cost operator

This is not a matter of 'We work lousy, but we work cheap', and it goes beyond low-cost production. A low-cost operator (LCO) strives to achieve lower costs than its competitors for similar products, on all elements built into the final delivered entity. This requires low costs not only in operations, but also in selling, distribution, administration and even marketing. The LCO is striving for a cost advantage to provide a winning strategy of superior value.

Many Japanese international companies are LCOs. In the 1960s and 1970s they often competed in the lower-price market segments, providing, for instance, in cars, high reliability with mediocre styling at very competitive prices. The Japanese are now bringing the LCO approach up-market, while also greatly improving product design.

An increasingly common strategy among blue-chip companies is to combine LCO with superior product quality, and to market at premium prices. When successful, this strategy results in superior consumer value and high profit margins. IBM and Heinz are among companies pursuing this strategy.

There are a number of ways to develop a competitive advantage through low-cost operation, including:

- high productivity. As seen in the Introduction, Sainsbury achieves low-cost operation mainly because its sales per foot are much higher than its competitors'. American Airlines gains 64 per cent more revenue per employee than the IATA average.[5] Toyota's dense concentration of synchronized factories and suppliers – mainly in Toyota City, and turning out twice as many vehicles per year as Metropolitan Detroit – is one of the keys to its low cost and high productivity.[6]
- low overheads. Many small or medium-size companies have a competitive cost advantage on this count. There may be few staff – the owner may deal personally with major buyers, personnel/work study/engineering departments may not exist and accounting may be basic. By contrast, divisions of some major companies are charged 2 per cent for 'head-office overheads', in return for benefits which are not always apparent and on top of their own overheads.
- low labour costs. Here again, small companies are less likely to be unionized, and will often pay lower rates than their larger competitors, while also gaining greater flexibility in working methods.

156

- better purchasing. Underwoods, a chemist chain only a fraction the size of Boots, is reputed to buy from some suppliers at lower cost than Boots. Purchasing skill can be more important than theoretical bargaining power.
- limited product range. Kwik Save has the lowest branded grocery prices in the UK, but relatively high profit margins. One of the factors in Kwik Save's low-cost operation is its narrow range of under 1,500 products (against 7,000 in a large Sainsbury). These products can be bought and sold in high volume, and do not require individual price marking because the check-out operators carry all the prices in their heads.
- low-cost distribution and selling. Small companies with narrow ranges can often achieve a competitive advantage by concentrating supply on a limited number of large customers and by delivering to their warehouses. Their larger competitors covering the whole trade may need a fleet of trucks and scores of salesmen.

Some companies achieve low-cost operation by exploiting a number of advantages:

The Equitable Life, the oldest mutual life assurance company in the world, founded in 1762, is a low-cost operator compared with most life companies. As a mutual company, it has no shareholders to pay dividends to, and all profits are ultimately channelled back to its customers (i.e. policy-holders). In addition, the Equitable does not pay commission to agents or brokers, and generates new business through recommendations by financial journalists and policy-holders.

The Equitable's low-cost position assists it in achieving high investment performance, and this in turn produces new business. The strategy is circular. As long as the Equitable continues at or near the top of the investment tables, its low-cost structure can be sustained.

Legal advantages

Patents, copyrights, sole distributorships or protected positions can provide competitive advantages. Patent protection is important in pharmaceuticals, but can be achieved in other markets. Wall's Viennetta ice-cream has been successfully patented in the UK and is not available under store private labels.

Superior contacts

In most businesses strong contact with large buying organizations can be a competitive advantage, but this may be only temporary, due to changes in personnel or deterioration in the quality of the contact. Businesses where superior contacts have most importance are those where a single purchaser can influence very large orders, as in building or defence. In such cases the contact is most likely to be a competitive advantage if it is plugged in at many levels in both the buying and selling organizations, rather than dependent on one or two people. The old fashioned one-to-one link can easily break down, and a multi-plug set of contacts is more effective. Figure 18 shows a seven-plug contact between a manufacturer and retailer.

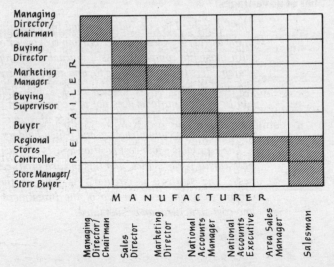

Figure 18. Multi-plug Contact – Manufacturer and Retailer

The principles of this model could also be applied to advertising agents and clients, defence contractors and governments, or frozen-chip producers and fast-food chains.

Superior knowledge

Competitive advantages can be built in by better business analysis, superior information systems, creative market segmentation or better understanding of costs. In many developing countries, Beecham has a strong position, created partly by use of market research, since few of its local competitors apply this effectively.

Scale advantages

Size can be a source of competitive advantage (or the reverse if it produces complacency or bureaucracy). In almost any business size can generate a financial advantage with the use of advertising. £1 million worth of advertising will result in a given impact whether your company is large or small. If your revenue is £100 million, £1 million of advertising is equivalent to 1 per cent of sales, whereas if it is only £10 million the same advertising effort accounts for 10 per cent of sales.

This principle applies to the costs of selling. To cover a particular retail trade, you need a certain number of sales representatives. If Company A has a sales force twice as big as its nearest competitor, but a market share three times greater, its sales-force cost ratio will still be lower. It therefore has a larger resource at less relative cost.

Scale advantages can also operate strongly in manufacturing and service operations. If you are a large retailer, property developers or investment groups are much more likely to contact you first about a hot development prospect than your smaller competitors.

The competitive advantages of scale largely explain why market leaders usually achieve much higher profit margins than the second or third contenders, and why market leadership is often an important objective for offensive marketers.

Attitudes

Any of the attitudes described in Chapter 3, 'Offensive Attitudes', can constitute an important competitive advantage.

● Can Any Company Develop Competitive Advantages?

The answer is clearly yes. Table 22 shows the five levels of competitive advantage. The objective of any company should be to move up to one of the top two levels. Those in the three bottom levels will struggle to survive in the long-term unless they step up. You may wish to consider which level your company or brand is on. Few companies are on levels 1, 2 or 5. Companies on level 5 disappear, or get sold off, like International Stores. Most companies inhabit levels 3 and 4, and probably generate the 70 per cent or so dogs identified in Booz Allen & Hamilton's portfolio analysis of American business units (see p. 153).

Table 22. *Five Types of Competitive Status*

Level	Competitive status	Examples
1	One or more large advantages	IBM
2	A number of small advantages adding up to large one	McDonald's
3	Advantages present, not recognized or exploited	Horlicks prior to acquisition
4	No significant competitive advantages	Midland Bank
5	Competitive disadvantages	International Stores

It is easiest for companies on level 3 to move up, since all that is required is good management. Prior to acquisition by Beecham, Horlicks was a convenience product inconvenient to use, directed at a declining consumption occasion (pre-bedtime), with an under-exploited brand name. Beecham eventually recognized the brand's potential advantages and did to Horlicks what it had already done to Ribena, Lucozade and Macleans:

> *Horlicks – made from wheat flour and malted barley – was invented by Arabella and William Horlick in 1883 in the USA, but had disappeared there by the time Beecham bought the brand in 1969. Eight years later, Horlicks had shown no*

volume growth in the UK and sales were stuck at around £6 million.

In 1978 the brand was repositioned as a relaxing hot drink, as opposed to a bedtime drink. The advertising used humans with keys in their backs. They were wound up during the day and relaxed with Horlicks.

In 1982 Beecham at last launched an Instant Horlicks, as a sister product to the traditional one. The advertising for Instant Horlicks stressed that the product could be enjoyed at any time of the day, and that it dissolved instantly with hot water.

Positioning was further refined and developed in 1985–6. Traditional Horlicks was directed at mothers who like the ritual and nourishment of a milk drink, while 'Instant' was relaunched as a low-fat drink for health-conscious consumers. Both versions of Horlicks continued to be marketed under the overall message of the 'relaxing drink'. Instant Horlicks volume has doubled in the past year and total brand sales are projected at £26 million for 1986.

So here we have a brand over 100 years old, whose sales in the past eight years have more than doubled at high profit margins.

● Offensive Strategies for Exploiting Competitive Advantages

Having completed the strategic groundwork and developed your competitive advantages, you are now at last in a position to carve out a winning strategy. Any company has at its disposal a wide range of possible offensive strategies. Some of the main ones are reviewed below.

Head-on

This strategy involves a direct frontal attack to drive back or overwhelm a competitor. To apply a head-on strategy successfully, a company needs strong products and heavy marketing support, since existing competitors are likely to counterattack in order to maintain their position.

161

A head-on strategy is most appropriate for a large, well-financed company, prepared to fight a battle of attrition, since it rarely produces quick breakthroughs.

IBM and Procter & Gamble are among the companies which frequently use the head-on approach. Procter & Gamble, for example, typically develops a product preferred on consumer blind test to leading competition, gains wide trade distribution, delivers product samples to most homes and out-advertises all-comers. Its entry to the chilled and frozen juice market in the USA demonstrates one of its less successful applications of this general approach, since it is doubtful whether Citrus Hill Select has a sufficient product advantage to justify its premium price:

> *Juice is a large market worth about $2·5 billion. Brand leader is Coca-Cola's Minute Maid with 24 per cent, followed by Beatrice Food's Tropicana with 15 per cent. Much of the remaining business is in store private-label brands.*
>
> *Procter & Gamble with a reputed target share of 15 per cent launched its Citrus Hill brand at the end of 1983, and launched an improved version, Citrus Hill Select, in 1985.*
>
> *Citrus Hill Select uses new processing technology, which is claimed to result in superior taste. It is premium-priced against other brands, including Minute Maid.*
>
> *Advertising spending in 1984 was estimated at $100 million for Citrus Hill, and the 1985 level may well be similar. By contrast, the brand leader, Minute Maid, only spent $14·6 million on advertising in 1984, and the number two, Tropicana, spent $12·2 million. Citrus Hill also distributed samples to consumers.*
>
> *By mid-1985 Citrus Hill had achieved only a 9 per cent market share, but there were no signs that Procter & Gamble's determination was weakening.*[7]

In the UK package-holiday market the leaders, Thomson and Intasun, have utilized their competitive advantages of lower-cost operation to attack competitors head-on with a lower-price strategy. This has succeeded not only in raising brand share, but also in expanding the total market.

In the USA the 3M Company has launched a head-on attack against Japanese competitors in the videotape market, and the strategy is a mixture of offence and defence:

In the late 1960s 3M pioneered magnetic recording tape, but during the 1970s Japanese producers such as T D K virtually took over the market through low pricing, and by 1982 3M had become a minor player.

3M has taken steps to ensure that this story will not be repeated in videotapes. Its 3M tape, already ranked number one in quality, is being joined by E X G, a higher-quality tape which is premium-priced.

3M is capitalizing on its distribution advantage by putting its video cassettes into a wider range of vendors, from office suppliers to discount stores. And it appears to be matching the Japanese blow for blow on price, in the knowledge that the video-tape market is likely to be worth $7 billion by 1990. The National Sales Director of T D K's U S subsidiary commented: 'I have never seen an effort of this magnitude.'

3M's aim is to maintain market leadership in the U S A and to become number one in Japan, where it already has a 10 per cent share.[8]

Flanking

This strategy involves attacking a competitor on a flank which is weakly defended. The competitor may lack skills in this sector, regard it as a low priority or be committed to a 'milking' strategy. In any event, a flanking attack is likely to draw a much weaker response than a head-on offensive, because the defender may not feel directly threatened, at least in the short-term.

Flanking strategy follows the classic approach of attacking the competitor's weakest point with your strongest weapon. It needs to be followed through at pace, because the threat posed by the flanker becomes clearer over time and can eventually lead to a strong competitive response. The flanking strategy will be illustrated by examining the attacks made on 'fortress' Birds Eye over the past twenty years.

Birds Eye saw off head-on attacks in the 1960s and 1970s, but has increasingly been flanked in the past decade:

Birds Eye innovated the frozen-foods market in the UK, and has remained one of the best-known brands in the grocery market. In the 1960s Birds Eye's share was over 60 per cent,

Findus's 20 per cent, and smaller brands plus private label had the rest.

Findus, employing an identical marketing approach to Birds Eye, of superior quality/premium price, attempted a few head-on attacks, but these were half-hearted and made little progress. The dominance of Birds Eye discouraged would-be attackers.

In the 1970s there were two successful flanking movements against Birds Eye, one by store private labelling, the other by Ross Foods.

Store private labelling at first concentrated its flanking efforts in market sectors of low interest to Birds Eye – low-price/moderate-quality commodity sectors like peas, fish fingers and burgers. It made strong progress, but Birds Eye continued to dominate the higher-quality and added-value sectors.

In the past few years the private-label attack has changed from flanking to head-on, as operators like Sainsbury have moved up-market, strengthened their own brand name and innovated their own new products.

In the early 1970s Ross Foods was a marginal operator in retail frozen foods with only a 2 to 3 per cent share, although it was strong in catering outlets. Over the next decade, Ross displaced Findus as number two brand by employing two flanking strategies.

The first was the development of a broad range of reasonable-quality products in large economy packs. This was an un-attractive route for Birds Eye or Findus, since they made much higher margins on smaller, premium-quality packs. The second was vigorous pursuit of private labelling, led by the economy range. Again Birds Eye and Findus had little interest in competing, since they did not wish to fuel the growth of private labelling.

By the mid-1980s Ross had begun to move away from the flank into more of a head-on position against Birds Eye.

In 1985 Birds Eye remained clear brand leader though with a reduced share. Ross had about 9 per cent, Findus has been squeezed down between the two to 3 per cent, while store private labelling now holds 34 per cent of market value.

This process can be illustrated as shown in Figure 19. McCain appears for the first time in the 1980s. Its strategy of the mid-1970s was to create a 'niche' in the market, but this became a flanking strategy in the early 1980s and could develop into a head-on attack in the later 1980s.

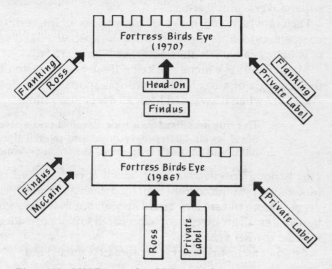

Figure 19. UK Frozen-food Wars in the 1970s and 1980s

In general, more companies use a flanking rather than a head-on strategy, and flanking tends to be lower-risk with a higher probability of success. This appears to apply in both business and in war. In an analysis of 280 campaigns from the Greek Wars to World War I, Liddell Hart concluded that in only six (2·1 per cent) did a head-on assault produce decisive results.[9]

The classic flanking moves in business tend to involve price (high or low), neglected segments or product innovation. Bic flanked Gillette in razors by innovating the low-priced disposable sector. Knorr and Batchelor flanked Heinz soups by introducing low-price packet soups after Heinz had seen off an earlier head-on attack by Campbell's. In each case the 'fortress' was slow to react, aware that strong reaction would accelerate the growth of a new lower-margin sector.

Niche or focus

The words 'niche' or 'focus' are used interchangeably to describe this strategy, which involves entering markets or segments which are too small or specialized to attract large competitors. Ideally, niche markets are small harbours which the supertankers cannot enter.

Factors which can make niche markets uninteresting to large competitors include the need to acquire specialized skills or the lack of volume against which to amortize high overheads.

Morgan Cars is a niche marketer. It caters for a customer seeking the nostalgia of a hard-riding pre-war sports car, as described by *What Car?* when it awarded Morgan a four-star rating:

> The ride's as hard as a rock, comfort and space minimal, noise levels deafeningly high, and overall the sports car has about as much refinement as a tractor. Wonderful![10]

This is not a specification with much appeal to Ford or General Motors, and yet the current wait for delivery of a new Morgan is six years.[11] Morgan cars lack broad appeal, but they have great attraction for a small group of people prepared to pay a considerable price in order to own a Morgan.

Another niche marketer is W. Jordan (Cereals) Ltd.

> *Jordans had been a small family milling business for 125 years until, in the late 1970s and early 1980s, it pioneered the UK markets for cereal bars and granola breakfast cereals. It has since found itself in direct competition with the likes of Quaker, Weetabix, Northern Foods, General Mills, United Biscuits, Lyons Tetley, Mars and Rowntree. That it has prospered in the face of such exalted opposition is perhaps confirmed by the countless 'inquiries' it has received from prospective purchasers in recent years.*
>
> *The Jordan family have long been advocates of the merits of wholefoods, and their granola and cereal bar products are therefore high in whole grains, seeds, nuts and fruit; low in sugar and other bulking agents; and totally devoid of artificial additives. These products were also among the first in the UK to carry nutritional labelling, and initially they were sold only through health food stores – a distribution channel which still accounts for around a quarter of their sales.*

This approach is not without its drawbacks, in that high product specifications necessitate high prices, and the absence of preservatives shortens shelf-life. In addition, the taste and texture of the finished product are not universal in their appeal.

Their larger competitors have only more recently come to recognize the 'healthy eating' phenomenon, and in any event are seeking to develop brands with much greater volume potential. Thus, they must compromise the strict canons of the wholefood movement in order to market products with much broader consumer appeal.

Like Morgan cars, Jordans is aiming at a limited audience with a distinctive product and benefit. In doing so, it achieves great loyalty and high frequency of usage among its target consumer group. It now appears to be taking further steps along its chosen niche path with the recent launch of a new muesli product based on Conservation Grade cereals – these grains are grown under a farming regime which prohibits those chemicals which leave a toxic residue in the crop or in the soil.

Almost without exception, niche products are premium-priced, to compensate the marketer for lack of scale in production and distribution. In addition, they usually command above-average profit margins.

A niche strategy can lead in a number of directions. The niche may be an end in itself, as in the case of Morgan or Jordans, or it may be a means to establish a toehold in a larger market. The Japanese often use a niche strategy as an entry point and subsequently expand across the larger market to which the niche is a small opening. In motor cycles the original niche was 50cc 'toys'; in cars it was small vehicles; and in TV sets it was miniaturized portables.

When does a niche become a mass market? Some niches grow steadily over time and convert into mass markets when they attract competition attacking the original niche product or company. Lager was a niche market in the 1960s, and now it is a crowded sector worth over £3 billion at retail prices.

Volvo started off as a niche product, appealing to the minority of customers who wanted a safe, functional, long-lasting car, and who were not particularly interested in styling or performance. It appears to have recently moved from niche producer to mass marketer, with the improved styling and performance of its latest range.

One trap to avoid is deceiving yourself that small brands in third or fourth position in their markets are niche products. The fact that a brand or company is small does not mean that it has found a niche. On the contrary, it may be a vulnerable follower in a mass market. Questions which clarify this issue include:

1. Is the niche or segment recognized as such by consumers and distributors or is it just a figment of marketing imagination?
2. Is your niche product distinctive, and does it appeal strongly to a particular group of consumers?
3. Is your product premium-priced, with above-average profit margin?

Anyone can find a niche, and they are discovered by deep understanding of how markets segment. The secret is to ensure that it is the right size – large enough to be profitable, but not sufficiently large to attract the supertankers, at least not in the early days when you are establishing a position. Some niche marketers are small companies. Others are large but have developed the knack of operating with many small-volume products. Two of the most skilful exponents of niche marketing – American Home Products and Reckitt & Colman – are major companies.

Guerrilla strategy

The best book on this topic is by Che Guevara,[12] who defines the main elements in guerrilla strategy as:

1. Defeat of the enemy as the final objective.
2. Use of surprise.
3. Tactical flexibility.
4. Concentration of attacks on ground favourable to the guerrilla.

The analogy with business is inexact, since the business guerrilla does not aim to defeat its large competitors overall and is quite satisfied to win small skirmishes. However, the three other elements mentioned by Guevara have some application to the small business competing with larger operators.

Typical guerrilla tactics involve attacking a competitor's weak product, his status with a specific retailer or distributor outlet, or a small geographical area. Whereas guerrilla tactics are usually employed by small companies because they require speed of reaction and flexibility, they are sometimes used by larger operators in the form of 'fighting brands':

> *The cream cracker biscuit market is dominated by Nabisco, with Jacob's. United Biscuits has a small entry through Crawford's Cream Crackers. Crawford's is never going to be a major factor in this market and may indeed be unprofitable. But it is used tactically to harass Jacob's, with periodical low-priced activity.*

Lever Bros. responded imaginatively in guerrilla style many years ago when Procter & Gamble introduced an improved formulation of Daz, justifying a claim of superior whiteness:

> *The whiteness performance of Daz was greatly improved by adding more bleach and fluorescer. A major element in the relaunch was the ability to claim superior whiteness, the Golden Fleece for anyone operating in the washing-powder market.*
>
> *Procter & Gamble developed the claim: 'New Energy Daz washes whiter than any other soap or detergent product made by any other manufacturer.' The claim did not exactly glide off the tongue, but it pleased Procter & Gamble and was approved by the ITCA, the TV copy authority. The Daz pack was strongly flashed with the 'New Energy' phrase, and the copy claim boomed out on TV.*
>
> *The cost of the product improvement was considerable, but the price of Daz was not increased. Daz was banking on the assumption that its major competitor, Omo, would be deterred from following its product improvement because of the profit-margin penalty involved.*
>
> *As Procter & Gamble expected, Lever Bros. did nothing with Omo. Instead, it responded by improving Surf, a small fighting brand. Lever therefore managed to invalidate the Daz claim of superior whiteness, at relatively low cost. Daz had to*

stop its new campaign, but continue to absorb the higher cost of the new formulation.

Product range

Market saturation through offering a very wide product range is sometimes described as an 'encirclement' strategy. The principle is that you offer retailers or distributors every conceivable product type and option, absorb a high proportion of stock and display space, and thereby limit opportunities for competitors. The Seiko Watch company is one of the most skilful practitioners of this strategy, with its worldwide range of 2,300 models.

There are obvious dangers in a strategy of product proliferation. It may create major manufacturing diseconomies, and is vulnerable to a focused attack by a supplier with a narrow range.

The Mars Group's strategy is the opposite of Seiko. Mars believes in a very limited range of 'power brands', strongly advertised and very efficiently produced in high volume.

Regional concentration

The principle behind this strategy is that it is better to be a large fish in a small pond than the reverse. In addition to local market knowledge, regional concentration can give a marketer the advantages of brand leadership in miniature, allied to a speed of reaction and market responsiveness unavailable to the national operator.

Like a niche strategy, regional concentration can be used as an entry point to a market. Walkers Crisps started in the UK as a regional brand in the Midlands and has gradually expanded to become national market leader. Regional concentration can also be used as a permanent strategy, as was the case with Finefare Stores:

> *On a national basis, Finefare ranked only seventh in grocery market share, behind Sainsbury, Tesco, ASDA, Dee, Argyll and Kwik Save. This was a distinctly unpromising position, especially since Finefare's relative market share against the leaders, Sainsbury and Tesco, was only 0·3 to 0·4.*
>
> *However, Finefare was number one or number two in Scotland and Tyneside/Teesside, and, through concentrating*

> *effort and expenditure on these regional strengths, it managed to maintain its national share while still returning good profit margins.*

Finefare is now a part of the Dee Corporation and its name has been discontinued.

Diplomacy

A strategy of diplomacy covers any form of external development, such as acquisitions, joint ventures, licensing or cooperation with third parties. Acquisitions are covered in Chapter 17. However, arrangements which fall short of acquisition are gaining in popularity, especially as offensive strategies in overseas markets. Their value is to fill gaps in knowledge or skills of each of the parties or to pool compatible resources, as in these examples:

- Sainsbury's joint venture with British Home Stores in Savacentre, described in the Introduction (see p. 23).
- IBM's joint venture in Japan with the state-owned Nippon Telegraph and Telephone to develop computer-communications services.
- when Glaxo's anti-ulcer drug Zantac was successfully launched in the US market, achieving the highest-ever Year 1 sales figure for a prescription-only drug, the small Glaxo field force was combined with the large Hoffman La Roche force in a joint effort.

Extension of existing assets

This strategic approach is fully covered in Chapter 1, under asset-led marketing.

● Picking the Right Strategy to Win

In selecting the right strategy, it is important to be aware of the repertoire available, to consider alternatives and to make clear choices. All of the strategies outlined above are possibilities for any size of company, except the head-on strategy, which is recommended only for large and very seasoned companies.

The main factors affecting your choice of strategy will be size and resources, strengths, competitive weaknesses and market opportunities. A careful consideration of these will enable you to select a winning strategy and avoid the lethargic middle of the road favoured by less successful companies.

In most markets, there is room for a brand leader, a differentiated number two, a low-price product and niche brands. If your company or brand is a 'me too' number three or number four, you do not have a strategy and will not survive for long unless you develop one.

● Winning Strategies Can Wear Out

Winning strategies need to be nurtured, updated and modified to meet changing consumer needs and competitive challenges; otherwise they will soon wear out and become losers.

Companies with winning strategies in the 1960s, such as Polaroid and Avon, lost their touch in the 1980s. In the case of Polaroid, slow growth in amateur photography and improved product performance from non-instant competitors blunted the edge it had enjoyed. Avon was slow to respond to the challenge to its distribution system posed by the growing number of part-time jobs available to women and the falling numbers staying at home during the day.

Factors which contribute to strategic wear-out include:

- changes in customer requirements.
- changes in distribution systems.
- innovations by competitors.
- poor control of company costs.
- lack of consistent investment.
- ill-advised changes to a successful strategy. (A speciality of galloping midgets.)

Caterpillar Tractor Co., the world's largest manufacturer of giant construction equipment, had a successful strategy for decades, but it began to wear out in the late 1970s:

> *Caterpillar was frequently cited in the book* In Search of Excellence[13] *as an example of an 'excellent' company. It was praised for its commitment to quality, hands-on management, reliability and a high-calibre dealer network. The book was*

published in 1982, the year in which Caterpillar reported a loss of $180 million, its first loss since 1932.

In the next two years Caterpillar accumulated further losses of $773 million. It was not until the third quarter of 1985 that the light began to show at the end of the tunnel, with a profit of $3 million. However, the weakening of Caterpillar's position had been apparent since the late 1970s. Table 23 tells the story:

Table 23. *Caterpillar Sales and Profit Trends*

	1984	1983	1982	1981	1978
Sales ($bn)	6·6	5·4	6·5	9·2	7·2
Profit/Loss ($m)	(428)	(345)	(180)	579	566
Percentage profit/loss	(6·5)	(6·4)	(2·8)	6·3	7·9

Caterpillar's strategy was to offer a broad product range of high-quality machines at premium prices, using a dedicated dealer network. All parts were standard worldwide. Superior service was an important peg in the strategy. Caterpillar guaranteed 48-hour delivery of parts anywhere in the world and did not charge for the parts if it failed to meet this deadline: '48-hour parts service anywhere in the world – or Cat pays'.

In 1982–4 Caterpillar was affected by a strong dollar, the decline in many heavy construction markets and low prices. Despite herculean efforts in reducing costs – down 22 per cent from 1981 to 1985 on a basis adjusted for inflation and volume – losses continued. Caterpillar was either not offering the right balance between quality and price in its products and service, or it was not responding sufficiently quickly to market changes. Or perhaps both elements of the strategy were wearing out in the face of evolving markets and competitive conditions.

Caterpillar is a company with major strengths and there are signs that it is on the way back, with adjusted strategies. In the past it had tended to come in later with new products, which were trouble-free, allowing competitors to suffer the pains of innovation. Now it has an ambitious programme of new and improved products, almost one a month for the next five years, and is driving for world technical leadership in certain areas.

But its most visible change in strategy is the decision to move into the smaller end of the construction market. The new Caterpillar backhoe loader retails for $42,000 against $500,000 for one of its large dump trucks. It is grouping all its smaller machines into a range called the Century line.

Caterpillar is aiming for a 20 per cent share.[14] In adjusting strategy to enter this sector, it will be competing in a much more price-sensitive market, to customers of whom it has little experience (small contractors) and against entrenched competition (J. I. Case and Deere).

No doubt the British firm J C B, whose machines Caterpillar distributed in the U S A until recently, will watch the results with interest.

Distillers in the U K is a classic example of strategic wear-out, and its change in approach appears to have come too late. Many of its brands are over 100 years old, but in the past twenty-five years its share of the U K Scotch whisky market has dived from 75 per cent to 15 per cent.[15] In the early 1960s it presumably had a winning strategy based on strong branding. Since then it has failed to respond to changes in consumer requirements, distribution channels and competitive thrust.

When companies are enjoying the benefits of winning strategies or growing markets, they tend to assume that they will continue for ever. The truth is that they never do.

● Winning Strategy in Action – Tetra-Brik Aseptic Packaging

Tetra-Pak is the international leader in packaging liquids for human consumption, with worldwide sales of $1·9 billion. It has a full management set-up in forty-five countries and sells direct in ninety-four. There are twenty-nine factories producing packaging machines or materials worldwide, including one in Wrexham.

A landmark in the history of the company was the development of the 'Tetra-Brik Aseptic' carton, in 1969. In the U K this is most familiar as a long-life fruit-juice carton. This new carton was a breakthrough. The product was sterilized and aseptically packed. The main benefit was that products like fruit juice no longer had to be refrigerated in store or at home. Product life was extended from a few days to over six months. Tetra-Pak built a number of other advantages around this core (see p. 178).

Tetra-Brik accounts for over two thirds of Tetra-Pak sales. It is used to package the majority of fruit juices in the UK. Outside the UK it is also the major package for UHT (ultra high temperature) milk. This type of milk accounts for over 50 per cent of total milk sales in all major European countries except the UK, where milk is still sold mainly in glass bottles and delivered door to door. World-wide, around 70 to 75 per cent of Tetra-Pak packages are used for milk, and 20 per cent for fruit juices.

Tetra-Pak was founded by Dr Ruben Rausing in Sweden and remains a family-controlled private company. Dr Rausing founded his first business in 1930, specializing in flexible packaging. By 1965 he had six companies, but against the advice of many of his friends sold five of them. He decided to concentrate all his assets on one company – Tetra-Pak. This decision was based on his philosophy of 'minimizing risk via risk maximization'. His reasoning was that by focusing heavy effort on one major market, and establishing a leadership position there, risk was minimized. As a philosophy, it is the opposite of spreading one's eggs across a number of baskets. Dr Rausing died in 1983 at the age of eighty-eight, and his sons, Hans and Gad Rausing, have continued his successful strategy.

How did Tetra-Pak manage to build up a large worldwide business very quickly, without acquisition, from its original base in a small high-cost European country? In answering this question, we shall look at Tetra-Pak's attitudes and its competitive advantages, and then focus on the winning strategy for Tetra-Brik.

Tetra-Pak's offensive attitudes

Tetra-Pak has a number of clear viewpoints about its business, and these can be summarized as follows:

1. Tetra-Pak is in the business of packaging liquids for human consumption. It does not sell packaging for non-edible use, e.g. motor oil or washing powder, since its packaging must be clearly identified with liquid foods and drinks only.

   The company believes in concentration of effort (see

p. 175), and has no interest in expanding into packaging solids.

2. Tetra-Pak views packaging broadly, to include filling systems, transportation, storage and handling in stores and warehouses, as well as the container. Its role stretches from raw-material procurement right through the cycle which ends with a consumer purchase of milk or juice. It leases unique machinery and sells packaging for it.

3. An efficient package, as defined in (2), 'should save more than its cost'. This was one of Dr Rausing's original mottoes.

4. Tetra-Pak develops only packages which are initially distinctive and superior in their target markets. It avoids 'me too' copies and protects the results of its R & D by patent wherever possible.

5. The company spends heavily on R & D, as a basis for innovating new products (10 per cent of Tetra-Pak employees are engaged in R & D). A substantial portion of profit is recycled into innovation and development.

6. The business approach is international. A fully staffed local country management is always set up as soon as feasible, comprising marketing, selling, administration and, in some cases, production. The vast majority of managers are local nationals, but production directors may often be Swedish.

7. Local country managers have a high degree of autonomy in day-to-day operation. Staff positions are generally avoided. Speed of decision-making is the norm and bureaucracy despised. 'The Company is allergic to too much bureaucracy and almost dangerously free of it.'[16]

8. Tetra-Pak's role is to satisfy four customer types – direct customers (e.g. dairies, juice marketers), the retail trade, the final consumer and society (i.e., environmental factors). Each product is likely to be a compromise, because what is optimum for one of the four may not suit the others. However, no product must 'turn off' any of the four.

9. The whole company focuses on customers. Country managers are expected to consider themselves sales-

men and spend at least half their time talking to customers. Top Tetra-Pak management in Lausanne is also committed to visiting all major customers worldwide.

10. Involvement with customers is active, not passive. Rather than just leasing machines and selling packaging, Tetra-Pak management will contribute to raising machine efficiency, and feed in market research and creative ideas to help with customer's selling and marketing.

Tetra-Pak's competitive advantages

Tetra-Pak's main direct competitors are Ex-Cello Corporation in the USA, Cherry-Burrell, and Combi-Bloc.

Ex-Cello's main package is the gable top, a tall package used widely for refrigerated milk and fruit juice (e.g. all St Michael fruit juice is in gable tops). It operates mainly through licences – Elopak is the UK licensee.

Cherry-Burrell sells machinery for gable-top packaging. Its UK agent is Bowater. Combi-Bloc is the most direct competitor to Tetra-Pak. In the late 1970s it managed to avoid Tetra-Pak's patents in developing machinery which produced an aseptic pack almost identical in appearance and function to Tetra-Brik. In terms of quality, efficiency, and reliability Combi-Bloc was a viable competitor. Combi-Bloc works mainly through agents, and the UK agent is also Bowater.

Glass, cans and plastic packaging are important though indirect competitors. Many of Tetra-Pak's competitive advantages stem from its attitudes and structure. Its assessment of its competitive advantages, which may well differ from Ex-Cello's or Combi-Bloc's view, is as follows:

1. **Greater customer orientation**. This is achieved through the broad definition of the four types of customer, internal emphasis on customer contact, autonomy of local management and speed of decision-making.

2. **More integrated structure**. Tetra-Pak has no agents or licensees. There is a close link between customers, packaging and machinery production.

3. **Concentrated market focus**. Many competitors com-

Developing Winning Strategies

pete in a much wider range of markets. Tetra-Pak specializes in packaging liquids for major food products.

4. **Market position**. Tetra-Pak has by far the leading market position in aseptic packaging for UHT milk and fruit juices.

5. **R & D investment**. Tetra-Pak's market success and private status enable it to spend a much higher percentage of sales on R & D than any of its major competitors can.

Winning strategy with Tetra-Brik

The basis for the winning strategy was matching offensive attitudes and competitive advantages with a good understanding of future market trends.

From the 1960s Dr Rausing appeared to anticipate the growing size, concentration and power which retailers were to develop, although he may have been surprised by the speed and extent of change. Identification of the retailer as a key customer was an important element in the winning strategy. Tetra-Pak applied a different strategy to each of its four main customers, as follows:

1. **Retailers**. The strategy was head-on, mainly against glass and refrigerated cartons. Benefits were lower cost of operation, greater convenience of handling, better utilization of space and no breakages.

   Tetra-Brik was highly appealing to retailers. It stacked well, was palletized and made efficient use of space in the warehouse, on the floor and on the shelf. The product did not require refrigeration. This saved the costs of daily delivery, and freed scarce refrigerated space in the store for other products.

   Finally, by offering lower-priced alternatives to refrigerated juice and fresh milk, the Tetra-Brik opened up fast-growing new markets for retailers, providing both branded and private-label opportunities.

2. **Producers**. The strategy was to offer producers access to new market opportunities – a flanking approach. Tetra-Brik had particular appeal to two types of producer. The

178

regional dairy wanting to expand its scale of operations found the package attractive for milk because the long-life UHT version enabled it to operate on a much wider geographical basis. It could also extend its product range into long life juice, using similar machinery.

The second type was the dry-goods producer wishing to expand into fruit juice, but previously deterred by the entry barrier of refrigeration. Tetra-Brik removed this entry barrier and allowed dry-goods marketers like Coca-Cola (Five Alive) and Del Monte in the UK to enter the fruit-juice category.

3. **Consumers**. The strategy was superior value. The consumer appeal of Tetra-Brik is a 25 per cent lower price on the shelf than a refrigerated gable-top pack, and long life. Drawbacks are some loss in flavour and inferior ease of opening and pouring compared with gable-top packs. The consumer has generally accepted the trade-off as giving good value.

4. **Society**. The strategy was to use facts and research to establish with opinion formers that one-way packaging (as opposed to re-usable containers like glass) was less wasteful than it appeared and to identify ways in which used packages could be converted back into energy (e.g. use as fuel).

Is the strategy wearing out?

Despite Combi-Bloc's directly competitive product, the winning strategy appears to be holding. Tetra-Pak has achieved compound volume growth of at least 20 per cent per year in the past five years. However, the company is heavily reliant on Tetra-Brik and could use more successful new products.

Future strategy is built around a number of approaches:

1. Gain more growth from existing packages, especially Tetra-Brik, by penetrating new liquid categories (e.g. soup, wine, mineral water), by building share in milk and fruit juice in existing countries (especially the USA and Japan) and by opening new countries. (A joint venture has just begun in India, and a plant is being

built in China in cooperation with the government.)
2. Broaden packaging range into new materials, like extruded polystyrene, to reduce reliance on paper as a raw material. This would make Tetra-Pak less dependent on paper, and polystyrene offers more scope for unique forms and shapes. It will also facilitate establishment in certain countries with their own plastics industry, supplying materials locally. Many countries have no local paper industry and dislike importing paper.
3. Improve existing packaging systems and introduce new ones.
4. Develop a unique package for carbonated drinks (Tetra-Brik cannot be used for carbonated products) to penetrate beer and soft drinks.

● Summary

A company should set realistic yet ambitious objectives, which at minimum achieve real growth in earnings per share.

Offensive strategy to meet objectives involves the development of competitive advantages, concentration of resources into areas of best return, and selection of the most effective points to attack. The ideal offensive concentrates your strongest resources against your competitors' most weakly defended areas.

Portfolio analysis is a useful graphic device for determining resource allocation by product or business unit, but is no substitute for the rigorous analytical framework described in the previous chapter.

Competitive advantage is the ability to do something better than your competitors. At least one competitive advantage is necessary to build a winning strategy.

Many types of competitive advantage can be developed, including superior product benefit, perceived advantage, low-cost operation, legal advantages and superior contacts, knowledge, scale advantages, or attitudes.

When a company's or a brand's competitive advantages are collated, a few have one or more large ones, and rather more have a number of small ones which can be sewn together to create a significant competitive edge. Some companies have potential competitive advantages which are not recognized or exploited, but many have none. The latter need to develop some competitive advantages as a prerequisite to building a winning strategy.

The strategic groundwork (see Chapter 6) and development of competitive advantages are the essential foundation of winning strategies.

In selecting a strategy to win, a company or brand should choose the most appropriate one from the wide repertoire available. Possible offensive strategies include head-on, flanking, niche, guerrilla, product range, regional concentration, diplomacy, or extension of existing assets.

With the exception of head-on strategy, which is reserved for companies with large purses and strong stomachs, all the strategies in the repertoire can be used by any company. The exact strategy selected will be influenced by your size, resources and strengths, by your competitors' weaknesses and by market opportunities.

Winning strategies will wear out unless they are nurtured, updated and modified in response to changing market needs and new competitive moves.

5 | *Effectively Executed*

8 | *Offensive Product and Packaging Development*

It is difficult, if not impossible, to find anyone who doubts the prime importance of product appeal. The need for top product quality is a universally acknowledged truism among companies. However, the fact remains that there are vast differences in the extent to which individual companies actually *do* something about this belief. It is also a fact that the largest profits generally go to those businesses which most devotedly follow a policy of insisting on a competitive advantage, no matter how small, for every product or service they market.[1]

The most important principle of product development, beside which all others pale, is that no other corporate activity matters more. Consumers buy product benefits, not advertising and promotions, and the surest, and sometimes the easiest, route to corporate growth is through product superiority. All the other factors of the marketing mix – advertising, promotions, pricing and packaging – respond most amiably to a superior product and will work hardest on its behalf.

With this track to an eldorado set out so clearly, one would expect it to be as crowded as the M1, jammed with businesses accelerating their powerful vehicles to the promised destination. But few companies follow it with full dedication. For example, one recent American study on 1,900 businesses indicated that in 38 per cent little or no new product development takes place.[2]

There are many reasons for this, such as the difficulty of judging how much to spend on product development, the ease of cutting spending and the time-lag effect of R & D activity. Perhaps the most important reason of all is that managing the R & D function, and integrating it with marketing and operations, are often very demanding.

● Background to R & D

Before listing the seven principles of offensive product development, here are some facts and opinions about R & D.

There are many thoughts on R & D, but few of the kind of facts marketers would like to have. It would be useful to see R & D spending as a percentage of new product sales generated by R & D activity – or some indications as to the financial returns of basic as against applied research.

As in many areas of marketing, there are few signposts and much ambiguity. R & D, like advertising, is to some extent an act of faith and an investment in the future. The time lag between input and output in R & D is longer than in any other business function. And there are uncertainties in achieving the planned technical result, in converting it to mass production at the required quality and cost and in gauging consumer reaction.

This section covers the various types of research, how much to spend on R & D, differences in attitude between marketing and R & D people, and ways of evaluating R & D effectiveness.

Types of R & D activity

R & D activity can be looked at from a number of angles. The R & D scientist would define it by type of technology – *development* research, which uses technology known to the company, and *basic* research, which explores technologies new to the company though not necessarily new to the world.

The managing director might categorize R & D into market-driven projects, where the impetus stems from market analysis, and technology-driven ones, where the idea originates from R & D. Finally, the marketing director usually defines R & D by type of product – existing or new.

All this is inevitably an oversimplification, and there is a certain artificiality in dividing research into market-driven and technology-driven projects, since it should be possible to point technology at market opportunities.

With these provisos, Table 24 sets out a map of the various ways of looking at R & D and attempts to relate them. The ratios of the types of research in the first two columns are pure guesstimates, although development and market-driven research are certainly more heavily funded than basic or technology-driven projects. Indeed, Western marketing people have been criticized for concentrating too much effort on minor product improvements and for neglecting the more difficult opportunities requiring new technology.

Table 24. *Map of R & D Profile*

Type of Technology	Origin of Product Concept	Relation to Business
Development (Technology known to company)	Market-driven (Marketing Department)	Existing products
		New products
Basic (Technology new to company or new to world)	Technology-driven (R & D on own initiative or in response to Marketing brief)	New Business
		New Technology

Table 25 is based on a study of 103 companies in Europe, and this breakdown is credible except for the ratio of minor improvements, which looks on the low side.

Table 25. *Allocation of R & D Expenditure**

Existing business: minor improvements	34%
Existing business: major improvements	47%
Planned business diversification	12%
Basic research to generate new technology	7%
Total	100%

*European Industrial Research Management Association, 'How Much R & D?', in *Research Management*, May/June 1985 issue.

What is the correlation of R & D expenditure to profit?

R & D spending as a percentage of sales varies greatly by industry. It could be as high as 10 per cent of sales for a pharmaceutical or computer company and as low as 0·5 per cent for a food manufacturer.

The secret of success in R & D is integration with marketing and customer needs. This applies even to 'big-bang' research of the kind needed by a large computer company like Intel or Apple:

> The raw materials for the big bang are detailed understanding of customers, competitors, markets and technologies, and the implications of how they are changing.[3]

A number of attempts have been made to relate R & D spending to sales and profit growth. One of the more determined efforts analysed 310 American firms in twenty-four industries and concluded that

> in general, R & D expenditures have fairly strong associations with profits and sales, although evidence also suggests some differences among industries.[4]

The effectiveness of R & D broken down by industry is shown in Table 26. On this basis, R & D expenditure appears most effective in growing markets with rapidly changing technologies.[5]

In summary, it seems that a substantial commitment to R & D will pay if combined with the right attitudes. But for every small company which overcomes barriers through the *right* attitudes, there are larger companies with great technical and financial re-

Table 26. *Correlation of R & D Expenditure to Profit and Sales Growth*

High Correlation	Low Correlation
Appliances	Building materials
Chemicals	Food
Containers	Beverages
Electrical	Machinery
Electronics	Machine tools
Natural resources	Instruments
Office equipment	Paper
Computers	Textiles
Oil service/supply	Apparel
Personal care products	
Telecommunications	

sources which rarely develop even minor product innovations, because they have the *wrong* attitudes.

Differences in attitudes between marketing and R & D people

To get the most out of R & D people, it helps to understand how they think. They usually think very well – just differently from marketing people.

Some of the differences in language and outlook are shown in Table 27. To create compatibility in language and outlook, marketing people need to brief R & D fully on markets, customers and competition, and make an effort to grapple with the more important technical issues. Equally R & D people can learn a lot by accompanying sales people and visiting customers.[6] This interface is an important part of the I of P O I S E – Integrated.

Table 27. *Marketing and R&D*

Marketing Outlook	R & D Outlook
Risk/Reward ratios	Technical orientation
Speed/timing urgent	Pressure undermines insight
Focus on fact	Focus on creativity
Desire for certainty	Acceptance of uncertainty
Short-/medium-term	Medium-/long-term
Profit-related	Focus on projects

Evaluating R & D effectiveness

R & D is only one element in product development. For example, a well-known UK grocery manufacturer has launched over twenty-five advertised new products in the past ten years, and not one is regarded as a success by its competitors. This consistent record of failure was due primarily to poor use of R & D by marketing.

The most common way to evaluate R & D is 'performance versus task'. The R & D department agrees a certain number of projects with the marketing department, specifying the product benefits to be developed and a timetable for achievement. Longer-term and more sophisticated calibrations can also be used, such as 'R & D spending as a percentage of new-product sales and profits'. This is one of the methods used by General Electric in the USA: 'Profits earned today by businesses directly based on [General Electric] corporate R & D run some 4 to 5 times the annual cost of the General Electric lab.'[7]

A final ratio which is sometimes more interesting than useful is to give R & D expenditure as a percentage of sales against main competitors and the industry average. This is usually ascertainable for large competitors and major industries.

 ## The Seven Principles of Offensive Product Development

Now that the background to R & D has been covered, we can move on to the seven principles of offensive product development.

1. Give priority to priority-setting

R & D work involves risks and some inevitable waste. Only a minority of R & D work results in commercial applications. *Business Week* reported many years ago that out of 100,000 patents applied for annually in the USA, only 3 per cent see the light of day as commercial products. However, the tantalizing thing about R & D is that the riskiest projects tend to result in the 'block-buster' new products.[8]

The setting of clear priorities in R & D concentrates effort and reduces waste. The first decision is how much time to spend on genuinely innovative work and how much on maintenance work such as making minor improvements or cost savings on existing products.

The pressure for the immediate is as strong in the R & D area as in any other and, unless a clear priority is set, short-term projects with a low potential pay-off are likely to clamour for attention and receive it.

Filling in the R & D Profile Map in Table 24 (see p. 187) is a useful exercise. It identifies whether the allocation of your company's R & D effort by type of activity is both what you think it is and what you want.

In balancing innovative projects against short-term ones, future cash-flow requirements must not be forgotten. Few businesses can afford to launch more than one block-buster new product in any one year, and short-term/low-risk projects produce useful extra cash to help finance more innovative projects.

Once a division between genuinely new work and maintenance or replacement effort has been determined, priorities should be set for individual projects. This is a continuous process and very much a matter of judgement. Obviously, the highest priority should be given to those projects with the best profit potential, and this is affected by marketing, technical and cost variables.

The three questions that should be asked about any product development project are:

1. Assuming technical success, what is its profit potential in the market-place?
2. What is the chance of technical success?
3. How much R & D time and cost is it likely to absorb from start to completion?

The answers will obviously be quite rough, but each question should be considered and an eventual priority arrived at, based on a balance between them.

A useful device for bringing some order to these generalities is the Product Development Priority Table, which is shown on p. 192. Scores are allocated for market potential and likelihood of technical success and a priority is set, based on these factors plus likely cost and time-scale. Six fictional projects are included in the table for the purposes of illustration.

191

Table 28. *Product Development Priority*

	Project Number					
	1	2	3	4	5	6
Market potential (max. 100)[a]	90	25	40	20	60	95
Percentage chance of technical success	55	100	70	40	20	10
Likely time-scale (years)	5	0·25	2	1	4	4
Estimated cost (£000)[b]	265	10	15	20	89	50
Priority Rating (AD)[c]	A	A	B	C	D	D

a. The score ranges from 0–100. 0–25 is a marginal improvement in consumer benefit; 26–50 is a significant improvement; 51–100 is a major breakthrough.
b. This column refers to R & D departmental costs.
c. Priority rating A is best, D worst.

An analysis of this table shows that Project 1, which offers a breakthrough opportunity with a reasonable chance of success, gets priority A, even though the gestation time is five years. Project 2 also gains top priority because, despite its marginal market potential, it involves no technical challenge and can be developed very quickly. Project 3 is worth pursuing too, but Projects 4, 5 and 6 would be dropped.

An orderly approach to priority-setting will reduce waste but will not eliminate it, because research is a creative rather than a mechanical process.

2. Turn uncertainty into risk [9]

The system just described for allocating priorities works well in most situations, but needs to be adapted when R & D is working on the frontiers of knowledge. Suppose, for example, that the head of R & D approaches you with this kind of proposition: 'We've just come across some developments written up in technical journals that might enable us to radically increase the life of our leading machine-tool range, by using a new type of metal and miniaturizing the product. But the project would be very expensive and the time-scale would be at least three years.'

You ask the obvious questions and the response is: 'The development cost would be over £1 million, the likely time-scale is two to four years and we can't give you any idea of the probability of success because there are too many variables.'

This presents an interesting dilemma: interesting because you know that a 50 per cent increase in product life would provide a major competitive advantage for your main product range, especially if cost does not increase much; difficult because you certainly cannot authorize R & D expenditure of over £1 million on a project the success of which is totally uncertain.

The answer is to sit down with the R & D department, familiarize yourself with the technological issues and then dismember the project into manageable chunks. Each of these can then be individually authorized, and evaluated, before moving on to the next. In this kind of project the earlier steps are fortunately usually less expensive than the later ones. A possible dismemberment sequence is shown in Table 29. Your likely action would be to authorize Steps A and B at a cost of £30,000, and to evaluate results with R & D before agreeing to Step C.

Table 29. *Project Dismemberment*

Steps	Estimated Cost (£000)	Time-scale (Months)	Probability of Success
A. Meetings with key academics and technical writers	5	3	100%
B. Visit operators in other industries abroad with pilot plants	25	3	100%
C. Determine by experiment whether new metal will work	35	6	80%
D. Build miniaturized pilot model	150	12	90%
E. Pilot tests	100	6	80%
F. Build first production plant	1,150	12	80%
Whole Project	1,465	42	46%

3. Product development is a continuous process

This principle is well understood by marketers operating in businesses where product life-cycles are short, such as computers and consumer electronics. It is less well grasped by some marketers in fast-moving consumer goods or services.

For any products except 'dogs', there should be a vigorous programme of product improvement and cost reduction. Products which stay still, even in stable markets like food, tend to get left behind:

> *A grocery manufacturer, brand leader in a large market, had been slowly losing share to private-label brands for some years. Equally seriously, its price premium over private labels had reduced from 20 per cent in the early 1970s to only 10 per cent in the 1980s.*
>
> *Although the brand had a perceived advantage over private labels, on consumer blind tests it only broke even, whereas five years previously it had won by 60:40 or more. This was because private labels had improved while the brand leader stood still.*
>
> *This particular manufacturer had a belief that if it maintained its 'traditional' standards of quality and acceptance, it would retain market dominance. In reality, maintenance proved insufficient and an important competitive advantage was lost.*

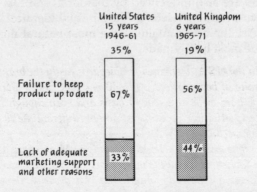

Figure 20. Percentage of Brand Leaders Losing Leadership
Source: James O. Peckham, *The Wheel of Marketing*, 1981.

194

The penalty for failing to keep products up to date is exposed in Nielsen studies of flagging grocery brands in the UK and USA. The main reason for being swept off the pedestal as brand leader was failure to keep the product up to date, as shown in Figure 20.

4. Products are pathways to consumer benefits

A technical success may be of no interest to the consumer. Irradiation of food at low and safe levels lengthens product life, but is likely to stumble on the emotional resistance of consumers. Technical performance is certainly important, since every consumer wants a product to fulfil its purpose well, but it should not be viewed in isolation. Consumers are emotional as well as logical beings.

A product which is regarded by scientists as being at technical parity with its competition may nevertheless be regarded by consumers as superior for non-technical reasons:

> *Most people prefer brown eggs to white ones although they taste the same. That is why they buy brown eggs even though, in a free-supply situation, these can cost rather more than white eggs. Our urban society nostalgically associates the brown colour with country wholesomeness and is therefore prepared to pay more for brown eggs.*

Consumers are also influenced by the derivation of a product. Faced by two products which are technically identical, they are likely to prefer the one containing the most natural materials or appearing the most home-made.

> *In the USA, Heinz white vinegar is easily the brand leader in spite of being priced 30 to 40 per cent higher than its competitors on a unit weight basis and even though in a blind-test situation consumers cannot differentiate it from the competition.*
>
> *The basis for Heinz's leading market share is its long establishment and the natural derivation of its raw materials. Heinz is the only brand that can describe its vinegar as 'natural' on the label, being made from natural grain – mainly corn, barley and rye – whereas the majority of other producers*

195

> *derive their vinegar from industrial alcohol, synthesized from petroleum.*

Finally, technical superiority may be achieved at the expense of some non-technical emotional benefit. This can add up to inferior *consumer* acceptance:

> *Technically Campbell's condensed soup offers much better value than Heinz ready-to-serve soup. It tastes good and is a lot less expensive – a bowlful of Campbell's costs 25 per cent less than a bowlful of Heinz. Yet Campbell's share lags far behind Heinz. Consumers have reservations about its product form, which involves adding milk or water. They are not convinced that it has the wholesomeness, richness and natural qualities of the ready-to-serve form.*

5. Superior product benefits can always be developed

> 'Our trouble is we're in a commodity market* – all that matters is price.'
> 'No, we don't aim for product superiority because we have tied distribution.'

In certain markets – for instance, some industrial goods, cars and consumer durables – it is easy to see how, with skilful marketing and R & D, superior products can be developed. But in many others, superior product benefits are hard to come by.

One can either accept the difficulties as insoluble, and the remarks with which this section opened take that line, or one follows a basic belief that product superiority can always be developed. There is more hope in the latter approach and it often pays off:

> *The major petrol companies in the UK (and elsewhere) have made little attempt to build superior consumer benefits into their petrol or oil products. They have tended to regard them as commodities and, with tied distribution, different brands of petrol rarely compete head-on.*

* 'Commodity market' is marketing slang for a market close to nature, where it is hard to build in product differences. Typical commodity markets in this sense are canned fruit, flour, tea, petrol, etc.

In the motor-oil market, they have shown a similar lack of initiative. The only two brands to build up distinctive positions were independents – Duckhams and Castrol. Prior to acquisition by B P in 1969, Duckhams innovated multi-grade oil, developed a distinctive product colour and aimed at the motoring enthusiast. Castrol, owned by Burmah Oil, has a strong branded position, despite its lack of tied outlets, thanks to a high-performance image well supported by distinctive advertising.

By contrast, the oil products marketed by major petrol companies are undistinctive. Nor have the majors done much better as service marketers or as retailers. Quality of service on British forecourts compares poorly with the USA. Only recently have the petrol majors begun to wake up to the opportunity to exploit high traffic sites as retail outlets, and in some of the better forecourt convenience stores sales of groceries now exceed sales of petrol.

The UK performance of the major petroleum companies as consumer marketers of petroleum/oil, as service marketers and as retailers, has been truly pitiful over the past twenty years.

On the other hand, marketers of bottled water have shown imagination in building brand images and product differences – surely the ultimate achievement. The bottled-water market in the UK is worth £40 million per year and is led by well-established brands like Perrier, Vichy, Evian and Malvern.

Finally, product differences in so-called commodity products can be created by surrounding them with superior services. Take hamburgers, for example. It is debatable whether McDonald's has a better product than its competitors. However, its back-up services of convenience, speed and cleanliness add value to a rather pedestrian product and combine to produce a superior customer proposition.

Table 30 outlines an inventory of consumer benefits which can be used as a check-list when searching for ways to differentiate or improve products. Although it is oriented towards consumer markets, it is by no means exhaustive, even for this category. Many of the benefits listed merely summarize a cluster of possible improvement areas. For instance, 'protective finish' covers non-stick, non-scratch, non-staining, heat- or dirt-repellent and flavour-sealing.

Table 30. *Inventory of Product Improvement Benefits**

Category	Examples	Benefits
Convenience	Bank cash tills – speed/ ease of use Microwave ovens – speed of preparation Zantac – lower dosage frequency McDonalds – speed of service	Speed/ease of use, preparation, serving, disposal or dispensing from packet, lower frequency of usage, saving of time, space, or effort
Physical dimensions	Yorkie chocolate – thickness Durabeam range – styling Sony Walkman – miniaturization Next – store design	Thickness, size, shape, layout, styling of product/pack, miniaturization, design
Objective physical characteristics	Caterpillar farm machinery – durability ABS braking – safety *Financial Times* – colour Nike 'Waffle' sole – springier VF Jeans – fit Jaguar cars – smooth ride Duracell batteries – longevity J. Sainsbury stores – cleanliness, lighting	Durability, shock-resistance, consistency, protective finish, stain removal, cleaning, water-proof, colour, strength, absorbency, viscosity, safety, perforation, mildness, elasticity, smooth/lumpy, portion control, easier storage, transparent/opaque, insulation, longevity, protection, fit
Subjective physical characteristics	Wispa – texture Lee & Perrins – flavour Toyota cars – reliability Comfort fabric softener – softness Claridges Hotel – ambience	Softness, taste, texture, freshness, crispness, comfort in use, smell, hotness, sweetness, purity, enriched, lightness, fashion, aesthetic appeal, more reliable results, versatility, personal hygiene, ambience.

* I am indebted to Joel E. Smilow, Chief Executive of International Playtex Corporation, for this basic approach.

6. Believe that small differences can matter

Even apparently minor differences in product performance, which may be spurned by a company's management as being unimportant, can be significant to the consumer, especially in product categories with high purchase frequency.

The expertise of consumers is often underrated, especially by consumer protection agencies, which are too prone to regard them as naive and easily deceived. On the contrary, consumers can develop an expertise in evaluating frequently purchased products which rivals that of the industrial buyer.

Small differences matter, however, only if they are in areas of importance to the consumer and are well exploited in advertising. A classic example of this is Spillers' flour, relaunched in the mid-1960s, with the 'flour men' campaign, and still in good health today:

> Spillers' flour was relaunched as a marginally superior product under the new name Homepride, which was preferred to McDougalls by 55 people out of 100 on blind test. The basis for the slight preference in favour of Spillers was its better texture.
>
> The relaunch advertising for Homepride stressed the traditional benefit of the baking result, with only secondary emphasis on fineness of texture. At this time Homepride had a 7 per cent share of the market, compared with McDougalls' 30 per cent.
>
> A new product management team arrived the following spring. After analysing a major consumer usage and attitude study on the flour market, it concluded that Spillers' advertising was based on the wrong strategy.
>
> This research showed that consumers did not regard flour as an important influence on the baking end result (usually scones or cakes). Factors like oven temperature, age of eggs, the balance of dry and liquid ingredients and the use of butter rather than shortening were the ones that mattered most. The new team concluded from this that advertising which positioned flour as having a major effect on the end result was not credible to the consumer and was therefore ineffective.
>
> Another conclusion drawn from this research was that fineness of texture and absence of lumpiness carried most weight with consumers in determining their choice of brand. This tallied with technical tests, which showed that a finer

flour improved the rising, texture and taste of baked products, though only slightly.

The previous launch had produced unimpressive results for Homepride and, by the end of the summer, the brand's share had lifted only marginally, despite a major increase in advertising level, which confirmed the diagnosis the new team had already made. Consequently, the advertising was changed to a 'texture' strategy in the autumn and brand share began to lift dramatically.

But Spillers was still not satisfied with the quality of the advertising execution and changed its agency. The new one developed the 'flour-graders' campaign and this has been running ever since. The main claim was 'graded grains make finer flour', and the small cartoon flour men in bowler hats, who were a central feature of the commercial, became immensely popular characters.

In 1970 Spillers' Homepride gained brand leadership of this declining market. Sixteen years later Homepride remains the brand leader, though private-label brands have made strong incursions. Spillers continues to be the only major miller with a process which grades the grains, and is still using the 'flour-graders' advertising. Homepride has recently launched a new self-raising wholemeal flour, which is also selling well.

7. Look for profit improvements

One should, of course, be continually seeking profit improvements in every part of the marketing mix, but there is often a reluctance to reduce the cost of the product in case quality is affected. This reluctance is understandable, because examples of brands which have downgraded quality and have therefore lost sales are not uncommon. However, it is not valid, because there may be opportunities to reduce the cost of a product without affecting consumer acceptance.

The reformulation of Andrews Liver Salt illustrates the combination of bold thinking with the cautious but persistent testing that is necessary to carry out such a move successfully.

Andrews Liver Salt was first sold in 1894 by Phillips Scott & Turner in Newcastle upon Tyne. It grew steadily throughout the 1920s and 1930s but slowed down in the 1940s and by the mid-1950s had begun to decline in volume terms. However, it remained the brand leader of the 'stomach-remedies' market, followed by Alka-Seltzer.

The Andrews formula, consisting of a mixture of sugar, tartaric acid, bicarbonate of soda and Epsom salts, had remained basically unaltered since the 1890s. Phillips Scott & Turner did not think it could be significantly improved, since it was very efficient both as a laxative and as an indigestion remedy. So they concentrated on seeking lower-cost formulations which would achieve an equally good result. This approach helped stave off price increases, an important factor for Andrews since low prices had been a key element in its past success.

The attempt to substitute citric acid for tartaric acid is one example of this approach. By the early 1960s tartaric acid was becoming increasingly expensive and in short supply. From a technical viewpoint, citric acid seemed to be a good substitute, and a reformulated version of Andrews using citric rather than tartaric acid was tried out in one part of the country.

When letters came in from consumers, complaining that Andrews was 'not what it used to be', the company decided to carry out a sensitive consumer-research comparison between the two alternative formulations. This research showed a clear rejection of citric acid by the Andrews user, and it was decided not to use it. However, further testing with a 50:50 combination of tartaric and citric acid proved acceptable, and this new formulation was adopted, giving a worthwhile saving in cost.[10]

● Offensive Product Development in Action: Hydrovane Compressors

Market background

Hydrovane is a medium-sized British company, run autonomously as a wholly owned subsidiary of Siebé, which also owns Compair (UK).

Hydrovane markets air compressors, which act as energy

sources for machinery. The bulk of air-compressor sales are in stationary (as opposed to portable) models. They provide power for machines in car-body repair, packaging, farm equipment and even dentistry.

There are two main technologies in air compressors – screw-rotary and sliding-vane. Screw-rotary machines are the most common. Hydrovane is the world leader in sliding-vane technology, and has refined this over the years while would-be competitors fell behind. Among the advantages of sliding-vane compressors are low noise levels, long life, greater reliability, high output and low maintenance frequency.

Hydrovane competes in world markets with 50 per cent of its sales overseas and its major competitors, all of which primarily market screw-rotary machines, include: Atlas Copco (Sweden); Compair (UK); Ingersoll Rand (USA); Hitachi (Japan); and Kayser (Germany).

The problem

Sales were buoyant during the 1970s, but fell back heavily in 1980–81, as the industrial recession hit the air-compressor market in the UK and overseas.

Profits were badly affected and by 1982 had fallen to one third of the level of 1980. The Hydrovane range was looking dated and sustained its high premium price (up to 100 per cent) only with difficulty.

The product development plan

In 1981 Hydrovane decided that its best chances lay in product improvements. It therefore decided to accelerate product development activities, while also raising manufacturing capacity and productivity to cope with extra demand resulting from the planned product initiatives.

The Managing Director sent out two of his engineers to research the market. They talked to customers and distributors and bought competitive compressors to analyse. A comparison of all competitive products was made based on the engineers' analysis and a review of sales brochures.

A price/volume map was then constructed for Hydrovane and its competitors, showing comparative price levels and volumes, and plotting the relationships. From this it became even more apparent that Hydrovane's products did not justify their price premium.

It was agreed to start the product development programme on the Hydrovane 5, since this was the smallest product in the range and the most difficult to improve. The product brief called for improvements in design and performance, and much lower costs. It was necessary to increase margins as well as to reduce price, since in future lower-margin export sales were expected to grow fastest.

The result

The Hydrovane 5 range was launched in the UK in September 1984. Price premium over competitors was reduced from about 100 per cent to 40 per cent, but the profit margin was increased since product cost was cut by 54 per cent. The design (assisted by the Design Advisory Service Scheme) and performance were both improved. In order to justify the production investment, Hydrovane 5 had to achieve at least 5,000 units per year, about three times the level of the product it replaced.

By late 1985 it was running at 7,000 units annually in four major countries and a volume of 10–15,000 units is expected when it is launched in all Hydrovane's major markets.

Between 1983 and 1986, Hydrovane will have remodelled its total product range. Sales in 1985 will be almost double the 1980 level, return on capital employed has risen to 30 per cent and the future outlook is promising.

● Offensive Packaging Development

Packaging will be covered briefly, not because of any feeling that it lacks importance, but because functional packaging is governed by the same principles as product R & D and because package graphics follow many of the same rules as advertising.

The purpose of packaging has changed greatly in the past twenty years. Its original function was to protect the package contents and it discharged this function in a utilitarian way. With the advent of self-service shopping, packaging became an important selling vehicle in its own right. In addition to its more basic purpose, it was used to create impact for the brand on the shelf and to make the product appear attractive to the consumer. The package was also an appropriate and inexpensive device for carrying promotional messages.

Now, some progressive companies are taking packaging a stage further and making it into an inseparable part of a product's performance. This trend is likely to continue, since, in certain markets, it is becoming increasingly difficult to develop products which are superior in their own right. New combinations of packages and their contents can also turn up novel product ideas which would not have been apparent if the product had been viewed in isolation:

> *Companies marketing to the catering trade have innovated more convenient forms of packaging over the years. Jam, cream, mayonnaise and ketchup are all sold in individual portions to the consumer, who gets extra convenience, at a price.*
>
> *For the manufacturer, profit margins on individual-portion packs are much higher than on bulk packs of the same products, and there is the opportunity to promote the brand name direct to the consumer – a rare luxury in the catering business. The caterer also benefits through higher margins and savings in labour, since the portions are pre-measured.*
>
> *A more recent innovation in catering is the sale of 'pub grub' – complete frozen meals initially packaged in earthenware dishes – to licensed outlets. The publican microwaves the meal and serves it in the dish. The empty dishes are returned to the manufacturer for refilling. For the publican the package is convenient and labour-saving. The manufacturer gains by retaining greater control over the final presentation to the consumer.*

Functional improvements can provide large pay-offs and boost whole product categories.

Examples of packaging innovations which have enhanced product convenience and performance include:[11]

> – toothpaste pump dispensers. These are less messy and easier to use. They started in Sweden and have already

captured 12 per cent of the American toothpaste market.
- pen containers. These have been successfully used for nail polish, and for dispensing insecticide in areas which cannot be sprayed.
- aseptic cartons. Their impact was demonstrated in the case of Tetra-Pak in Chapter 7.
- more convenient, new shapes. Elefant, a liquid toilet cleaner from Germany, comes in a squeeze bottle with a curved top. Consumers can clean toilet-bowl rims without putting their hands inside the bowl.
- pre-measuring devices. Liquid Tide, in addition to a drip-proof spout, has a bottle top which doubles as a measuring cap.

Table 31. *Check-list for Packaging Development*

	Points to check
Offers protection against	Moisture, air, heat, cold, separation of product, tearing, explosion, leakage, staleness, breakage, crushing, dirt, corrosion, scuffing
Consumer convenience	Ease of opening, disposal, storage, dispensing and handling, safety in use, re-usable, re-closable, clear instructions for use, light to handle, stands easily
Trade appeal	Ease of stacking, shelving, displaying and identification of both individual products and outer cases, economic utilization of space and good protection
Consumer sales appeal	Good size impression, attractive shape and design, easily identifiable, distinctiveness from competition, appearance ties in with product purpose
Environmental	Ease of disposal, absence of litter, biodegradable, safe after use, non-bulky, compressible

Package graphics is one of the lowest-cost and highest-leverage areas of marketing activity. Changes in design are relatively inexpensive but can bring quite large business gains, especially on small brands which do not normally catch the attention of either the consumer or the trade (e.g. Terry's Neapolitans in 1985).

Packaging, unlike advertising, can close a sale, since it operates at the point of purchase. In the case of lesser-known brands, it may even trigger off the whole cycle of interest, attention, desire and action by itself. Most often, however, it will work hand in hand with the other elements of the marketing mix – especially advertising.

A package should protect the product, appeal to the consumer and the trade and, ideally, enhance product performance. Table 31 shows a check-list of points to note in package design and development.

● Summary

Product or service development is the single most important corporate activity. Every company believes that top product quality is essential, but few actually do something about this belief.

R & D is in general valuable, provided it is backed by the right systems and attitudes. It can be categorized from a number of angles – development v. basic, market-driven v. technology-driven and existing v. new products.

There is no exact correlation between R & D spending and sales or profit growth, but one definitive study suggests that R & D expenditure produces the best returns in growing markets with rapidly advancing technologies.

Marketing and R & D people have different attitudes. It is important to understand these differences and to ensure that R & D is integrated within the offensive marketing approach (the I of POISE).

R & D effectiveness can be evaluated by using the task method or by relating past R & D expenditure to profits generated on new products developed via R & D.

The seven principles of offensive product development are summarized below:

Summary

1. **Give priority to priority-setting**. Decide the R & D priority allocation between genuinely innovative work and maintenance activity. Priorities should then be set for individual projects.
2. **Turn uncertainty into risk**. In evaluating high-risk R & D projects involving new technology, reduce the risk by dismembering the project into component parts.
3. **Product development is a continuous process**. For any products except 'dogs', the proper approach is to constantly improve product acceptance or to reduce cost without loss of quality. Failure to keep products up to date carries dire consequences.
4. **Products are pathways to consumer benefits**. Technical product performance should not be viewed in isolation, since consumers have emotional as well as logical needs.
5. **Superior product benefits can always be developed**. This principle applies to any market, however 'natural' and unprocessed the product may seem.
6. **Believe that small differences can matter**. They can be powerful profit builders if they are in performance areas that matter to the consumer.
7. **Look for profit improvements**. Even if the product cannot be improved, its cost can often be reduced without impairing performance.

Functional packaging has much in common with product development, while packaging graphics follow many of the same rules as advertising (see Chapter 12).

In many markets where product innovation has become difficult, packaging is being used to improve convenience and function. Taken together with its role in product design, packaging is becoming an inseparable part of product performance.

Packaging graphics is one of the lowest-cost and highest-leverage areas of marketing activity. Changes in design are relatively inexpensive but can bring large business gains, especially on small brands.

A package should protect, appeal to consumer and trade, and, ideally, enhance product performance.

9 | *Offensive Market Research*

● Basic Principles

Market research is about facts and impressions extracted from customers. It leads to better business decisions. It helps a company to keep in touch with what consumers think of its products and those of its competitors, and it monitors their actions in the market-place. Of course, research is not a way of guaranteeing success, but its effective use makes success more likely.

The key questions which market research can answer quite well are:

1. How do consumers evaluate our products or services against those of competitors?
2. What are they looking for in this market and how far are we providing this effectively?
3. How are consumer tastes changing?
4. What are consumers buying in the market-place, from whom and why?
5. How do consumers react to these new ideas we have thought up?

Market research is a complex industry. At the risk of oversimplification, it takes three forms:

208

1. *What consumers buy.* The word 'consumer' is used broadly, since it covers grocery-multiple buyers and shoppers, fund managers and industrial purchasing agents. We are all consumers.
2. *What they know and think, and why.* The raw material for this is consumer awareness, attitudes, images and reactions.
3. *How they react in a simulated situation.* What is consumer reaction to possible future marketing initiatives like new advertising, new products or new services?

Table 32 elaborates on these categories of research. This table is also a rough league table of the reliability of research. What people are buying is a fact and is therefore quite easily ascertained. What they think about existing products or markets is also a fact, but opinions are volatile. There is both art and discipline in choosing whom to interview and in making certain that interviewers are consistent.

Simulated situations are the least reliable, because they deal with the future, rather like peering into a crystal ball. However, the techniques used, though perhaps not the insights, are superior to those of Gypsy Rose Lee. But the interpretation of simulated research requires experience, caution and the occasional pinch of salt.

The most frequently used research types are market-share panels, usage and attitude studies, product tests and discussion groups.

Market-share panels measure consumer purchases in the market-place. There are two main techniques for doing this. The **retail panel** reads sell-out in a nationally representative panel of stores, through store auditors who compare purchase invoices with stocks. The **consumer panel** traces the same picture by recording the purchases of thousands of customers. This used to be done by getting customers to fill in a diary of what they had bought, but increasingly a 'people meter', which records the data electronically for each family member, is replacing the diary.

Usage and attitude studies question consumers about their habits and reactions to particular products in the market. They sometimes come up with rather predictable information, but at least give the marketer a solid base of fact to work on.

Table 32. *The Main Types of Market Research*

Type	Purpose	Most Typical Method(s)
What People Buy or Do		
Retail-store panels (e.g. Nielsen)	Measure market position	Auditing retailer purchases
Consumer panels (e.g. AGB)	Measure market position	Diaries, people meters
Activity studies	Measure shopping trips, leisure pursuits, etc.	Telephone interviews
What People Think and Why		
Usage and attitude studies	Profile of products/ services	Telephone or in-home
Market segmentation studies	Identify market sub-segments	Telephone or in-home
Continuing advertising/usage studies	Trend data on awareness and attitudes	Telephone or by post
Opinion-former studies	Get views of opinion-formers	Personal interviews
Product tests	Compare products	Hall, van or in-home testing
Advertising recall studies	Measure recall of advertising	Telephone
Buyer/Distributor studies	Get buyer attitudes	Telephone or in person
Employee attitude studies	Measure employee attitudes	Personal interviews
Exploratory research	Probe consumer motivations	Small discussion groups
Simulated Situations		
Simulated test markets (STMs)	Test new products or services	'Sales' van or simulated retail store
Advertising tests	Persuasiveness of advertising	Various
Concept tests	Test advertising, product, packaging or promotion ideas	Small groups with concept drawings
Trade-off research	Forecast consumer behaviour	Personal interviews

The **product blind test** is a long-established technique in which two competing brands are evaluated by consumers in blank packets so that their reaction to the product itself, shorn of packaging, advertising and all other attributes of the brand image, can be assessed. It is worthy but indispensable and is sometimes neglected or misused.

A variant of the product blind test is the **named-packet test**. Some brands with very strong images may lose a blind test but easily win on a named-packet basis. A named-packet test is also a good way of testing new package designs. The product is a constant, but the preferred pack produces a 'halo' effect on perceived product performance.

Group discussions involving, say, four to eight groups of six to nine people are a very popular research method, not least because they are inexpensive and can be set up quickly. Sometimes they are used just to get a 'feel' for consumer reaction to advertising concepts or new ideas, or they may be run as a preliminary to a larger study.

Groups provide a fast hotline to the consumer and are helpful in screening hypotheses, identifying the questions to ask in a larger study and providing guidance on consumer language. Insurance companies often use obscure jargon in their advertising, which shows they are out of touch with the consumer. However, group discussions should not be used as a basis for key decisions – these deserve the backing of quantitative research conducted on a representative sample of target consumers.

● **The Changing Face of Research**

The research techniques described above have been around for thirty years or more. There has been no shortage of innovation on the research front, but most of the new methodologies have failed to last the pace.

Now, however, the combination of new computer applications, in-store scanning, cable TV and shopper-identification cards is likely to radically change the face of research over the next ten years.

The market-research industry is already exploiting new computer uses, such as computer-assisted interviewing, on-line data access to clients and immediate data feedback.[1] For the client, this means greater flexibility in data use and faster receipt of results.

The most important new technology affecting market research is the store check-out scanner. This is an electronic device which reads a barcode on each product and gives an itemized print-out of every item purchased, with prices paid. Scanning is not yet widespread in the UK but will be by the 1990s. Here are some of its likely effects:

- retail auditing will no longer be conducted by field workers laboriously counting stock and studying invoices. Participating stores will send their check-out tapes to a central data processor – in the UK, the A. C. Nielsen Company – to churn out market shares for all products audited. Market-share information will therefore be available more quickly and in more detail than at present. Nielsen has already invested heavily in scanning, both hardware and software, on a worldwide basis.
- retailers will have access to a massive bank of information about the performance of all products for each of their stores, by linear foot of space, by size and so on. This will improve the efficiency of retailers and increase their bargaining power compared with manufacturers.
- check-out scanning has already been combined with a customer 'demographic card' and the ability to transmit different commercials to matched homes within an area.

For the first time it is becoming possible to get definitive answers to the questions which businessmen, with growing irritation, have been asking for decades – questions like: 'What effect will this advertising have on my sales?', 'What happens to my sales if I double advertising weight or cut it in half?', 'How much extra consumer trial do I get with a 20p coupon rather than a 10p coupon?'

Nielsen, with its Testsight and ERIM models, and Behaviorscan in the USA, are in the forefront of this new type of panel technique:

The Behaviorscan technique is to take a test area of, say, 100,000 people, living in homes equipped with cable TV. It then ensures that all grocery stores in the town install check-out scanners, if necessary helping with the cost of installation. A panel of approximately 2,500 consumers is selected and given plastic customer cards containing name, address and demographic details.

Each time the panel customers go shopping, they insert their cards in a slot at the check-out. Consequently, for each transaction Behaviorscan can relate the itemized list of products bought to the demographics of the purchaser. Thanks to cable TV, Behaviorscan is also able to vary the type of commercial screened and its weight, within its consumer panel. It can then relate these variants to sales.

Figure 21 shows the difference in sales level between one part of the panel, which received heavy advertising and home sampling, and the other part, which was exposed to a lower weight of advertising and promotion.

However, use of these techniques is unlikely to become widespread in the UK until the 1990s.

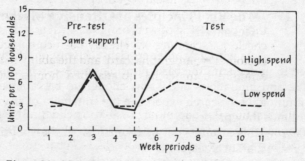

Figure 21. New Brand Sales – Heavy vs. Light Introductory Advertising and Promotion*

Quite apart from scanning, progress has been made during the past few years in econometrics (see Chapter 12, 'Offensive Advertising'). Econometrics attempts to put a value on the effect of changes in advertising weight, prices and sales promotion. A data

* Source: Behaviorscan, internal publication.

base of three years' monthly or ten years' quarterly sales, market shares, advertising weights and price differentials is desirable.

Using a technique like multiple linear regression, the computer provides the best fit between the variables. Market testing of different TV advertising weight by area and pricing tests in matched store panels can improve the data base. Time lags can also be incorporated into the program to allow for the delayed effect of advertising.

A validated econometric model can be used to ask questions about the future. Should we increase or cut advertising weight? Does price-cutting work on this product and to what extent? What happens to our business in the next three years if the number of teenagers declines?

A number of companies, such as Unilever and Beecham Foods, treat econometrics as a standard analytical tool, and usage is spreading rapidly.

However, no matter what new developments come along in methodology or technology, the basic principles of offensive market research will remain constant.

● The Six Principles of Offensive Market Research

As with any other specialist activity, marketing people need to understand the basic principles of research, appreciate its value and limitations and know enough to be capable of cross-examining the research experts on the suitability of any particular technique they propose.

Bearing this in mind, let us take a look at the six principles of offensive market research:

1. Research produces data, not decisions

Research is a device for improving the quality of the information on which decisions are based. It is not a substitute for decisions, although it can make decisions easier and more certain.

Market research is sometimes wrongly regarded by executives as a kind of 'answer machine' into which they can drop any questions or problems which bother them, in the hope that it will make judgement unnecessary. Applied in this way, research is doomed to misuse and will be stretched beyond its capabilities:

> *A few years ago a UK food company, which is now trading quite successfully, got into a terrible fix. After doing no product blind-testing for five years, it had a shock when its largest brand, second in its market, lost by a 30:70 margin on blind test against the brand leader. What is more, its inferior product was premium-priced.*
>
> *The product was rapidly improved and some research was undertaken to try to provide guidance to the sorely worried management team. The big question, of course, was whether to reduce the price and, if so, by how much?*
>
> *Three research studies were carried out and these purported to show the following results:*
>
> *– there was little consciousness among retailers of the brand's unfavourable price.*
> *– consumers had little awareness of the differences in prices between the various brands in the market. This deduction was based on direct questioning of consumers about their knowledge of prices, through interviews conducted in the home.*
> *– an experimental study also apparently suggested that price was unimportant. Two packets of the brand were exposed to the consumer, each marked with different prices (there was a 10 per cent difference between the two prices). Consumers were asked which one they were most likely to buy, and showed no preference between the two differently priced packets.*
>
> *This strange result was probably due to consumer confusion about the question. Consumers no doubt thought the interviewer wanted to know if they saw any difference between the two products and therefore ignored the obvious price difference. It was a bad piece of research and opinion within the company was divided as to what action should be taken; it was undoubtedly a critical decision.*
>
> *One camp was opposed to cutting the price. They argued that a price-cut would be viable only if volume increased substantially, and they instanced the three research studies as clear evidence that it would not. In addition, they felt that the brand's higher prices had in the past helped it to establish a feeling of premium quality among its own users.*

The other camp strongly favoured a price-cut. They agreed that a large increase in volume was necessary to justify a price reduction, but felt confident that this would happen. The arguments they put forward were based on general principles. The product was frequently purchased and in a high-turnover food category. It could therefore be assumed that consumers would be sensitive about price. In addition, a marketing policy based on premium-pricing a number two brand, whose product acceptance was at best on a par with the brand leader, was untenable. Moreover, the premium-pricing would not enhance the image of a fast-moving brand (unlike a cosmetic or fashion product).

They also dismissed the three research studies as useless and misleading, since they dealt with a speculative future situation, and predictions for researchers and actual purchase decisions were two entirely different things. Finally, the inability of consumers to recall actual prices in the home did not prevent them from observing them in the store.

Fortunately, the second camp won out and the prices were reduced. As expected, volume rose sharply and the company moved back into a profitable position.

The moral is that the decision could have been made without doing any research, just by following general business principles and using common sense, as the group whose opinion held sway did.

Research can also be wrongly exploited as a delaying tactic for postponing hard but obvious decisions. The weak manager uses research in the same way as the politician sometimes uses Royal Commissions.

2. Look for the action

Every market raises questions which it would be interesting to research. But unless the research is likely to lead to action, it is not worth doing. Some research, such as continuous retail or consumer panels, is useful as a background to effective marketing. You could live without detailed information on market size or brand share, and many smaller companies do, quite successfully.

However, for those able to afford it, this kind of data tells how you are performing in the market-place, how well the competition is doing, what your position is by account, service or product, and area. It also holds clues as to why brand shares are changing. Is your share rising because of distribution gains, extra advertising weight, pricing changes, sales promotion or all of these, and what are the relationships?

All this is quite basic, and continuous panel data is very rewarding to those who are thorough. Two competing companies may be receiving almost identical panel information from the same research organization, but one might derive twice the value from it. However, because the need for continuous research is accepted without question by some companies, it can become part of the wallpaper – there, but taken for granted.

Non-continuous research – 'ad hoc' as it is inelegantly called – is carried out to answer particular questions, and this should also lead to concrete action. The marketing department is usually the customer for ad hoc research. To ensure that research projects result in action, most companies write a formal brief, and some insist on a subsequent report from the marketing department, outlining action taken.

The brief for a major piece of research such as a usage and attitude study deserves at least the same degree of attention as an advertising strategy. It should outline the purpose of the research and relate this to the business decisions influenced, then summarize the method to be used and, finally, list the expected use of results. This can usually be condensed into a single page. The great value of the 'expected use of results' paragraph is that it forces the sponsor of the research to think about the various outcomes *before* the project begins.

Once the research is completed, an internal summary and an action report, perhaps two pages long, should be written by the marketing person sponsoring it. This would apply even if, as usually happens, the researcher also writes a report. Increasingly, researchers are also recommending action steps, but only marketers have the authority to transform action into reality – which is why they should write their own reports.

Unfortunately, this discipline is often ignored, as in the example below:

> *This major company has a large market-research budget of over £1 million. Its Market Research Manager is technically excel-*

lent and has pushed forward the frontiers of knowledge with some pioneering studies.

However, his primary interest is in very sophisticated research and he has little patience for bread-and-butter projects, although some are carried out.

Integration between the Marketing Department and Market Research is weak. The marketing people are not knowledgeable about research, and the impetus for many projects comes from the Market Research Manager. Market Research briefs are sketchy, and when reports are issued, Marketing rarely, if ever, writes its own internal action memos.

The result of this is that too much pathfinding and too little pedestrian work is done, so that simple but important questions are left unanswered; the value derived from the research is limited, mainly because Marketing is not sufficiently disciplined to confront the action issues raised by it; and finally, because there is not a consistent approach to market research, methods and questionnaires change and opportunities to compare different studies or to check trends over time are lost.

3. The best information may cost nothing

Potentially first-class internal company facts about sales, consumer complaints or selling efficiency may never see the light of day just because they have not been analysed.

Every organization keeps records of monthly sales on a national basis. There are numerous ways in which this data can be usefully broken down: by sales district or unit, by T V area, by major outlet type, by size of customer or individual products and by sizes and varieties.

Some companies have invested heavily in 'user-friendly' internal data systems. These enable brand managers, with little knowledge of computers, to key into central computers via desk V D Us, using very simple yes/no question-and-answer techniques.

Regular analysis of internal raw data often pinpoints new problems and opportunities, as the example below shows:

Following two quite stable years, sales of a U S product began to fall away and during the period from January to June they were 16 per cent below the previous year.

> *The company in question had excellent internal data break-downs, and sales were analysed by territory. It was discovered that five territories (out of 150 in the whole country) accounted for three quarters of the product's national deficit.*
>
> *The five salesmen involved had excessively loaded the trade on a bonus the previous December and consequently had to accept a large amount of returned product in the period from January to June. Outside these five territories, the brand was only 3 per cent behind the previous year and, in relation to its very limited marketing spending support, reasonably healthy.*

There are other basic yet fruitful sources of internal data. A careful tabulation of consumers' letters of complaint and appreciation can provide a gauge of quality-control effectiveness. Analysis of sales representatives' reports yields stop-press information on average daily-call rates, sales per call, distribution gains and losses, and display levels. A great deal of potentially actionable financial data is often left unprocessed or is circulated to the wrong people.

In addition, there has been an explosion in the amount of low-priced 'off-the-peg' data about companies and markets. It varies from government statistics and syndicated reports to trade journals. The variety is such that one can often initially screen the potential of a possible new market without spending more than £1,000. Some of this data is available on-line. For instance, one financial service company can provide every trade-press reference to specific companies or markets over the past four years, immediately, on-line.

Most firms could probably make better use of internal and low-priced external data, but one hopes that the horror story below is untypical:

> *A large American company had no sales breakdown of its products by variety, geographical area or type of account. There was no data on the minimum break-even volume for new lines, nor any information on profitability by type of product or account. Facts about who bought the product, attitudes to the company and its brands, and reasons for purchase were entirely lacking. Nor did the company know its market share, even on a national basis.*

4. See the people behind the numbers

The impact of a legal case, especially one involving a jury, can be only dimly communicated in the Law Reports. Many of the incidents will have been omitted, the atmosphere of the court is absent, the appearance and manner of the participants are not described and there is no reference to the demeanour of the accused or the witnesses.

Equally, a research report can be fully appreciated by marketers only with up-to-date and first-hand knowledge of their company's customers. Marketing people are sometimes justifiably accused of being out of touch and more in tune with the executive lifestyle than with the typical consumer. It is important to get out 'where the rubber meets the road', to talk frequently to consumers and the trade, if only to gain a background 'feel' in interpreting formal research.

Marks & Spencer, with its northern origins, keeps very closely in touch with its customers. As Lord Sieff put it: 'Most of our stores are in places like Wigan, and middle-aged men in Wigan do not wear yellow shirts.'[2]

Professionally conducted research and informal customer contacts should be run in harness, since each has limited value in isolation.

Senior management, especially the Managing Director and Marketing Director, also need to retain access to raw data. In large organizations, research results often reach marketing directors in predigested reports which have been minced, blended and filtered through the layers of management. These reports will gain a much richer texture if marketers can also get their hands on occasional chunks of raw information – unedited videotapes of group discussions, computer tabulations and direct access to research field-workers.

For example, at one company the Managing Director spends at least one hour a month flicking through some of the previous week's orders. At Colgate, management regularly conducts 'consumer checks' by personally calling on homes at random to get a reaction to company products.

5. Good research requires imagination

The objective of most research is to uncover consumer attitudes and feelings. Although the means of measuring these may be mechanical, the thinking behind the technique and the questioning must be imaginative. Consumers rarely analyse their real reasons for buying even major commitments like insurance policies and houses, never mind instant coffee and yoghurt.

For example, if you ask consumers a direct question about why they buy a particular brand, you are likely to get the kind of feedback shown in Table 33, which is not very nourishing.

Table 33. *Non-actionable Consumer Playback.*

Reason for using last brand	%
Always used	20
Relative used/recommended	15
Saw advertising	10
Recommended by friend/neighbour	14
Bought on special price offer	12
No particular reason	21
No answer or don't know	8
Total	100

Finding out what consumers really think involves more than throwing a broadly directed question at them. In order to bring out real, as opposed to surface, motivations, the interviewer has to stimulate interest, and this requires a creative approach.

The need for imagination in research is often overlooked by marketing people who reserve all their creativity for advertising, promotions and packaging. One of the most difficult areas to research is products new to the world which create new usages, like the first Apple personal computer.

Research should not only be imaginative but also sympathetic, since the researcher may in the early stages be working with a product which only half solves the problem, and with consumers who have difficulty in envisaging how they would use the product.

Combining imagination with sympathy and objectivity is no easy task, and the example below features a product strong enough to survive the absence of this combination, 3M's 'Post-It' notes, which have now achieved sales of over $200 million a year:

> *In 1970 Dr Silver was working in 3M Central Laboratories to develop adhesive with maximum holding power. Instead, he discovered one that would stick but could be easily lifted off.*
>
> *He sent out samples, but nothing happened for several years. Then a colleague, Art Fry, a keen chorister who sang in two church services every Sunday, needed markers for his hymn book. Fry knew of Silver's work, and developed a peelable hymnal marker in the 15 per cent of R & D time 3M allowed for his own projects. He felt there was potential for the product, but he 'didn't have the words for it'.*
>
> *The marketing people did surveys of potential customers, and results were very poor. Consumers had managed without such a product and couldn't see the need for it. Fry reasoned that people would have to use the product to discover what it was good for. So he distributed samples to colleagues and asked them to come back for more when they ran out. He recorded usage and found that it exceeded usage of Magic Tape by the same people. Magic Tape was 3M's biggest-selling office product. Meanwhile, surveys conducted by the Marketing Department continued to show that consumers had low interest in the product.*
>
> *However, 3M began selling Post-It notes in four cities, with advertising support but no sampling. The test failed. A new test was opened in Idaho, with a heavy advertising and sampling plan. Results were sensational and the product was launched in the USA in 1980, and internationally in 1981.*
>
> *Post-It notes are still growing and in 1984 the product was included in the exhibition of 'The World's 100 Best-ever Products', in the Boilerhouse at the Victoria and Albert Museum.*
>
> *The lesson is clear. It was pointless to use traditional research techniques to evaluate this totally new product, as the marketing people had attempted to do. The informal research technique used by the scientist, Art Fry, was in fact the right one.*[3]

6. Blind-test . . . with your eyes open

A blind-test result is very important. It tells you whether or not your product has that much-prized asset, superiority. If the answer is positive, you are likely to make important investment decisions on the basis of it.

For a new product, a blind-test win represents 'permission to move into the market-place'.[4] For an existing one, a blind-test result may determine the amount of marketing support received, since companies are rightly prepared to back superior products more heavily than parity ones.

Blind-testing is also simple and inexpensive. Any logical by-stander knowing nothing about marketing will be astonished to hear that many large consumer-goods companies do either very little blind-testing or none at all. And some of those which do employ it use invalid techniques. Here is an example of the latter:

> *An American food company conducted a blind test, which purported to give its new product a 70:30 win over its competitors. It was invalid because the base of consumers was only 100, the test was conducted in a hall rather than in the consumer's home and the method of use specified bore no relation to normal consumer habits.*
>
> *Based on this blind-test 'win', the company decided to deliver samples of its 'superior' product to some millions of homes at a cost of $2 million. The sampling operation proved a total failure because, having tried the sample, only a very small proportion of consumers subsequently purchased the product in a store.*
>
> *The poor response of this brand to sampling, its inability to transform new triers into regular users and the results of technical assessments all indicated that the product was at best on parity with competition. A properly run blind test would have shown this and enabled the company to save the money it wasted on sampling.*

While this is probably an exceptional example, invalid blind-testing is by no means restricted to a few unfortunate cases, and the main errors made are as follows:

– blind-testing is done in halls on small samples of customers and is used as a basis for important decisions;

this is a false economy. Hall testing is inexpensive and useful for pilot testing or short-listing the most promising alternative formulation. Quantified in-home blind-testing should precede any new product launch or major change in product formulation.

– consumers are given special usage instructions, instead of being allowed to use the product according to their normal habits. For example, telling a mother to taste a babyfood would be invalid, because many mothers never do this but give the product to their babies straight away.

– consumers are prompted and their attention directed to particular performance areas. This type of direct questioning is less valid than the consumer's unprompted response to products.

– products of uneven age are compared. Sometimes the company product is taken fresh from the factory, while samples of the competitive one are bought in the market-place. This naturally favours the company product.

The products tested must have had a comparable life. This means they should be picked off the shelf in a representative sample of retail stores, since it is impossible to obtain factory-fresh products from a competitor. Furthermore, the consumer purchases products from the store, not from the factory.

The manufacturing or R & D departments should *not* have the opportunity to examine the product picked up or to reject it as being untypical of normal production methods.

Assuming the sample of stores used for the pick-up is representative, the production methods *will* be typical and, anyway, the competitor's R & D department would have no opportunity to examine its blind-test product for typicality:

> *A company started to use the market pick-up system of acquiring blind-test products for the first time. The R & D Department was rather apprehensive and gained the right to examine the company products picked up and to reject them if they represented 'untypical' production methods.*
>
> *The R & D Department rejected the first three pick-ups*

conducted by the market-research group, as they contained examples of 'untypical' production methods. As a result, it took nine months to set up this product test and, when it was eventually completed, the Marketing Department was deeply sceptical of the results.

Offensive market research in action: launch of 'new Coke'[5]

Coca-Cola was invented in 1886 by John Pemberton, a pharmacist in Atlanta, Georgia. He sold the rights to another pharmacist, Asa Candler, for $2,300 and died destitute in 1888.

The formula for Coca-Cola syrup remained unchanged for ninety-nine years, except for the removal in 1901 of the minute quantity of cocaine originally included. Candler mixed the formula himself. It was kept in a safe to which only he and his book-keeper were allowed access. Over the years, a great deal of mystique built up regarding the secrecy of the formula, which was housed in a vault at the Trust Company of Georgia Bank and which was accessible only to a handful of very senior executives.

From the early 1980s Pepsi-Cola began to attack Coca-Cola with a superior taste strategy. It conducted hundreds of blind product tests in shopping centres and advertised the winning performance of Pepsi on taste. Pepsi-Cola began to eat into Coca-Cola's market share, especially in grocery multiples, although the success of Diet Coke and Cherry Coke ensured that, on a company basis, Coca-Cola gained share.

In 1981 Coca-Cola started to test new formulae and between 1982 and 1985 it spent over $4 million in blind-testing various products among a total of almost 200,000 consumers. The pace of testing quickened in late 1984, when two Atlanta research firms, with the final formula for 'New Coke', took taste tests to thirty American cities and sampled 40,000 people.

Nearly all this testing was done on a blind product basis. Overall, the consensus of blind tests showed a preference for the 'New Coke' formula, at 55:45 vs. Coca-Cola and 52:48 vs. Pepsi-Cola. When the drinks were marked as Coca-Cola or Pepsi-Cola, though not identified as 'new', the products tied. But when the participants were told that Coca-Cola was a new formula, they chose it by almost 55:45. However, it appears that *only one* of the many tests was on a 'named' basis – the rest were 'blind'.

While this massive programme of product testing was in progress, Coca-Cola continued its regular research studies – such as national and regional store audits, and telephone surveys tracking consumer usage, attitudes and advertising awareness. But it apparently did not at any point get consumer reaction to replacing Coca-Cola with a new formula and this was reputedly due to a concern over security.

The outcome is well known. Coca-Cola was replaced by New Coke on 23 April 1985, and three weeks later, in response to public outcry, Coca-Cola Classic was reintroduced as a sister brand. Now Coca-Cola Classic is heavily outselling New Coke, whose future is questionable, but only about half of those drinking Coca-Cola Classic think it tastes like the original flavour.[6]

So what went wrong? Here we have a product improvement which was preferred on blind test, and yet is rejected in the market-place. Was the research unreliable? Or was the wrong kind of research carried out? Only Coca-Cola executives know the real answer to these questions. But observers have the impression that the most important issues – the effects of a widely announced formula change on brand image – were not researched. Coca-Cola is not only strongly branded. It is part of the American heritage, a national institution almost on a par with the Stars and Stripes and the Statue of Liberty.

What should Coca-Cola have done? The blind-testing was worthwhile although the extent seemed unnecessary. If Coca-Cola was so concerned about security as not to research reaction to the replacement of Coca-Cola by New Coke, it could have checked response indirectly by floating a range of attitude statements such as: 'I'm happy with Coca-Cola as it is'; or 'I'd hate to see Coca-Cola changed'; or 'I'd certainly prefer a new, better-tasting Coca-Cola.' In addition Coca-Cola presumably has roomfuls of research on its brand image, going back many years.

It is easy to be wise after the event, and Coca-Cola's speed of reaction, plus the success of the other brands in its range, have still enabled it to continue to build company share in the American soft-drinks market.

● **Summary**

Market research falls into three main categories, covering what consumers buy, what they think and how they react in simulated situations. The reliability of research is greatest when measuring facts, such as purchases, and least in evaluating speculative possibilities.

New technology is changing the face of market research, and the pace of change is likely to be greater in the next ten years than in the previous thirty. Techniques are already in place which make it possible to measure the effect of individual marketing inputs on sales much more precisely than in the past.

Six principles of offensive market research are summarized below:

1. **Research produces data, not decisions**. Research is a device for improving the quality of decisions. It should be used as a torch, not as a crutch to bolster weak decision-makers.

2. **Look for the action.** Unless research results in action, it is not worth doing. Precise research briefs and subsequent action reports by the marketing person responsible are aids to this. Research sponsors should have a clear idea as to how they will use the results of the project before it starts.

3. **The best information may cost nothing.** Every company possesses a great deal of processed and raw data, which may be neglected or be in the wrong format.

4. **See the people behind the numbers.** Professionally conducted research and informal customer contact should be run in harness, since each has a limited value in isolation.

5. **Good research requires imagination.** In order to bring out real, as opposed to surface, motivations, the interviewer has to stimulate interest and this requires a creative approach. Marketing executives should apply more of the creativity to research which they reserve for advertising and packaging.

6. **Blind-test . . . with your eyes open.** Blind-testing tells you whether you have that much-prized asset – product superiority – but, as a research tool, it is sometimes misused.

10 | *Offensive Pricing*

You have a distinctive and exciting product or service to offer the world. How should it be priced? Faced with your offering, consumers will ask themselves: 'How do I rate this compared with the alternatives?' 'What is the relative price?' 'Which is the best value?'

Advertising and promotions play their part in influencing the consumer, and really good packaging or presentation can have an important impact. However, for most brands the rating of product/service and price is what matters most.

Pricing is one of the most difficult areas of marketing in which to make decisions because there are so many variables involved. The reaction of three groups has to be considered before setting or changing a price: consumers, the trade and competitors. Their interreactions are hard to read.

Pricing decisions often have to be taken quickly without testing, but usually have a major effect on profit, one way or the other. It is a lonely feeling, having forged ahead with a price increase, to find that your competitors do not follow after all. All this places a high premium on good management.

● The Background to Offensive Pricing

Economics of pricing

A sound grasp of the effect of volume changes on cost per unit is basic to any pricing decision and it may be possible to construct a volume/cost graph, especially if operations and finance are cooperative.

The economics of pricing vary greatly by product category. The comparison in Table 34 between a high margin category (cosmetics) and a low one (frozen foods) demonstrates this.

In the table each product has sales of £1 million and the volume gain needed to finance a 10 per cent price cut is analysed. For the

Table 34. *Additional Sales Needed to Pay for a 10 per cent Price Cut – Cosmetics Brand v. Frozen-Food Brand**

	Cosmetics Brand		Frozen-food Brand	
	Pre-price Cut	Post-price Cut	Pre-price Cut	Post-price Cut
Sales (000 units)	100	117	100	160
Sales (£000)	1,000	1,052	1,000	1,440
Fixed cost of goods (£000)	40	40	130	130
Variable cost of goods (£000)	260	304	670	1,072
Total cost of goods (£000)	300	344	800	1,202
Gross Margin (£000)	700	708	200	238
Advertising/promotions (£000)	350	350	60	73
Selling/distribution (£000)	100	106	70	90
Administration and financing (£000)	50	52	20	25
Operating Profit (£000)	200	200	50	50
Percentage Volume Gain Needed	—	**17%**	—	**60%†**

*The key figures in this table are indicated by bold type.
†It is assumed that 60 per cent extra volume can be accommodated without building new manufacturing capacity.

cosmetics brand only 17 per cent extra volume is required, but for the frozen-food product a mighty 60 per cent is needed, as the table shows.

The situation is different when it comes to a price rise. The economics are more favourable for both brands and especially so for the low-margin frozen food. If a 10 per cent price rise only caused a 5 per cent volume loss, the frozen-food brand would more than double its profits, as shown in Table 35. The lesson is that price rises are relatively more attractive for low-margin products. The catch can be that low-margin brands may also be more price-sensitive. (The relationship between price levels and consumer demand is covered later in this chapter, see p. 232.)

Table 35. *Effect of 5 per cent Volume Loss Following 10 per cent Price Rise**

	Cosmetics Brand		Frozen-food Brand	
	Pre-price Rise	Post-price Rise	Pre-price Rise	Post-price Rise
Sales (000 units)	100	95	100	95
Sales (£000)	1,000	1,045	1,000	1,045
Fixed cost of goods (£000)	40	40	130	130
Variable cost of goods (£000)	260	247	670	636
Total cost of goods (£000)	300	287	800	766
Gross Margin (£000)	700	758	200	279
Advertising/promotions (£000)	350	350	60	60
Selling/distribution (£000)	100	97	70	68
Admin/financing (£000)	50	50	20	20
Operating Profit (£000)	200	261	50	131
Percentage Profit Gain	—	+30%	—	+162%

*The key figures in this table are indicated by bold type.

Cost-plus versus demand pricing

The most favoured approaches to pricing are cost-plus and demand pricing.

Cost-plus involves taking your costs and adding on a fixed percentage for profits. The advantages are simplicity and less price competition between companies. But the drawbacks are overwhelming for manufacturers in highly competitive markets, since 'cost-plus' does not take into account competitive reaction.

The other problem with cost-plus is that it ignores the demand curve for the brand or the category. A rise in price due to cost pressure could reduce profit if sales revenue fell heavily.

Demand pricing is the better method because it takes market response into account. The only justification for a price increase is that it will increase profit and, unless a company is badly strapped for cash or is deliberately milking a product or service, profits should be looked at from a long-term viewpoint.

With this method of pricing one wants to know what would happen to the sales-revenue trend if prices were increased by 10 per cent – whether it would remain stable or fall so heavily that a price increase would reduce profit.

If a price increase could be expected to deflate profit, it should obviously not be pursued. And if rising costs are a big problem, the solution should be found through means that seem more likely to increase profit, like cutting costs or increasing volume.

In essence, demand pricing ignores cost. If an increase in price looks likely to raise long-term profit, it should be adopted even though costs remain stable or decline. Value rather than cost is what determines pricing.

● The Eight Principles of Offensive Pricing

No one faces pricing decisions with 100 per cent confidence, but the pursuit of the eight principles of offensive pricing outlined below should facilitate decision-making.

1. Know your price dynamics

Although pricing decisions often have to be taken quickly, the quality of decision-making can be enormously improved by taking a hard look at the price dynamics of a market beforehand. You should never be in the position of not really knowing whether price matters in your market, as in the example from the food industry on p. 215.

Before embarking on the details, the important distinction between markets and products should be underlined. A total market may be insensitive to price changes, while consumers may be very price-conscious about individual products, or vice versa.

Any analysis of price dynamics should therefore query not only the effect of price changes on the volume of a product, but also the effect on the total market. The application of general common-sense principles is a good start:

- **frequency of purchase** has a major influence on the sensitivity of individual products or services to price changes. Those in markets where frequency of purchase is high – like babyfoods, fast foods, petrol, bread and tea – tend to be very price-sensitive.
- **degree of necessity** affects markets rather than products within them. If a product category is very necessary to its users, changes in the prices of all products are unlikely to affect its size. But discretionary markets – like crisps, consumer credit, clothing or cars – are adversely affected by general price increases.
- **unit price** is another factor. High-priced items like holidays, cars, furniture and consumer electronics tend to be subject to long deliberation and considerable price-consciousness, although status and styling may also affect the outcome.
- **degree of comparability** also influences the price sensitivity of brands – consumers are less price-conscious about insurance policies than about grocery products, because they are more difficult to compare.
- **degree of fashion or status** affects pricing, but sometimes in reverse; fashion or cosmetic brands may use high prices as a way of establishing quality.

The operation of these general principles is illustrated in a number of different markets by Table 36 and, by applying these broad principles, you can draw some general conclusions about the likely price sensitivity of certain products/services and markets in about five minutes flat. With this under your belt, you can then analyse price/volume relationships in your market.

Table 36. *Factors Influencing Price Sensitivity by Market*

| | Mass Markets | | | |
	Babyfoods	Clothing	Motor Insurance	New Cars
Purchase frequency	Very High	Low	Low	Low
Necessity	High	Medium	High	Medium
Unit price	Low	Medium	High	High
Comparability	High	Medium	High	Medium
Fashion	Low	High	Low	High
Effect of pricing:				
on markets	Medium	Medium	Low	High
on brands	High	Medium	High	Medium

Your first step is to choose competitors against whom to check prices. A mutual life assurance company, like NPI, would be sensible to compare its premiums to brokers and accountants with those of competitors, like Equity & Law, Scottish Amicable and UK Provident, for comparable policies.

A chart for a grocery product is shown in Figure 22. If the price differential between this brand and its competitors moves from 2p to 3p, market share declines dramatically. Once the differential exceeds 3p the effect on share is more gradual, because hard-core users will continue to buy – despite the extra cost.

The optimum price differential for this brand is about 2p more than the competition. Unfortunately, this particular brand spent two years at a 3p to 4p price differential (and a 12 per cent market share) before moving up to a much more profitable 16 per cent market share.

This chart was constructed by relating market shares to price differentials for four competing brands, using Nielsen bi-monthly data for the previous four years. Some judgement had to be used in allowing for the effect of new products, but changes in advertising weight and sales promotion by brand were also fed into the analysis. The answer on pricing was clear-cut and proved correct when applied.

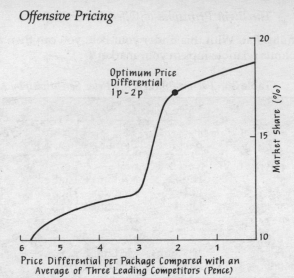

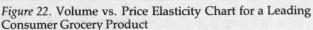

Figure 22. Volume vs. Price Elasticity Chart for a Leading Consumer Grocery Product

2. Strengthen your pricing muscles

The shape of the price/volume graph just analysed is not fixed. The objective of offensive marketers is to change the graph in their favour, ·by strengthening their consumer proposition. This can be achieved by product or service improvement and by changes in strategy, packaging or advertising.

With the proliferation of low-price operators and store private labels, every brand needs to build its muscles and improve its relative position. The hypothetical example in Figure 23 illustrates this process with a brand which improved its relative customer proposition in 1980–86.

Priced at 2p above its leading competitors, this brand earned a 15 per cent market share in 1980, but built to 18 per cent in 1983 and 18·5 per cent in 1986, at a better price differential. Higher prices are the reward which marketers gain for consumer satisfaction.

In food, Marks & Spencer is an example of a brand which succeeded in widening its price premium by steadily strengthening the appeal of its products over time. Its food products earn a premium because customers perceive them as fresher, of higher quality and more exciting. They also generate net profits of around

234

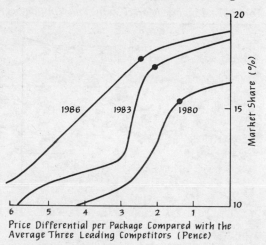

Figure 23. Strengthened Price Realization 1980–86

8 per cent on sales against only 5 per cent for Sainsbury, the most efficient grocery supermarket operator.

3. Choose your price segments

Every market is segmented by price brackets. In general, stronger brands occupy the upper pricing half, while commodity products and store private-label brands are in the lower half.

The bar chart in Table 37 illustrates price segmentation for a lingerie market. Note that the top price sector accounts for only 9 per cent of volume but 18 per cent of value, while the bottom price sector is almost the reverse.

It is important to set a price sector strategy. Is your strategy, like that of Seiko Watches or Pedigree Petfoods, to compete at every price point and to blanket the market with your products? Or is it to focus on the top 20 per cent of selected market sectors, like BMW and Nike shoes?

Perhaps your strategy is to concentrate on the lowest price sector, like Kwik Save Stores, Freshbake frozen pies or Amstrad computers, exploiting efficient low-cost operation. Or, like many Japanese global marketers and store private-label brands, you may

235

Table 37. *Lingerie Market Value and Volume Segmentation*

Price	Value	Volume
£8 and over	18%	9%
		19%
£6–£8	27%	12%
£5–£6	13%	40%
£3–£5	32%	20%
Under £3	10%	
Total	100%	100%

use low price as an initial entry point and, once established, widen your coverage of price segments by moving upwards.

There are many alternative strategies for pricing. What matters is having a clear one, which has been fully thought-out, rather than drifting across the price segments. Obvious considerations are:

- **profitability**. Some price sectors are very much more profitable than others. For example, in the car market the top 10–15 per cent of the pricing band is highly profitable, while the bottom 20 per cent is overcrowded and produces lean returns.
- **fit with your company**. What price sectors best capitalize on your strengths? Are you a sophisticated marketer with strong brands and heavy R & D backing? Or does your expertise lie in low-cost operations, fast reaction and a limited range of high-volume products?

  Companies which have been successful in one price sector often have difficulty in moving into new ones. In general, though, it is easier to move up than down. Companies attempting to move down can suffocate in high overheads and wither in the absence of large marketing budgets.
- **competitive intentions**. Watch out for the Japanese

trick. When the Japanese entered the motor-cycle market with small machines, Harley Davidson with its 750–1000cc superbikes hardly noticed. Now Harley Davidson is in a possibly losing battle with Honda in the exalted price sector it once owned.

4. Consider the alternatives

Pricing is often regarded as a somewhat mechanical aspect of marketing, but in fact it provides plenty of opportunity for creativity and this can pay off handsomely. For a start, price is only one part of the marketing mix, and the profitability of a change in price should be compared with all the other viable alternatives.

Suppose, for example, that a 10 per cent increase in price was being considered and was expected to bring in £500,000 extra sales revenue and £200,000 additional net profit. Before recommending such an increase, it would make sense to consider whether various other possible combinations would raise profit by more than £200,000, like these:

– increase the price by 5 per cent and run an extra promotion.
– hold the price and reduce the advertising by £150,000.
– raise the price 15 per cent and adopt a major product or service improvement.

Even when it has been agreed to follow the price increase route, the alternative ways of implementing it may be numerous. You could:

– hold the price but reduce the product weight by, say, 20 per cent.
– maintain the weight and raise the price by 10 per cent.
– raise the price by 5 per cent and reduce the product weight by, say, 10 per cent.
– improve the package design and marginally improve the product (without adding much to its cost) concurrently with a price rise of 11 per cent.
– alter payment or delivery arrangements, change the conditions of free maintenance or technical assistance, or increase guarantee/warranty periods.

In selecting alternatives, be careful not to weaken the image of your product or reduce its appeal.

5. Manage the ripples

In competitive industrial or distributor markets, different prices are often paid by different buyers for the same product. This results from variations in volume purchased, delivery methods and servicing levels, all of which influence the cost of supply. But price is also affected by bargaining power and purchasing skills.

Consequently, situations can occur where Purchaser A, buying 1,000 units, can pay more than Purchaser B, buying 500 units. All this is well known to buyers and their managers, and is a potentially sensitive area.

It is especially sensitive in marketing to competitive retailers, and here is a familiar example:

You are Sales Manager of a coffee manufacturer selling to three major grocery multiples, which account for 35 per cent of its sales. Retailer B has the worst terms but will sometimes accept much lower margins on promotions than the other two. Retailer C is the smallest of the three, but has a very skilful and aggressive buyer, and the best terms.

The manufacturer runs a 15p per unit promotion, aiming to get retailers to reduce price per jar to £2·40. Retailers A and C do this, but Retailer B ignores your protests and comes down to £2·20. Table 38 shows how it looks.

You expect trouble and sure enough it comes.

First Retailer A and then Retailer C call you up in fury. In each case, the buyer's boss had stormed in and asked why Retailer B was being allowed to buy more cheaply.

You end up by giving both another 10p per jar promotion allowance, so they too can come down to £2·20. Your explanation to Retailers A and C that they are both buying very competitively is not accepted – they are both convinced that Retailer B is getting some special deal. In reality, it is Retailer C who is pulling off the best deal.

The next move sees your main competitor come down to £1·99 and so on . . .

Table 38*

	Retailer A	Retailer B	Retailer C
Percentage of Manufacturer's Sales	17%	10%	8%
Base cost of coffee jar (£)	2·60	2·60	2·60
Continuing discount percentage	10%	8%	12%
Continuing discount (£)	(0·26)	(0·21)	(0·31)
Promotion payment	(0·15)	(0·15)	(0·15)
Net cost to retailer	2·19	2·24	2·14
Promoted Retail Price	**2·40**	2·20	**2·40**
Retailer Profit per Jar	**0·21**	**0·04**	**0·26**

*The key figures in this table are indicated by bold type.

How do you manage your way through this tricky but familiar situation or, even better, how do you prevent it from happening? Here are some suggestions:

– work out precisely your operating profit for each account, after deduction of discounts, over-riders, promotion allowances, distribution, selling and merchandising. The last three cost areas should be based on work study and not just approximated or, even worse, allocated as a given percentage across all accounts.

Based on this analysis, you may wish to renegotiate delivery arrangements or reduce in-store servicing levels on low-margin accounts.

In any event, the analysis will enable you to develop a long-term trading strategy for each account, including maximum levels of discount below which you will not move under any circumstances.

– a clear trading strategy will make your dealings with buyers more effective, and communicate an impression of consistency. Buyers distrust 'wheeler-dealers' who constantly respond to pressure and seem desperate for volume. Be prepared to forgo short-term volume in defence of principles. That way, the more aggressive

elements in the trade will turn their attentions elsewhere.
- build strong relationships at three or four levels in the buying organization, so that a problem with one particular contact level can be absorbed.
- be willing to initiate moves which help the retailer without costing you much. Design packages to make efficient use of shelf space as well as having consumer impact; ensure you fully understand the buyer's information needs and meet them comprehensively; set up imaginative, tailor-made promotions.

Even the best-managed trade-pricing strategies will involve regular tactical skirmishes, which is why it is worth investing in high-quality account managers. Markets and bargaining positions regularly change and day-to-day calibration of a pricing strategy is essential.

6. Beware profit cannibalization

A company needs to guard against cannibalism breaking out in its midst. This may sound like a particularly nasty form of office politics, but it affects products rather than people.

Profit cannibalization occurs where a marketing initiative by one product or service severely damages the profits of other products in the *same* company. It can take place on four fronts, each of which is looked at below. As with all the more difficult marketing questions, there are no infallible golden rules, but general guidelines can help.

New products

The example below, which is true, but must remain anonymous, illustrates how profit cannibalization can blunt the success of new products:

> Company X had a leading position in a large and growing consumer market. Its market share was around 24 per cent. Half of this was accounted for by one large brand, the rest by smaller brands. There were two large competitive brands, each with market shares between 15 per cent and 20 per cent.
>
> Company X had developed a distinctive and appealing new

brand, which was designed to take business from the two large competitive brands. The new brand did very well and is regarded as the most successful innovation in its market over the past decade. However, cannibalization of the existing products of Company X, which was anticipated at 15–20 per cent, proved to be a disastrous 40–50 per cent.

On subsequent investigation, the reasons for this became clear. In order to finance the high marketing costs of the new brand, Company X cut back advertising spend on existing brands, while competitors unsurprisingly increased support, as shown in Table 39. In addition, Company X raised prices on existing brands 16–18 per cent faster than competitors, following the launch of its new product. This is shown in Table 40.

Table 39. *Advertising Weight (Indexed)*

	Two years Pre-launch	Year of Launch	Year after Launch
Company X existing brands*	100%	50%	35%
Competitive brands	100%	116%	103%

*Excludes Company X's new brand.

Table 40. *Retail Prices: Company X Existing Brands v. Competitors*

	Six months Pre-launch	Year of Launch	Year after Launch
Company X brands	93%	108%	110%
Competitive brands	100%	100%	100%

Following its investigation, Company X was quick to change its pricing and advertising strategies on existing brands and executed the changes well enough to recover much of the lost market share.

Lessons to be learned from this example and others, on how to minimize profit cannibalization with new products, are:

– accept and plan for some loss of business on existing products when you introduce new ones. Minimize the volume and profit loss by targeting new products at sectors or segments where you are relatively weak and ensure that profit per unit on the new product is higher than average.

– with existing brands, treat your own new products or services as competitors. Ensure that each one has a strong defensive plan to minimize any loss, including aggressive pricing, and maximize the effect against competitors.

– with consumer brands, make certain that your new product gets extra space for the company and does not 'borrow' from existing products.

Moving down-market

This exercise demands skill in both pricing and product positioning. The danger in moving into lower-priced segments is trading down existing users, rather than attracting new ones.

Mercedes avoided this trap with its 190 series:

Prior to the launch of the 190 series, Mercedes marketed mid- and large-size saloon and estate cars priced between £12,500 and £37,000, mainly in 2300 to 5000cc sizes.

BMW had for many years done well with the much smaller 3 series model, with high quality and performance. The price band was £7,800 to £11,500 and engine size from 1800 to 2300cc.

The Mercedes 190 series was targeted against the high-quality small-car segment and priced at £10,900 to £12,100. Apart from BMW, other competitors in the UK market included those shown in Table 41. In moving down-market,

Table 41

Competitor	Price Range (£'000)
Audi 80	£7·8 – £11·8
Montego 2·0	£7·9 – £10·5
Ford Sierra 1·8 to 2·3	£7·1 – £11·9
Peugeot 505	£7·7 – £10·5
Vauxhall Carlton	£8·3 – £10·6

Mercedes priced the 190 right at the top of the small-car range.

Worldwide, the 190 series has proved highly successful. Annual sales are 200,000 units, which is 40 per cent of all Mercedes sales. More importantly, there was little trading down and 50 per cent of 190-series purchasers had never owned a Mercedes before.[1]

A contrasting example of the failure to solve the problems of trading down was the IBM PC Jr computer:

IBM's PC was launched in the USA during the early 1980s, targeted at the business user and priced at the top end of the personal-computer market. It proved highly successful.

The lower-priced sector of PCs – at $500 to $1,000, mainly for home users – was dominated by Apple II. IBM decided to enter this market with the PC Jr. Unfortunately, the PC Jr was not a particularly good product and had some unattractive features like a rubber keyboard. In order to move it through, IBM promoted the product very heavily, especially in December 1984, when market share peaked at 17 per cent.

However, profits proved elusive and it was estimated that for 1984 marketing and manufacturing costs on the PC Jr were $887 per machine, against a retail price of $750 in December. In addition, there appeared to be heavy cannibalization of IBM's higher-margin personal computer by the loss-making PC Jr.

By early 1985 sales of the PC Jr had slowed to a trickle and IBM withdrew it. The inventory of 100k machines was to be sold over time to the education market.[2]

Perishable products

Let us suppose you are running a fresh-fruit stall in a covered market. Your customers come to you because your products are always fresh and prices are reasonable. Demand is not always predictable and sometimes by midday on Saturday you still have a lot of stock, which will be unsaleable on Monday.

You can either cut the price, sell off the stock to less scrupulous merchants for sale the following week or compromise between the two. If you make a practice of cutting prices on Saturday afternoon, your Friday and Saturday-morning customers may delay their purchases till then. You will be trading down customers who would otherwise have paid full price.

This issue emerges in more complex form in another type of perishable product: travel. Whenever an express train slides out of Euston, or an aircraft takes off from Heathrow, the empty seats are as saleable as rotting strawberries – their time has passed. Pricing these products calls for considerable skill:

> *In the passenger-train market, there are many customer segments. The three main ones are business journeys, leisure travel and commuting.*
>
> *Price elasticity on the London commuter services is relatively low. This elasticity varies by individual route, depending on comparative road v. rail journey time and quality of rail service. London commuter trains are in peak use for only four hours per day. Outside peak hours, there is a different customer – much more price-conscious leisure travellers – and prices are therefore very much lower.*
>
> *Business travellers are also less price-conscious than leisure travellers, because the company is usually footing the bill. But most trains still contain a mix of leisure and business travellers. That mix has to be studied by route and by time of day. Consequently, prices are set highest at peak times when most business people travel, and lowest at off-peak.*
>
> *Pricing a railway network is complex. A balance has to be struck between the restrictions on travel times necessary to maximize profits and the simplicity of fare structure required to attract the customer. The object of the exercise is to fill as many seats as possible with the highest ratio of full-fare payers.*

Pricing other perishable products like package tours and air travel involve similar principles. The temptation to cut price, in order to fill up spare capacity, is always considerable, because an empty seat or a vacant hotel room produces no revenue, while the extra cost of filling them is minimal.

Runaway larger sizes

In certain markets, like cars or earth-moving equipment, larger sizes are very much more profitable than smaller ones. In the grocery market, this is not usually the case.

Larger sizes often produce lean returns because the price economy the customer expects is less than the savings gained by manufacturers. Furthermore, they are most prevalent in grocery multiples which themselves generate below-average profits for manufacturers. Figure 24 illustrates this norm.

Potato crisps are an example of this:

> *Single bags of potato crisps cost 13p each and are sold mainly in small shops, catering outlets and licensed premises. Multipacks of crisps consisting of six small bags within a larger bag cost about 54p per unit, or 9p per small bag, and are sold mainly in grocery multiples. The price per individual bag is therefore around 30 per cent less in six-packs, yet these cost more to produce because the 'overbag' is an extra item. The dilemma for manufacturers is that large multiples and six-packs are the most rapidly expanding market sectors.*

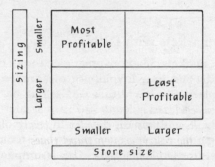

Figure 24. Profitability by Product Size and Store Size

For those in this dilemma, there are no easy answers. In many instances, larger sizes involve substantial additional costs in the short-term because of the diseconomies of shorter packaging and production runs. In the long-term these may disappear if sufficient volume is generated to reach the threshold for higher manufacturing efficiency.

Since most markets are moving towards larger sizes over time, manufacturers cannot afford to ignore the opportunities. Pricing should be determined based on expected volume in two or three years' time, once the new size is established on a 'going' basis, even though this involves a short-term diseconomy. The offensive marketer should lead the introduction of larger sizes and determine their price structure.

7. If you make a mistake on pricing, admit it and remedy fast

Anyone can make a mistake on pricing, and the important thing is to face up to it and put it right, fast. There is usually no practical reason why this cannot be done. But it is difficult to put into effect, because neither people nor companies like to admit they have made mistakes.

The irony is that mistakes do not matter too much if they are spotted and remedied quickly. This of course applies to every area of the business. As one executive with wide experience in acquisitions said: 'The key is to recognize a mistake early and then move quickly to cut losses.'[3]

8. Beware markets with falling prices

In certain markets, like consumer electronics or microchips, prices fall rapidly over time as volume grows and production costs fall. For example, a 64k RAM that was selling on the spot market at $3·50 in mid-1984 had fallen to $0·75 a year later.[4]

In categories like these, with rapidly developing technology, fast growth and declining unit cost, you may have to base today's price on the estimated costs in two years' time. The assumption is that the lower price will generate high volume and that your production people will be able to convert this into major savings.

The courageous but expensive experience of Texas Instruments in a number of markets of this type demonstrates the difficulties:

> *Texas Instruments has for years been in the vanguard of the American response to the Japanese challenge. It is strong on technology and production and, until the mid-1980s, had chalked up an outstanding record of growth and profits. In 1984 semiconductors (chips) accounted for 50 per cent of Texas Instruments' $5·7 billion sales and 80 per cent of its profits.*
>
> *A typical Texas Instruments strategy is to identify a growth market, design an acceptable product and then spend heavily on large plants operated to high efficiencies. The aim is to make*

Summary

Texas Instruments the lowest-cost operator, thus enabling it to achieve high market shares by selling mainly on price.

This strategy was applied in digital watches and hand calculators. It eventually failed because the Japanese entered these markets with a combination of low prices and product innovation. They offered new product features and met consumer needs more effectively than Texas Instruments.

The same trend is apparent in microchips, in that Texas Instruments' production cost curve for 8 RAM chips took a dramatic downturn, but the company was slow to pick up on the larger 16–64 RAM chips.

The lesson is that low-cost and trend-setting technology is not enough. In pursuing low-cost objectives, even the most sophisticated companies run the risk of losing sight of market needs or getting locked into high-volume production of yesterday's products.[5]

To compete successfully in markets with falling prices, companies need clear strategies and special skills. Requirements include:

- a reasonable confidence that ultimate success will lead to high profits, thus justifying the high risk.
- a competitive edge in technology and mass production.
- speed of reaction to changing market needs.
- a strong financial base and only limited involvement in rapidly changing markets with falling prices.
- an ability to combine innovative marketing with competitive pricing.
- a willingness and ability to take a long-term view.

 Summary

Together with product performance, pricing is the main determinant of a brand's value to the consumer.

Pricing is one of the most difficult marketing decision areas, because there are so many variables involved.

The economics of price rises are usually much more attractive than for price reductions, where large volume gains may be necessary to break even. Price rises can be especially attractive for low-margin brands, even if some volume is lost.

The two most favoured approaches to pricing are cost-plus and demand pricing. The latter is preferable.

There are eight principles of offensive pricing as follows:

1. **Know your price dynamics.** By applying simple rules, you can often draw general conclusions about the price sensitivity of your brands and markets very quickly. For many products or services it is possible to construct a volume/price-elasticity graph, using historical data and econometric analysis.
2. **Strengthen your pricing muscles.** The objective of all offensive marketers is to change the shape of the volume/price graph in their favour, by strengthening their customer proposition.
3. **Choose your price segments.** You should have a clear strategy as to which price segments you wish to compete in and why.
4. **Consider the alternatives.** The profitability of a change in price should be compared with other viable alternatives. Creativity in analysing alternatives can pay off handsomely.
5. **Manage the ripples.** Minimize disruptive ripple effects by accurately establishing your profit results for each major retail account, by building strong relationships at three or four levels, by responsiveness to genuine trade needs and by establishing a reputation for being prepared to bite the bullet.
6. **Beware profit cannibalization.** Profit cannibalization can occur on new products, when companies move down-market, on perishable products and on larger sizes. There are no magic rules, but general guidelines can help.
7. **If you make a mistake on pricing, admit it and remedy fast.** This speaks for itself.
8. **Beware markets with falling prices.** Leave them to others unless you have the unusual blend of strengths necessary to tackle them successfully.

11 | *Offensive Sales Promotion*

● **Basic Principles of Sales Promotion**

Description and role

Sales promotion means immediate or delayed incentives to purchase, expressed in cash or in kind. It has a temporary and short-term duration only, but can affect brand image in the longer-term.

A promotion has only three targets and two modes. The targets are the trade, the consumer and company employees. The modes are the immediate incentive and the delayed incentive to purchase. Incentives are *immediate* when they can be obtained concurrently with purchase, and straight price-cuts are the simplest example. Incentives are *delayed* when the purchaser has to take additional action (like mailing in an application leaflet) or has to await the outcome of chance (as in a competition).

In general, the purpose of advertising is to create awareness and improve attitudes towards a brand, while the objective of promotions is to translate favourable attitudes into actual purchase. Usage or experience of a brand also strongly influences attitudes.

No promotion is an island unto itself

Sales promotion is often mistakenly viewed in isolation from the other elements in the marketing plan and is sometimes utilized as a desperate measure to prop up sagging products.

Companies may also attempt to use sales promotion as a solution to problems of a more radical nature – like inferior performance – without recognizing that such a task is beyond its capabilities. In such situations, it only fulfils the function of heart massage and may render a disservice by temporarily obscuring the patient's serious condition.

The limited yet important role of sales promotion is not widely recognized. The objective of a promotion is to achieve a specific number of new or additional purchases during its currency. If it accomplishes this objective, it has fully completed its task. Whether or not the brand continues to grow and prosper after the promotion is over says little about the quality of the promotion – it is mainly a function of the brand's performance, pricing and advertising.

A promotion gets a product or service an 'interview' with the customer. Its long-term future with the customer will depend on how he or she assesses its performance against other product candidates previously 'interviewed'. Comments by marketing people like 'The promotion was not successful because it only achieved a temporary bump in business' demonstrate a clear misunderstanding of the role of sales promotion. It therefore follows that promotion will be most productive on new products or existing ones with a superior customer proposition.

Sales promotion is a valuable weapon in the offensive marketer's armoury, and its firepower is critical in launching new products. Speedy customer trial is essential to new product success, and the faster the better. Heavyweight weapons like in-home sampling or couponing can achieve early trial. This invests a new brand with all-important momentum which is sustained by the weight of launch advertising and the excitement of the distributor.

The contribution of sales promotion to new brand success is well illustrated by the launch of the Sony Compact range of hi-fi systems. This is also a good example of offensive marketing in action:

> *Hi-fi systems comprise radio, turntable, tape deck(s), amplifier and speakers in a single unit. Prices range from £120 to over £1,000 depending on quality and the number of 'add-ons'*

in relation to price. Hi-fi comes in tower systems or midi systems. The latter are smaller, will fit on bookshelves and are rapidly gaining market share. The hi-fi market is seasonal and centred around Christmas. Main outlets are Dixons, Rumbelows, Comet, Laskys and other specialist stores with very limited display space.

In early 1985 Sony held about 15 per cent of the midi market. Sony midi systems were on average 70 per cent more expensive than equivalent competitive products. Lower-priced competitors had more features and 'add-on' items, and Sony was relying too heavily on its name to justify its premium pricing.

Sony analysed the market very thoroughly, especially in terms of quality and add-ons against price, and designed a new range, priced from £299 to £999, covering seven different price points. While competitors expected no new initiatives until October, the traditional time for launching new products, Sony introduced the new 'Compact 7' series in June 1985. Quality and design were of a high standard, and Sony's price premium was cut from 70 per cent to 40 per cent.

The launch promotion in June/July was 'The Sony Compact Challenge'. There was a customer offer of a free high-performance Sony tape mailed to consumers who had listened to a Sony Compact hi-fi in the store. They were then invited to fill in a test report comparing the new Sony to their existing hi-fi.

This offer had a similar impact to a demonstration drive in a car, especially since the quality of tapes and hi-fis is continually improving, so that a new model will almost invariably outperform an older one. The customer offer also provided dealers with a strong selling opportunity.

There was also a trade offer of a display and sales incentive. Window-display kits, dispensers with test report forms and shelf strips were provided. Sony dealers were awarded prizes based on systems bought and displays observed by visiting Sony personnel. These were supplemented by a free draw for participating dealers. The new Sony Compact hi-fis and the Compact Challenge were also featured in a print advertising campaign running from June to October.

Sony share of the midi market rocketed to 30 per cent in July and reached 36 per cent in the peak pre-Christmas season.

Sony had broken industry tradition by launching a major new range with heavy support 'out of season' and combined product performance, pricing and advertising with sales promotion in a powerfully focused marketing plan.

On established products, a Nielsen study of eighty-three consumer offers in the USA confirms that brands enjoying long-term share growth benefit most from promotion. On these brands, sales volume increased by 10 per cent during the promotion, but retained a gain of 7 per cent in the period following. By contrast, on brands in decline sales promotion at best only temporarily cushions the fall. These results are illustrated in Figure 25.

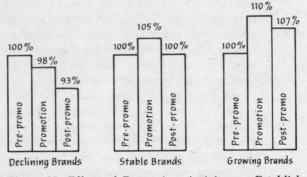

Figure 25. Effect of Promotion Activity on Established Brands

The wide variety of promotion types

Consumer promotions come in many forms. The nineteen main ones are described in Tables 42 and 43, which are intended to serve as check-lists for practising marketers. Most of these consumer promotions can also be adapted as incentives to distributors.

Some types of promotion techniques – like price-cuts, free gifts, coupons and samples – have been in use for over a hundred years. They still work efficiently when applied to the right situation. Others come and go, and some of the more transient promotion types, just like products, have life cycles.

Table 42. *Summary of Types of Immediate Consumer Promotion Incentives*

Promotion type and brief description	Advantages	Disadvantages
(1) *Reduced price packs.* Price reduction marked on package by manufacturer, e.g. 3p *off* Chum dogfood. Value of typical price reduction varies between 5% and 10% of retail price.	(*a*) Universal appeal of money. (*b*) Trade prefers price reductions. (*c*) Reliable results can be expected. (*d*) Can be mounted quickly without prior testing. (*e*) As effective for small as for large brand because no economies of scale.	(*a*) Undistinctive and easily matched by competition. (*b*) Price off amounts can escalate into mini price war. (*c*) Unless amount of reduction exceptional, most likely to be bought by regular users of brand and bargain-hunters who switch brands frequently.
(2) *Free merchandise packs.* Free premium item attached to brand package, e.g. free tool rack in every Polycell pack.	(*a*) Usually more effective in getting trial among non-users than equivalent value price pack. (*b*) If a set-building item, can attract new users and hold them for a number of purchases. (*c*) Usually possible to give consumer an item worth twice what company paid for it, due to purchase of thousands. (*d*) Distinctive and unique, hard to copy.	(*a*) Appeal hard to predict and requires prior testing. (*b*) Premium supply and quality control often time-consuming. (*c*) Limited number of high appeal items within affordable price range. (*d*) Extra costs for special packaging.

Table 42.   *contd*.

Promotion type and brief description	Advantages	Disadvantages
(3) *Re-usable container packs*. Containers may be free or involve extra payment by consumer. The product is packed inside a special container which has an intrinsic value, e.g. Maxwell House packed inside glass percolator.	(a) High consumer appeal if well done. (b) Consumer can be sold large quantity of product. (c) Unique and hard for competition to copy. (d) Strong visual impact even if not specially displayed.	(a) Limited number of possible items – usually have to be product-related, and must protect product quality like any other packaging. (b) Major manufacturing complexities and long lead times. (c) High risk and requires prior testing.
(4) *Bonus packs (sometimes called* free product packs). Consumer is given extra product at no additional cost, e.g. Cadbury's Marvel 10% extra free, or Jacob's Club, six for the price of five.	(a) Alternative to price pack. Offers incentive in form of extra product rather than lower price. (b) Costs less than equivalent value price packs. (c) Forces consumer to use up more product. (d) Can accustom consumer to using larger size, i.e. consumer can be traded up.	(a) Must offer quite large amount of extra product to make impact. Even more likely to be bought by regular users than price off pack. (b) Expensive and time-consuming to produce unless bonus pack is standard package size. (Economics versus a price pack depend on internal company accounting system.)

Table 42. *contd.*

Promotion type and brief description	Advantages	Disadvantages
(5) *Home sampling (distribution by hand or mail to individual homes).* Free sample of a brand (usually a new one) is delivered to the home. The manufacturer hopes that, having used the sample, the consumer will then purchase the product at a store.	(a) Strongest possible promotion for new or improved brand with superior performance to competition and a mass market appeal. (b) Helps force trade distribution of product. (c) Best technique for gaining trial among non-users. Virtually assures widespread trial usage of product. (d) Can be precisely targeted via ACORN or other demographic techniques.	(a) The most expensive available promotion. (b) Of little value to brand with minority or special interest market. (c) Hopeless for a brand without superior product performance. (d) Often requires development and production of special sample size. (e) Because of high fixed cost of distribution, usually only affordable by large brands.
(6) *Cross-ruff sampling.* Free sample of one brand is banded to another brand which is retailed at normal price. The two brands may come from the same company (e.g. free Silvikrin with Macleans toothpaste) or different companies.	(a) Very inexpensive way of sampling a product. (b) Has promotional benefit for brand carrying sample. (c) Carrying brand may penetrate specific minority group aimed for, e.g. young mothers via babyfood brands.	(a) Less controlled way of sampling than home distribution method. Effectiveness depends on how far target consumer of each brand fits. Carrying brand must have low frequency of purchase, otherwise consumers will each get a number of free samples. (b) Some wastage. A proportion of consumers will not even use sample, or will give it to a friend. (c) Trade may press for the margin they would have made if sample had been sold rather than given away free.

Table 42. *contd*.

Promotion type and brief description	Advantages	Disadvantages
(7) *Home couponing*. A valuable coupon, redeemable against a specified brand, is distributed to homes, e.g. 10p coupon. Value of coupons varies widely, from minimum of around 10% of retail value to a maximum of 100%. Redemption levels on mass appeal brands 5% to 15%.	(a) After home sampling, the best way to achieve trial for new or improved product. (b) Usually less expensive than sampling, but still an expensive promotion. (c) Requires no special packaging or factory handling. (d) Can be mounted quickly. (e) Can be very precisely targeted.	(a) Misredemption, i.e. consumers redeeming coupon against a brand other than that for which it was specified. This can run as high as 33% of all coupons redeemed. (b) Unpredictable cost, hard to estimate accurately ahead. (c) Wastage. Up to 95% of consumers may never redeem coupon at all. (d) Unpopular with trade, which has to handle coupons. (e) Inefficient for high share brands. (f) Hard to achieve effective display of a coupon promotion.
(8) *Magazine or newspaper couponing*. Same as in (7) above, but coupon has to be cut from magazine or newspaper. Redemption levels tend to be about 2% of all coupons printed (magazine 2·5%, newspaper 2%).	(a) Same advantages as in (7) above but at much lower level. (b) Publication may be tailored to target audience, e.g. teenage girls.	(a) Much less expensive than home delivered coupon, but often less economic on a 'cost per new user' basis because redemption is so low. (b) Limited regional flexibility for including or excluding specific geographical areas.

Table 43. *Summary of Types of Delayed Consumer Incentives*

Promotion type and brief description	Advantages	Disadvantages
(1) *Personality promotion.* A number of 'personalities' tour an area and call on housewives in their homes. Those called upon who can answer a simple question, and have the appropriate brand on hand, win a prize, typically worth £5–£10. Very rarely used today, due to expense, and legal restrictions.	(a) Most appropriate for large brands because of high fixed costs in administration and TV advertising support. (b) Generates trade excitement and high display levels. (c) Can significantly increase consumer sales. (d) Does not require special promotion packaging and is effective against existing trade stock.	(a) Prohibitively expensive except for major brands. (b) Housewives never called on (the majority) are sceptical. (c) Law restricts degree of noise (e.g. bell chiming) that can be made to attract attention in urban areas. (d) Complex to organize, and function usually delegated to outside firm. (e) Only small proportion of total promotion cost reaches consumer, as prizes. (f) Lacks immediacy.

Table 43. *contd*.

Promotion type and brief description	Advantages	Disadvantages
(2) *Free premium.* Consumer mailing in specified number of packet tops or labels (known as *proofs of purchase*) will be sent free premium by manufacturer. *Example*: Heinz Beans Free Coin promotion – 1983 Royal Mint Coin Collection for 25 labels. 235,000 applications.	(a) Manufacturer can pass on to consumer major savings in mass purchase of premium. (b) Can be useful loading promotion for holding regular users loyal to brand. (c) Manufacturer benefits from 'slippage': consumers collecting packet tops with view to mailing in and then not doing so. (d) Distinctive, hard to copy.	(a) Appeals primarily to existing users. Less effective in attracting new ones. (b) Low trade appeal and poor display cooperation. (c) Lacks immediacy. (d) Requires careful prior testing of effectiveness and redemption levels. Hard to judge likely cost. (e) Easy to misjudge redemption and be left with unwanted premiums or run out and cause consumer ill will. Only effective against proportion of users who start collecting for premium: at best 1 in 4.
(3) *Buy one and get one free.* Consumer sending in 1 packet top or label from a brand will receive coupon entitling him/her to free 2nd packet. A variant of this is *buy 2 packets and get 1 free*. Redemption usually high: 15–40% of special promotion packs put out, if offer featured on packet.	(a) Sound loading promotion for holding regular users. (b) Can be mounted more quickly than free mail-in promotion. (c) Less risk of failure than free mail-in, no problems of premium supply. (d) Most effective for brand with low market share.	(a) Undistinctive, easily copied. Lacks immediacy. (b) Even less effective than (2) above in attracting new users. (c) On equal cost basis, less effective than reduced price pack. (d) Low level of trade interest and display. (e) Prior testing to check redemption is prudent.

Table 43. *contd.*

Promotion type and brief description	Advantages	Disadvantages
(4) *Refund offer.* Consumer sending in specified number of packet tops will be mailed a fixed amount of money in return. Simple form of offer is 50p *for 3 labels.* Refund may, however, be escalated, e.g. 50p for 3 labels, 70p for 4, £1 for 5. Redemption varies, depending on proportion of all households using brand, value of offer and number of labels required from consumer.	(a) An alternative to (2) and (3) above for sustaining loyalty from existing users. (b) Cash has universal appeal. (c) Allows great flexibility in design. Offer can be escalated, and made high or low in value. (d) Can be mounted very quickly. Featuring on packet not essential.	(a) More distinctive than (3), less so than (2). Easily copied. (b) Limited trade appeal. (c) Prior testing wise to check redemption. (d) Appeals primarily to existing users: insufficient immediacy to attract many new ones. (e) Usually only applicable to brand with high purchase frequency since at least 3 or 4 labels have to be requested to make the promotion affordable.
(5) *Game promotion.* Two main types. (a) *Card and stamp games:* Involve skill but have appearance of chance. Answers look easy but are in fact difficult. Consumers usually given cards on which stamps from packets have to be arranged skilfully. (b) *Rub-off cards:* Consumer gets card and rubs with coin to reveal hidden symbols, e.g. BP Dallas oil game.	(a) Can be very effective in building extra consumer sales if well designed. (b) Apparent ease of winning creates high consumer involvement. (c) Consumer interest can be sustained over period of 6–8 weeks. (d) Most effective on brands with high purchase frequency, e.g. petrol, groceries. (e) Distinctive promotion, which can be tied in with brand advertising theme. (f) More effective in attracting new users than (2), (3) or (4).	(a) Complex to design or execute and requires assistance of outside promotion house. (b) Expensive and requires media support to be effective. (c) Better for retailer promotions than for manufacturer because of packaging complexities.

Table 43. *contd*.

Promotion type and brief description	Advantages	Disadvantages
(6) *Charity promotion.* For every label or packet top sent in, sponsoring company will contribute specified amount to named charity. *Example:* Ski Yoghurt Stoke Mandeville Appeal. 10p donated by Ski for every 10 pack foils mailed in.	(a) If really well done, can have significant effect on consumer sales. (b) Group collection by schools, scouts and women's organizations often a major factor. (c) Can generate significant trade support and display. (d) Charity may place organization and manpower support behind promotion.	(a) Can be difficult to find charity with necessary broad appeal. (b) Only suitable for large brand because major charities not interested in placing effort against small potential return. (c) Contact and negotiations with likely charities can be time-consuming. (d) Lacks immediacy.
(7) *Self-liquidating promotion.* Consumer mails in 1 or more labels plus some money and receives premium in return. Consumer has advantage of getting item in this way at below normal cost, since manufacturer passes on advantage of bulk buying and takes no profit. Typical cost to consumer is 50–70% of equivalent retail price. Redemption of special packet tops usually below 0·5%, or under 20,000 applications for premium. *Example:* Persil Royal 21st Birthday stamps offer.	(a) Very occasionally has measurable effect on consumer sales. (b) Creates impression of activity on package. (c) Low cost.	(a) Usually has no effect on consumer or trade sales. (b) Usually has nil level of interest for trade. (c) A very over-used promotion technique. (d) Absorbs management and sales force time to no object. (e) Very few housewives send in for self-liquidators. (f) Danger of being left with surplus stocks of premium, or of losing consumer goodwill due to delays in mailing out, if demand unexpectedly high.

Table 43. *contd*.

Promotion type and brief description	Advantages	Disadvantages
(8) *Skill competition*. Consumer has to fulfil simple test of skill (typically arranging 6 phrases about the product in order of importance) and mail in 1 or more labels, thereby entering a competition with prizes. *Example:* Adventure holidays with Weetabix.	(a) Very occasionally has measurable effect on consumer sales. (b) Does not involve premium supply problems and can be set up very quickly. (c) Usually attracts more entries than typical self-liquidator. (d) Low cost.	(a) Low level of consumer interest. Usually has no effect on sales. (b) Costs more than self-liquidator, though still an inexpensive promotion. (c) Even less display potential than self-liquidator. Nil interest to trade. (d) Absorbs management and sales force time to no object.
(9) *Sweepstake contest*. Similar to (8) above but no skill needed. It is illegal for manufacturer to require proof of purchase from consumer, in running sweepstake.	(a) Typically attracts more entries than equal value skill competition. (b) Less common than skill competition. (c) Otherwise, same as for skill competition.	(a) Proof of purchase cannot be requested. (b) Otherwise, same as for skill competition.
(10) *Cross-ruff couponing*. Brand A carries a coupon, either on label or inside pack, redeemable against Brand B. The 2 brands may be from the same or different companies. Average redemption rate for one-pack coupons is 25%, but varies widely.	(a) Very inexpensive method of coupon distribution. (b) Provides selling point for carrying brand at no cost. (c) Can increase consumer sales of carrying brand if a broad appeal, high value coupon is included (but this is unlikely). (d) Can enable the couponed brand to reach a specific target group (e.g. slimmers, if carrying brand is a low-calorie one).	(a) Little control over who gets coupons. The same consumer may gain 3 or 4 coupons from buying carrying brand frequently. (b) Coupon redemption tends to be slow in building up. (c) Usually has no measurable effect on consumer sales of either carrying or couponed brand. (d) No trade appeal or display potential.

Table 43. *contd.*

Promotion type and brief description	Advantages	Disadvantages
(11) *Coupon on next purchase.* A brand carries a coupon redeemable against consumer's next purchase of same brand. *Example:* Maxwell House 10p coupon on next purchase. Consumer tears coupon off the label and gets its face value deducted from subsequent purchase of same brand. Normally used as alternative to reduced price pack.	(a) Can offer higher face value than equivalent cost on reduced price pack: a 10p coupon redeeming at 33% will only cost company 1·65p per pack because 2 packs were moved at a cost of 3·3p. (b) Can increase frequency of purchase among existing users. (c) A suitable holding promotion to retain loyalty of existing users.	(a) Normally less effective in driving up consumer sales than reduced price pack because no immediacy, and appeal is almost exclusively to existing users. (b) Less trade appeal than reduced price pack.

Suiting the technique to the occasion

Faced with such a bewildering range of possible promotions to use, the uninitiated will naturally wonder how to choose the right one for each situation. This is indeed one of the key skills in promotion development. There are four stages in developing a promotion, as follows:

1. Work out the objectives and strategy for the promotion.
2. Run through a list of all the promotion techniques and draw up a short-list of those which fit the strategy and the budget.
3. Think up creative ideas, stemming from the half-dozen or so techniques short-listed.
4. Pick out the best idea and develop it in detail.

The first two stages are the ones which require some elaboration, since the other two are self-explanatory and simple to describe, though, of course, essential to the quality of the final promotion.

The aims and objectives of any given promotion vary, but will usually include a given percentage increase in sales to the trade and the consumer, accompanied by wider trade distribution, and there may also be merchandising and brand-image objectives.

The strategy specifies at which groups the promotion is aimed and what it is designed to make them do. If the target is the trade, which particular parts of it are to be given priority and how far are sales, as opposed to extra distribution, price-cutting or display, the main aim? If the consumer is the main target, is the promotion to be directed at non-users, occasional users or regular users? And is it designed to make them buy once or a number of times during the promotion? All these elements have to be weighed in the strategy, and priorities allocated to each one.

In building a strategy for a promotion, one of the most important issues, which affects the particular technique eventually chosen, is whether to aim for consumer *trial* or consumer *loading*.

Trial involves gaining a single purchase from a wide range of consumers, many of them non-users, whereas loading seeks a number of purchases from a smaller group of consumers, most of them probably regular users.

Trial is obviously the more positive of the two strategies and is followed by most brands with growth ambitions. The theory behind it is that if you have a superior product, and consumers can be persuaded to try it, they will be so impressed by the experience that some will continue using the brand even after the promotion is over.

Loading is most frequently used either by brands that are badly on the slide, or by perfectly healthy ones faced with a powerful competitive new-product introduction. But, in each case, the object is to hold on to your regular users and to prevent them from quietly slipping away to your competitors.

Most promotions can be categorized as either trial-getters or loaders. The difference is obviously not starkly black or white, because, to some extent, every promotion performs both functions.

Promotions with an immediate purchase appeal – like sampling, couponing or free gifts in the packet – are most likely to achieve trial. Those with a delayed effect – like skill competitions and money or gifts that have to be sent off for – usually appeal to regular users and have a loading effect.

The two lists of promotion techniques in Tables 42 and 43 (see pp. 253–62) are divided into two categories: immediate and delayed incentives. They also list the advantages and disadvantages of each promotion type. Anyone armed with a strategy, and applying it to the appropriate list, should therefore be able to quickly pick out the few promotion techniques that match it, before setting the creative juices flowing.

Should promotions tie in with advertising?

Fifteen years ago the answer would have been 'probably not'. Finding strong promotions was difficult enough without imposing such a restriction. Today, however, things have changed and the conventional wisdom is different, as shown in Table 44.

Promotions, like every other business function, have been affected by the reduced resources available and the greater emphasis on effective use of funds. Costs of advertising have escalated well ahead of inflation.

Table 44. *Conventional Wisdom on Promotions*

	1970	1987
Division between advertising (above the line) and sales promotion (below the line)	Strict	Blurred
Promotion tie-in with advertising	No	Preferably
Advertising of promotions	Rare	Frequent
In-store material	Easy	Difficult
Marketing budgets	Large	Restricted

In the past ten years TV media cost has risen by a factor of 5·2, all advertising by 4·2 and inflation by a mere 3·2. For a grocery brand, the minimum TV advertising budget required to achieve a threshold of communication is over £1 million. By contrast, much can be done with a promotion budget of £100,000, or even £50,000.

Under these circumstances, the rapid growth of sales promotion is not surprising. Its scope has also broadened, so that it not only provides temporary incentives to purchase, but also carries brand messages to enhance the effect of the advertising.

The old divisions of 'above the line' (advertising) and 'below the line' (sales promotion) are becoming blurred and, increasingly, the two are working hand in hand. Advertising agencies and sales promotion consultancies now cooperate more closely, as in this example:

> *A new advertising agency was appointed by Weetabix and developed a campaign centred around 'The Weetabix', animated characters shaped like Weetabix biscuits.*
>
> *At an early stage the agency recommended that the sales promotion consultancy be briefed on the advertising. This was done and Weetabix now meets twice a year with both external agencies to review advertising and promotion.*
>
> *The sales promotion agency also gets early warning of any new commercials. For example, when 'The Weetabix' were doing break-dancing commercials, there was a pop-music sales promotion. Other recent promotions – free adventure books and adventure holidays – underlined the 'toughness' of Weetabix users.*

The majority of Institute of Sales Promotion award-winners in recent years combined a purchase incentive with brand-image enhancement. Sales promotion may also be used to sustain a campaign already established by advertising:

> *For two years the Chunky dogfood character 'Henry', and his 'owner' Clement Freud, were supported by sales promotion alone, since advertising had become too expensive. Among promotions run were Henry aprons, Henry dog awards, Henry limited edition prints of dogs, Henry dog blankets and so on.*

However, there have been many highly successful promotions with no relation to brand advertising or usage. A promotion with broad consumer appeal – like the Shell 'Make Money' campaign (see p. 267) – will succeed whether or not it ties in with the advertising. And close relevance to a brand's advertising theme will not save a low-appeal promotion from disaster.

● **The Seven Principles of Offensive Promotion Development**

There are seven principles of offensive promotion development. Trade promotion is covered separately in Chapter 14, 'Offensive Trade-channel Marketing'.

1. Set clear strategies

A common mistake can be either to start thinking about detailed promotion ideas without the benefit of a strategy, or to develop a strategy which sets no clear priorities and is merely an inventory of all the things a brand would like to achieve. A clear strategy provides the discipline necessary to develop a strong promotion.

2. Give promotions the same priority as advertising

Most consumer-goods companies spend more money on promotions than on advertising.

Sales promotion is becoming widely applied in retailing, consumer durables, financial services, consumer electronics and certain industrial products. Yet it is a strangely underrated marketing tool. Top management will spend a great deal of time on advertising and packaging, but is not particularly interested in promotions even though the promotions budget may be as high as 10 per cent of company sales. And few writers on marketing subjects give much attention to sales promotion in their books.

Many marketers, especially the more senior ones, still regard promotions as a rather grubby area of business. Sales promotion continues to lack status within companies, and remains the province of the product manager rather than the managing director. This relatively low status gives the offensive marketer a chance to gain an edge by giving promotions the priority they deserve. At present, the amount of genuinely innovative thinking applied to promotions *within* companies is minute compared with that lavished on advertising and R & D. This leads us to the next point.

3. Aim to innovate new promotion techniques

New promotion techniques are not often developed and, even when they are, there is of course a risk that they will lack appeal. Companies inventing or exploiting successful new techniques gain the large rewards due to innovators.

Shell pioneered the 'matching-half' promotion with 'Make Money':

Make Money was a very successful promotion and paid for itself many times over. It enabled Shell to increase its sales by 50 per cent over a ten-week period. When the promotion was over, sales remained above the pre-promotion level for several months because some motorists who had changed to a Shell station during the promotion stayed with it afterwards.

Make Money was very simple. Every time motorists bought Shell petrol, they received a half-note with a 50p, £1, £10 or £100 denomination. Anyone able to match the two halves of a similar face value won the amount printed on the note. The cost was controlled by making available only a limited number of winning halves. The reason for the promotion's success was its simplicity, immediacy and apparent ease of winning.

The promotion was first run in the late 1960s, but has been repeated in adapted form a number of times since.

The Kellogg's Cornflakes Diamond Jubilee promotion was innovative in that it combined a consumer offer with a completely new temporary pack. It is also a good example of the integration of advertising, promotion, public relations and packaging:

Research showed that Kellogg's Cornflakes had become a victim of its own success. It was so familiar as to be no longer noticeable, and children thought cornflakes were boring. The objective of the promotion was to regenerate consumer interest and attract new users, while at the same time reinforcing the brand's traditional qualities.

1984 marked Kellogg's Diamond Jubilee and it was decided to replace the regular pack with a 1924 pack design for a limited period.

For four packet tops the consumer could get a toy replica of a 1924 Kellogg's delivery van. This offer was supported by a TV commercial and a 10-million door-to-door leaflet drop. In addition, a second commercial showed the evolution of the Kellogg's Cornflakes pack over sixty years, emphasizing product improvement. Finally, there was a diamonds competition in the TV Times as part of a comprehensive PR campaign.

The results were impressive. Kellogg's gained 2·3 million kilos of extra business, and 1·9 million applications for the toy van were received.[1]

4. Creativity can build dramatic results from old techniques

An original exploitation of an ordinary promotion technique can produce remarkable gains. A low-budget consumer competition rates as a lightweight offer, unlikely to have any impact on sales. But the 'Invest in Miele' promotion was so thoroughly planned and well executed that it proved an exception:

> *Miele markets high-quality domestic appliances and kitchen furniture, and distributes through department stores, kitchen specialists and independent retailers.*
>
> *The objective of Miele's promotion was to get displays in the high-traffic areas at the front of the selling area, where its products would be visible to dealers and consumers.*
>
> *The consumer offer was the chance to win five prizes of £1,000 share portfolios, and the first 2,000 entrants gained a collector's share certificate worth £5.*
>
> *For the participating dealers, there was a framed share certificate, worth £25, together with regular mail-outs related to the promotion, which was advertised in the national press.*
>
> *This type of offer would not produce a flicker of interest in the highly promoted arena of grocery retailers, but in Miele's trade sectors it proved successful. Of all Miele dealers, 93 per cent participated and sales increased by 23 per cent.*

Another example of good results from traditional techniques was the Milk Marketing Board cookbook offer in late 1983. A self-liquidating premium* is usually ineffective as a promotion technique, but in this case was used to good effect:

> *The objective of the Milk Marketing Board's promotion was to increase demand for whole milk, sold door-to-door, by encouraging existing consumers to buy more. To achieve this it was essential to gain the active participation of dairies.*
>
> *Dairies were offered supplies of the* Dairy Book of Family Cookery *for £2·35 each. The roundsmen would then distribute 11 million leaflets inviting customers to buy the book for*

---

* A self-liquidating premium is not a KGB device. It is a premium offer in which the consumer sends in the cost of the item to whoever is making the offer.

£2·95 if they purchased two extra pints of milk. The promotion was supported by TV advertising.

Of all roundsmen 87 per cent participated, and 12 million extra pints of milk were sold, together with 1·4 million copies of the cookbook.

Among the factors contributing to the promotion's success were the profit on the books offered to dairies and the lack of any need for consumers to send off for it – they merely paid the extra cost as part of their weekly milk bill and received the book.[2]

5. Do not waste time on ineffective lightweight promotions

For every Miele and Milk Marketing Board promotion, there are still thousands of skill competitions and self-liquidating premium promotions which sink into merciful obscurity without having the slightest effect on a brand's business, even though they may have brought in over 200,000 applications.

Most marketers would acknowledge that, with the occasional exception, skill competitions and self-liquidators are weak promotions, and yet they continue to be widely run. The justifications for persisting with them are unconvincing, the most common being: 'They give the sales force a talking point'; 'They will gain us some display'; or 'They provide a change of pace'.

Retail buyers, especially in grocery, are knowledgeable about the effectiveness of promotions, and 'talking points' of this kind can lead to very uncomfortable conversations for salesmen.

The essence of offensive marketing is to concentrate as much time as possible on development projects which, if successfully concluded, will have a measurable effect on the business. In this context, time spent on working up self-liquidators or skill competitions of the normal mediocre standard is wasted time.

6. Research your promotions and analyse the results

It has recently been estimated that while 1 per cent of *advertising* expenditure is allocated to research, the equivalent figure for *sales promotion* is less than 0·1 per cent.[3]

The main argument against researching promotions is that,

unlike advertising, they have a short-term effect on sales and market share. They can therefore be easily measured without the need for research.

The argument falls down on two counts. First, although the information to assess sales promotion does exist, it is rarely used. Outside a very small minority of effective companies, profit-oriented analyses of completed sales promotions are as rare as new Rembrandts. Second, the argument does not address the issue of pre-testing promotion ideas. If advertising can be successfully pre-tested, surely sales promotion is a simple research challenge?

Group discussions or hall tests are quick and inexpensive ways to test the relative pull of premiums, the most appealing structure for a competition, the strength of alternative promotion concepts, comprehension of promotion mechanisms and so on.

Offensive marketers who research promotions and analyse the results, both in total and by account, will inevitably make superior use of their promotion funds and gain an edge over competitors.

7. Plan, plan and plan ahead

Promotions should be planned in outline by brand and month for at least a year ahead, be firm six months ahead and be completely prepared four to eight weeks in advance of D-Day.

● Summary

Sales promotion means immediate or delayed incentives to purchase, expressed in cash or in kind. Its main role is to achieve a specified number of new or additional purchases over a limited period, but it may also be used to widen distribution, gain display, build traffic or enhance brand image.

Sales promotion is most effective on new, growing or recently improved brands. Its long-term success is dependent on the relative product performance and value of the promoted product or service.

There is a very wide repertoire of promotion types to choose from; to ensure that the most appropriate type is selected, clear objectives and strategies should be developed for each promotion.

The old distinctions between 'above' and 'below the line' spending are breaking down and promotions are increasingly integrated with advertising and public relations.

The seven principles of offensive promotion development are as follows:

1. **Set clear strategies**. These provide the discipline necessary to develop strong promotions.
2. **Give promotions the same priority as advertising**. Expenditure on sales promotion exceeds advertising spending. Give this underrated marketing weapon the attention it deserves.
3. **Aim to innovate new promotion techniques**. The rewards for those who try and succeed are large.
4. **Creativity can build dramatic results from old techniques**. An original exploitation of an ordinary technique can also produce remarkable gains.
5. **Do not waste time on ineffective lightweight promotions**. They absorb time and money, irritate the trade and lead nowhere.
6. **Research your promotions and analyse the results**. Marketers who research and analyse their promotions will gain an edge over competitors.
7. **Plan, plan and plan ahead**. Effective planning enhances the quality of promotions. It saves time, money – and psychiatrists' bills.

12 | *Offensive Advertising**

There is probably no other part of the business to which we allocate resources that provide so little justification for their use.[1]

Basic Principles

How advertising works

Advertising creates awareness of the existence and advantages of goods and services. It is a form of personal salesmanship designed to make consumers see a brand in a more favourable light.

With a familiar brand, consumers will have formed a number of different impressions, both favourable and unfavourable, based on previous usage, recollections of past advertising, attitude to packaging and price, opinions of friends and so on. Advertising will add to this set of impressions by attempting to reinforce

---

* This chapter concentrates mainly on TV advertising, due to limitations of space. However, the principles of developing and assessing TV advertising can also be applied to other forms.

favourable attitudes and to loosen or eliminate unfavourable ones.

The devices used are information, reason and emotion. Advertising interacts with all the other elements that make up the image of a brand and contribute to its performance, which is why its effect is so difficult to pin down.

Consumer attitudes are in a continuous state of flux. Table 45 is a purely hypothetical illustration of the changing attitudes of a car buyer over a three-year period. The buyer is a self-employed builder, who bought a new BMW 520 three years ago. The other brands within his range of preference were a new Audi 200 and a second-hand Mercedes 280. His changes in attitude and the factors contributing to this process are tracked at six-monthly intervals over three years, culminating in the purchase of a new Rover 800 (see Table 45). On a frequently purchased brand, like tea or washing powder, this process would be speeded up.

Table 45. *Changes in Buyer Attitude over a Three-year Period*

Time (Months)	Product Experience	Advertising and Communication	Range of Preferred Brands	Competition
0	Buys new BMW 520		Audi 200 Mercedes 280 BMW 520	Nil
6	Service costs more than expected	Reassured by BMW advertisements. Direct mail on Mercedes 190	Audi 200 Mercedes 190 BMW 520	Mercedes 190 launch
12	Water pump goes on M1. Emergency repair	Dislikes Audi advertising. Reads *Which?* report on cars. Sees advertisements for Rover, Volvo, BMW	Mercedes 190 BMW 325 BMW 520	Neighbour buys Mercedes 190. Launch of BMW 325

Table 45. contd.

Time (Months)	Product Experience	Advertising and Communication	Range of Preferred Brands	Competition
18	Another expensive repair	Reads comparison of 520 and Audi in *What Car?* Sees advertisement for Toyota Celica	Mercedes 190 BMW 325 Toyota Celica	Toyota Celica launch
24	Good experience with car, but service costs continue higher than expected	Invited to test-drive Mercedes. Direct mail from Rover re 800 launch	BMW 325 Toyota Celica Mercedes 300	Tries out neighbour's Mercedes 190.
30	Car fails to start in garage. Decides to replace	Sees advertisements for BMW, Volvo and Rover. Test-drives Rover 800. Orders provisionally	Toyota Celica Mercedes 300 Rover 800	Rover 800 launch
36	Buys Rover 800	Heavy Rover advertising. Favourable reviews in press	As above	Nil

The varying effectiveness of advertising

Advertising is usually most effective on new brands, because people take time to form definite opinions about them and are not deterred from buying by previous poor experience.

Once a brand has been on the market for some time, it becomes harder for advertising to make an impact. Most consumers will already have a firm opinion about the brand. The advertising has to change and reinforce existing attitudes rather than create fresh ones. Its role in strengthening the commitment of existing customers is also important.

Not surprisingly, advertising is most effective on products with superior performance, since customer experience with the product reinforces the favourable attitudes built up by the advertising. Various special analyses by A. C. Nielsen confirm this.[2]

Advertising expenditure is more efficient than promotion spending for large brands, and the reverse is generally true for small ones. A price reduction of 10p costs the same amount (per unit sold) for any brand whatever its size. But a £2-million advertising campaign will have a lower cost per unit for a large brand than a small one, because the lump sum can be spread across a much higher sales volume.

In the hypothetical example given in Table 46, the same advertising budget costs 5p per unit on the large brand and 50p per unit on the small brand.

Table 46*. *Comparative Advertising/Promotion Costs per Unit*

| | Net Sales | | Advertising/Promotion Cost/Unit | |
	Units (million)	Value (£ million)	£2 million advertising	10p price cut
Brand A	100	50	**5p**	10
Brand B	10	5	**50p**	10

*The key figures in this table are indicated by bold type.

The limitations of advertising

Advertising is not the all-powerful persuader which many of its critics imply. The average consumer is present at the showing of over 10,000 commercials every year. An advertiser spending £1 million in that period would buy less than ten of those viewings, or 0·01 per cent of the total.

To make your £1-million investment pay, you have to establish a presence in the minds of consumers. Each person has only finite mental storage space and, with only a 0·01 per cent share of exposure, your advertising will have to work very hard to get through.

From the viewpoint of the advertiser, the consumer's mind resembles a filing cabinet.[3] The file contains sections like 'tea', 'banks', 'cars', 'building society', 'washing machines' and so on. File contents change weekly as new messages enter and others are disposed of.

All the time the number of messages is increasing, but only a small proportion will enter the cabinet. Most individual file headings contain four to seven messages, and as a new one comes in, an old one is likely to move out. Some files contain quite old material like 'the sunshine breakfast', 'Guinness is good for you', and the 'real thing', because new messages have lacked the power to dislodge them. Most individual messages are quite thin, but a few like Persil, Mars Bar or Heineken have more detailed entries.

Here are just three examples of the limited effect of advertising:

- before the wearing of seat-belts was made compulsory, efforts were made to persuade people to use them by advertising. All cars contained seat-belts. Most people favoured them and the evidence justifying use on safety grounds was strong. The product was unique and there were no alternatives. Prior to advertising, 28 per cent of people wore seat-belts. After a £5-million advertising campaign, the proportion rose to only 33 per cent.[4]
- The toothpaste brand Crest was launched in the USA following an eight-year R & D programme and claimed effectiveness in preventing tooth decay among children.

  The claims were fully justified and backed by extensive clinical tests, but the brand achieved only a 14 per cent market share. Then, some years after the launch, the American Dental Association publicly endorsed the results of Crest's clinical tests. Within six months brand share soared to over 30 per cent, and has stayed there for the past twenty years.

  Heavy advertising helped to communicate the ADA endorsement, which in turn gave the message a credibility and substantiation that it had previously lacked.
- When charities advertise appeals for disasters widely

reported on TV, funds raised exceed advertising costs by a multiple of five or ten. But advertising for yesterday's disaster or for projects not in the news, though highly necessary, usually produces dramatically poorer response.

The credibility of advertising, even though backed by charities of impeccable reputation, is insufficient on its own.

How advertising differs from other outside purchases

Advertising is purchased from an outside supplier, called an advertising agency. It is intended to add value to the product *after* manufacture, by increasing the consumer's perception of its value.

It cannot be equated with the raw materials that go into a product, even though it is purchased externally and also carries the brand name, as Table 47 shows.

Table 47. *How Creative Advertising Purchase Differs from Raw Material Purchase*

	Advertising	Raw Materials
Buying specification	Broad and subjective	Detailed and objective
Cost	Same, irrespective of quality	Varies with quality
Assessment of quality	Difficult	Easy
Correct amount to buy	Not known	Exactly known

It might be fairer to compare advertising with the purchase of capital equipment, since advertising is generally accepted as a long-term investment. But no accountant is prepared to depreciate this year's advertising campaign over two years, never mind five, since its effect on sales cannot be precisely measured.

These analogies illustrate the uniqueness of advertising as a form of expenditure. It is an investment but it cannot be depreciated. Its quality cannot be evaluated objectively. No one is quite sure how much or how little it is best to buy. And, most unusual of all, advertising costs the same whether it is of the highest quality or the lowest.

Advertising percentages

Now we come to the question of advertising expenditure.

Advertising is a much more important cost ingredient in some markets than in others. Based on figures from the USA, which accounts for over 50 per cent of world advertising expenditure, toys have the highest ratio of advertising spending to sales, followed by toiletries/cosmetics and pharmaceuticals. Car and office-equipment manufacturers both spend quite large *absolute* sums of money on advertising, but these represent only a very small proportion of sales.

Table 48 summarizes advertising spending, both in absolute cash levels and as a percentage of sales, for a number of selected product categories in the USA.* Advertiser gross-profit margins have an important influence on advertising spending as a percentage of sales – high-margin categories like pharmaceuticals, toiletries/

Table 48. *Advertising Spending by Selected Product Categories in USA, 1984**

	All media Advertising Spend ($ billion)	Advertising as Percentage of Sales (%)
Food	4·8	6·1
Automotive	2·4	1·4
Pharmaceuticals	2·1	9·9
Retail	1·9	2·6
Soaps and cleaners	1·7	9·7
Electronics/Office equipment	1·4	2·0
Toiletries/Cosmetics	0·9	13·9
Toys	0·2	17·2

*The key figures in this table are indicated by bold type.

* Adapted from '100 Leading National Advertisers', in *Advertising Age*, 26 September 1985. The table referred to covers only the 100 largest advertisers in the USA, but these accounted for 53·5 per cent of all national advertising spending in 1984.

cosmetics and cleaning products tend to have high advertising/ sales ratios. The two companies with the highest advertising/sales ratio were Warner-Lambert (23 per cent) and Mattel (19 per cent).

In 1985 three American companies exceeded $1 billion in advertising expenditure for the first time: Procter & Gamble, Philip Morris and R. J. Reynolds.

How much to spend

'I know that half of my advertising budget is wasted, but I'm not sure which half' is a comment that was made many years ago and has now passed into advertising folklore.[5] Accountants particularly enjoy repeating it.

Setting advertising budgets and assessing the effectiveness of advertising campaigns remains an approximate art and although techniques are available for making the whole business more scientific, some have serious weaknesses. The evaluation of advertising still relies heavily on the personal judgement of experienced executives.

Every company would give a lot to know the effect of advertising on its sales, but this can rarely be done with precision, except in the case of mail-order sales. The trouble is that advertising is only one of the many variables which affect sales. Indeed, an advertising campaign is itself influenced by four variable factors: the content of the message, the amount of money placed behind it, the choice of media and the amount of competitive activity.

Tradition and guesswork play an important part in the setting of advertising budgets. Any sharp accountant in search of corporate cost savings could have a field day in challenging the basis of advertising appropriations in most companies.

The overwhelming majority of companies use either arbitrary or subjective methods and the main approaches can be categorized as follows: task; historical; percentage of turnover (or case-rate); share of market; 'match competition'; residual. Because none of these methods is ideal, they are not elaborated upon here, but Appendix 4 contains an examination of each one.

Of all the approaches, that based on percentage of turnover looks to be the best, provided allowance is made for the well-argued exception. The snag is, however, that advertising budgets cannot be effectively established by using mechanical guidelines and formulae on their own. These must be supplemented by the results of market-testing alternative advertising weights and of econometric analysis.

Techniques for assessing the strength of individual advertising campaigns are more advanced than those for establishing budgets, but still far from perfect. Campaigns or commercials can be evaluated before they have been produced (pre-testing) and after the cost of production has been incurred (post-testing).

Pre-testing is a way of checking out creative approaches, comparing alternatives, and fine-tuning. It enables the advertiser to bounce ideas off consumers and to have a dialogue with them at low cost. There is no denying its value, but it can be a time-waster when used to test mediocre ideas or to placate stubborn copywriters. Some of the most useful pre-testing can be done at a very early stage, using verbal concepts or simple pictures.

Post-testing occurs after the event. The advertisement will have been made, the campaign will be running and large amounts of money will already have been spent. Some would argue that testing at this stage is too late. But for those who see advertising as a continuous and long-term investment, post-testing can check the strength of the strategy, pinpoint whether the execution is effective and even provide genuine clues about the effect on sales. The main methods of evaluating advertising are summarized in Table 49.

Table 49. *Techniques for Evaluating Effectiveness of Advertising Campaigns*

| Type of Testing | Factors Which Each Technique Can Measure | | |
	Strength of strategy	Strength of execution	Effect on sales
Pre-testing			
Group discussions	Sometimes	Yes	No
Persuasion/Interest studies	Yes	Yes	No
Concept studies	Yes	Yes	No
Post-testing			
Recall and playback	No	Yes	No
Awareness/Attitude studies	Yes	Maybe	No
TV-area test markets	No	No	Yes
Econometric analysis	No	No	Yes

Basic Principles

Recall and playback involves interviewing consumers who were watching TV at the time of the first transmission of the commercial. Their recollection of any elements is recorded and compared with norms stored in a data bank consisting of hundreds of commercials. The limitation of the technique is that recall does not equate with persuasiveness.

Awareness and attitude studies (often referred to as 'tracking studies') call for more extensive consumer interviews and enable comparisons to be made between competing brands, both before and after the start of a new advertising campaign. Studies may be repeated at regular intervals to establish trends in awareness and product attitudes.

TV-area tests consist of an advertised area and a control area. Advertisers wanting to put their toe into the water can advertise in one TV area only and compare sales trends there with the rest of the country. Alternatively, in running a national campaign they can exclude advertising from one TV area and compare sales and market share with the rest of the country. In each case, they can start to analyse the effect of advertising on sales.

Wall's Viennetta ice-cream is an example of a TV-area test of advertising for a new brand:

> *Wall's Viennetta was a new patisserie-style ice-cream dessert, launched in the UK in April 1982. The product was a technical breakthrough, and the patent has since been successfully defended.*
>
> *Viennetta was introduced nationally with a lightweight colour-magazine advertising campaign. Success was such that it was decided to try out TV advertising in late 1982, and Anglia TV was selected as the test area.*
>
> *The test campaign ran for seven weeks from 1 November 1982 and covered 90 per cent of consumers, giving them 7·4 opportunities to see the commercial.*
>
> *Results were evaluated by calculating Viennetta sales in the Anglia region as a percentage of national sales in the three months prior to the start of advertising and comparing it with the three months following, as in Table 50.*
>
> *Wall's concluded that TV support trebled sales of Viennetta during the seven weeks of TV advertising and doubled them in the five weeks after it ended. The cost of the advertising paid*

281

Table 50. *Evaluation of Viennetta Advertising Campaign*

Period	Viennetta Sales in Anglia as Percentage of National	(Index)
August/October	6·3	(100)
November	14·8	(235)
December	23·4	(371)
January	13·0	(206)

back in extra trading profit after four weeks and the campaign was expanded nationally at the end of 1983.[6]

TV-area testing is becoming increasingly difficult to set up and measure in some markets. Retail multiples may be reluctant to stock a brand regionally and, since more deliveries are made through retailers' central warehouses, manufacturers' sales data has limited value. Furthermore, without a boosted area sample, market-share information may be unreliable for small brands or markets. Store-scanning, when it comes, should help.

Econometric analysis takes this process of evaluation further and is becoming more widely used. Its purpose is to isolate the effect of advertising as the dependent variable from other possible influences on brand share and then, using multiple regression, model the effect of such things as:

- price differential between analysed brand and leading competitors.
- share of category advertising.
- distribution levels and trends.

The model will help to identify the effect of each of these variables on brand share. (See pp. 213–14 in Chapter 9, 'Offensive Market Research'.)

 The Six Rules of Offensive Advertising

1. Set crystal-clear advertising strategies

What does offensive advertising mean in the context of offensive marketing? If a product has superior performance or distinctive attributes, the advertising strategy will almost write itself, emerging smoothly from the offensive marketing strategy.

The essence of offensive advertising is exactly the same as offensive marketing. The product will have a ready-made proposition; offensive advertising takes this and handles it distinctively to make it stand out from the crowd. In certain markets, like lager, where distinctive *products* are difficult to develop, the role of offensive advertising will be to add value, as in the case of Heineken.

In other markets, non-offensive marketers may fail to apply the effort or skill needed to engineer a product advantage and will expect the advertising agency to develop a strategy from scratch. They should not be surprised if, with such poor raw material, the agency has difficulty in fashioning a strong campaign.

Strategies are more essential in advertising than in any other part of the business. Advertising is unlikely to be effective unless its message stresses a benefit which is important to the consumer.

An advertising strategy forces client and agency to work out the overall impression they wish a campaign to convey. This involves setting priorities between the various communication aims – an important exercise, because a major cause of poor advertising is the attempt to cover too many points in too short a time. The strategy should be highly competitive and aim to establish an impression of superiority on at least one important score.

A good strategy will have simple communication aims, since complex or unclear benefits are simply not absorbed by the consumer.

One of the reasons for Fairy Liquid's success has been a clear-cut advertising strategy:

> *Fairy Liquid is a very successful branded product in a category dominated in most Western countries by cheap competition. It has held a market share of over 30 per cent almost since launch twenty-seven years ago and current value share exceeds 40 per cent.*
>
> *When it was first launched, other leading brands were following a strategy of speed/ease of use or cleaning. Procter & Gamble did extensive research on consumer attitudes and found that cleaning was a slightly more important benefit area than mildness. Fairy Liquid was strongly preferred by consumers on both counts, based on product blind-testing.*

The product group recommended that Fairy Liquid be advertised on a cleaning platform with mildness as a secondary claim. Procter & Gamble's senior management rejected this and instead approved the reverse – a strategy stressing superior mildness with reassurance on cleaning.

Procter & Gamble reasoned that consumer playback on cleanness as a benefit in the research was artificially inflated by advertising directed at it. It preferred to have a distinctive copy platform. It was influenced by the mildness reputation for the Fairy name built up by Fairy household soap and encouraged by the success of Ivory Liquid in the USA, also using the mildness angle. The decision proved to be a good one.

In this example, Procter & Gamble staked out important unoccupied territory (i.e. mildness), and exploited it with a proposition of superior mildness, backed by a product which delivered the promise.

The advertising strategy for Dulux Natural Whites is clear but comprehensive, and includes the important element of desired consumer response:[7]

- Marketing aim: *To increase Dulux share of the whites market in the face of heavy promotion from Crown – the main competitor – and the continuing threat from the cheaper paints, particularly own-label brands.*
- Advertising objectives: *To reawaken consumer interest in white paint, lifting it from a low-priority commodity area, where decisions are taken on the basis of habit and price, to assume a more important role in the decorating process, requiring a more conscious and positive choice.*

 Within this, to increase interest in and commitment to Dulux white paint by announcing the launch of a 'new range of whites from Dulux'.
- Target audience: *Users of white paint, whether premium or commodity. They are likely to feel less than happy about their continued use of white paint, but are not prepared to make a move into the more exciting but far riskier area of colours. In demographic terms this represents a very broad sample – BC1C2, under 55 years old – but women are likely to play the major role in decision-making.*

The creative strategy behind the campaign is as follows:

- Proposition: *Now there is an exciting but safe way to transform your home.*
- Reason why: *Dulux has developed a new range of whites. So now you can have a white with a touch of pink – Rose White; with a touch of green – Apple White; and with a touch of cream – Lily White.*
- Tone of voice: *Soft and reassuring.*
- Consumer response: *I know these paints are whites, so I can feel confident in using them; I believe they are colours, so I can take a real interest and pride in their effect in my home.*
- Executional consideration: *The unobtrusive inclusion of the Dulux dog, an extremely effective and emotive branding device, will enable us to concentrate on the overall proposition while indisputably linking Natural Whites to the Dulux brand.*

This example illustrates how the advertising strategy emanates naturally out of the marketing strategy.

The success of Dulux Natural Whites is well known. Dulux increased its share of the white emulsions sector from a low of 18 per cent in 1981 to 36 per cent in 1983, while maintaining its share of the colours sector at 29 per cent.

2. Run only outstanding advertising

Advertising is expensive and carries your product name. If you insist on top quality in your products, why accept less from your advertising? As long as you allow plenty of time for advertising development and make it very plain to the advertising agency that you want not just good, but outstanding material, you should succeed in getting it.

Never, like the American client in the example below, run advertising just to 'be on the air':

A distinctive new campaign was developed for a slimming product called Metrecal. It was built around consumer testimonials by people who had been fat. There was a strong analogy with Alcoholics Anonymous and the main copyline was: 'I am a Metrecalic.'

The test commercials consisted of broken-down-looking women in stark, limbo-like settings, recalling how they had lost weight after 'becoming hooked' on Metrecal.

The effect was depressing. The research even more so, with a substantial proportion of consumers saying it was the worst advertising they had ever seen. However, it was decided to run the advertising on the basis that some advertising was better than none at all and that no alternative campaign was available.

The result was that sales continued to decline, the money was wasted and, much worse, an unattractive image was conveyed of both the Metrecal consumer and the product.

3. Create a climate where creativity can flourish

Few would deny the desirability of this objective, but there is a diversity of sometimes conflicting opinion as to how it can best be achieved. The approach used by many large companies, that of formal agency presentations and tiers of approval levels, is unlikely to produce a creative environment. A new idea is fragile and easily crushed by traditional thinking or highly elaborate approval procedures.

A good starting point for clients is to tell the advertising agency that they value its freedom from the traditional thinking in which they are enmeshed and hope it will exploit this objectivity to develop radically new ideas. While they appreciate innovation involves risk, they are prepared to accept this, subject to appropriate testing.

No client ever tells an agency openly that it is not enthused at the prospect of breaking new ground and quite satisfied to ring the changes on humdrum and conventional approaches. It can, though, imply this loud and clear, through its reaction to new ideas.

No agency, however determined, will continue to generate radically new thinking for a client who is frightened by it. Many companies like the thought of new ideas in the abstract, but will not accept the iconoclastic approach which can make them a reality.

The caption to a *New Yorker* cartoon of a chairman addressing his board sums this up well: 'What we need, gentlemen, is a completely new idea that has been thoroughly tested.'[8]

Clients have to go further than giving the agency a charter to think freely. They have a part to play in bringing their knowledge of the consumer to bear on the communications task, and in approving the advertising.

4. Assess advertising sympathetically but ruthlessly

The advertising agency has just completed its first presentation of a new campaign. During the past two hours you have listened to the culmination of weeks of work. The account planner covered the strategic background, the account director developed it and the famous copywriter has just sat down after persuasively outlining the first two commercials in storyboard form.

Now they are looking at you and awaiting a response. The marketing director is deep in thought but nods at you absent-mindedly. How do you evaluate a new campaign? The agency is entitled to a professional response, and what follows is a suggested step-by-step approach for effectively assessing a TV commercial:

The right mental approach: Start by putting yourself in the shoes of your target customer and paint a mental image of him or her. What kind of houses do your typical customers live in, what are their interests and how do they see your product or service?

First gut reaction: What is your instant first response to the advertising idea? Will the advertising be noticed? Will it be received and enjoyed? Is it memorable?

Unless it passes these simple tests, the advertising is unlikely to work. Do not get into a detailed evaluation of advertising which follows strategy but is really boring.

Stimulus and response: Think what the consumer will take out of the advertising, not what is being put into it.

A classic example of miscommunication is where the pilot of a 747 in mid-journey comes out of the cabin, switches off the movie everyone is watching and says, 'Don't panic.' The response to this stimulus is the opposite of that desired: sheer panic. So ask yourself whether the advertising is likely to have the intended effect on the consumer.

The pictures:　Having adopted the outlook of your consumer, take the agency's storyboard and look through the pictures *twice*. Do *not* look at the words at all at this stage, because, for television the pictures ought to tell the story on their own.

When you have scanned the pictures twice put down the storyboard, close your eyes and recall the impression they have made on you in thirty words or less (consumers rarely have more than thirty words of recall for a commercial). What are the key elements you recall from the pictures?

At this stage, write your impressions down on a piece of paper. Then study it and ask yourself whether the storyboard is 'on strategy'. Your thirty-word recall should be right in line with the strategy, because otherwise the storyboard is *off strategy* and is therefore unacceptable in its present form. If you decide the board is on strategy, proceed, still ignoring the words, to debate whether it is likely to interest consumers. Here are a few checkpoints:

- is the situation likely to be interesting to consumers? Is it one with which they can identify or not? Is it totally static or does it have a story? Are the people in the commercial interesting? Is the commercial too 'gimmicky', exploiting the copywriter's latest fad?
- is the storyboard believable, or does it lack conviction?
- is the structure of the board simple and easy to understand? How many people are there? How many changes of scene? Does it proceed from point to point in a logical way?
- is this commercial different from most other ones on the air and likely to stand out from them, or is it another run-of-the-mill, uninspired effort?
- does the commercial strike the right tone? Is it appealing to consumers on their level, or is it patronizing or esoteric?

The words:　Now read the words – twice – in association with the pictures. Their job is simple: to supplement the pictures and to enhance their impact.

Having done that, ask yourself again whether or not this commercial is of interest to your consumer. And check that the words too are on strategy. Then look at each frame individually and check whether the words support the picture, or whether they are pulling in different directions – the words saying one thing and the picture conveying a different impression; audio and video must interlock.

Full understanding: At the two previous stages, you will obviously ask the agency to clarify anything about the pictures or words which is not clear. But now is the time to clarify things like:

- whether the agency envisages a musical accompaniment or not and, if so, what type of music is planned.
- what kind of 'characters' does the agency have in mind for the people in the commercial?
- can certain complicated optical effects be achieved in reality or not?

Initial response to the agency: This should cover all the above points, concentrating particularly on how far the commercial meets the strategy and how interesting and involving it is for the consumer. It should be confined to a broad evaluation and not dwell on details.

5. Run successful campaigns for decades

Once you have developed a clear strategy and strong execution, stick with it. Fight off marauding marketing or agency people who have become bored with it, want to try something new or wish to make a name for themselves.

By all means refine and update a winning campaign, just as you would a successful product. For example, Fairy Liquid's present market situation is very different from the one into which it was launched. Private-label brands are strong and low-priced competition has intensified.

To meet this, Fairy Liquid modified its strategy to give more emphasis to its value for money. This change started in the mid-1960s. Today the Fairy Liquid 'Mother and Child' campaign, stressing mildness to hands, runs side-by-side with separate commercials emphasizing how much further a bottle of Fairy Liquid goes.

A few strong campaigns have run for decades and occupy

well-established places in the consumer's mind, such as: 'Have a break, have a Kit Kat'; 'Chum. Top breeders recommend it'; 'Eight out of ten cat owners stating a preference choose Whiskas'; 'A Mars a day helps you work, rest and play'; 'It's the taste' (PG Tips).

It is no accident that all these brands have sales of over £100 million. The present Whiskas campaign has been running since 1969. The example below demonstrates that for a product with superior performance and a clear strategy the advertising almost writes itself:

> *In the spring of 1969 the Chancellor of the Exchequer imposed purchase tax on petfoods for the first time. Prices increased by 22 per cent, and the whole market was badly affected. Premium-priced products were under most pressure as consumers traded down to cheaper brands.*
>
> *At this time, Whiskas was in a bad way. It was a premium-priced cat food, but its product performance did not justify the higher price. Whiskas was the number three cat-food brand and share declined from 20 per cent to only 15 per cent within months of the general price rise. It lacked the strength to resist the pressure. The brand leader, Kitekat, a medium-priced product, and Kattomeat, supported by Arthur the white cat, fared better.*
>
> *Whiskas's management set about improving product performance and a new recipe was developed which, on blind test, beat the competition by 80:20. It was decided to relaunch the brand as Whiskas Supermeat in late 1969 and the advertising strategy focused on superior product acceptance. This led to the 'Eight out of ten cat owners prefer it' campaign, which has been used ever since.*
>
> *The combination of improved product with advertising stressing its superiority rapidly drove Whiskas to market leadership. Good marketing, consistent support and the development of flavour variants have sustained the momentum since. Whiskas's market share is now over 50 per cent.*
>
> *Whiskas's advertising may be criticized for being pedestrian, but it has succeeded where it matters most – in the market-place.*

Other simple but compelling ideas which are building up long-term campaign momentum are: 'Zanussi – the appliance of science'; 'Heineken refreshes the parts other beers cannot reach'; 'Mr Kipling makes exceedingly good cakes.' But some famous campaign ideas appear to be fading through lack of support, like 'Don't be vague – ask for Haig', and others dropped many years ago though still remembered.

If you happen to run a famous campaign and someone wants to change or ditch it, ask these questions:

1. Do we really understand the importance of the part of the consumer's mind which we are lucky enough to occupy?
2. Is the problem the strategy or today's execution of it? Do not change your strategy just because the execution is no good.
3. What is the motive for changing? Are people in the company bored with the same old thing? How do you know that the new approach is better than the tried and tested old one? Has its merit been thoroughly researched and tested in the market-place?

6. Never be satisfied with your advertising

Offensive marketers continually strive to upgrade and improve the performance of their products. The same applies to advertising. The launch of a successfully tested new pool of TV commercials is not the completion of a project, but merely part of a continuous process of advertising development. It is always worthwhile to test alternatives and to experiment with new approaches, as successive brand managers of Pedigree Chum, Whiskas, Mars Bar, Fairy Liquid and Kit Kat have done for years.

● **Summary**

Advertising makes people aware of the existence and advantages of goods and services. Its purpose is to create and sustain favourable attitudes, but it works hand in hand with other elements of the marketing mix, especially product performance. Advertising is most effective on brands with superior performance. The consumer's mind only retains and stores a very small proportion of the advertising to which it is exposed.

291

Advertising is difficult to evaluate, because it is only one of many variables affecting sales. The main approaches used to set advertising budgets are task, historical, percentage of turnover, share of market, and 'match competition'. Since none is ideal, a combination may be used. However, market testing of alternative weights and econometric analysis are more effective than any mechanical technique.

There is a wide variety of research techniques for evaluating the effect of advertising both during development and after production.

The six rules for offensive advertising are:

1. **Set crystal-clear advertising strategies**. Strategy should simplify communication aims, emerge from a marketing base and preferably incorporate distinctive positioning.

2. **Run only outstanding advertising**. If you insist on top quality in your products, why accept less from your advertising? Very good and very bad advertising both cost the same. Advertising is expensive and carries your brand name.

3. **Create a climate where creativity can flourish**. A new idea is fragile and easily crushed by traditional thinking or highly elaborate approval procedures.

4. **Assess advertising sympathetically but ruthlessly**. The agency is entitled to sympathetic support and professional judgements from the client. A step-by-step approach for assessing a TV commercial has been outlined.

5. **Run successful campaigns for decades**. Always look for campaign ideas, not individual advertisements. When you find a strong one, improve and update it, but stick with it for the long-term.

6. **Never be satisfied with your advertising**. The task of developing better advertising is continuous and never finished.

13 | *Offensive Branding*

Brands enable *consumers* to identify products or services which promise specific benefits. They arouse expectations in the minds of customers about quality, price, purpose and performance. A brand stands out from commodities because commodities lack identity.

A perfume in an expensive-looking bottle branded 'Chanel No. 5' will command a high price. If it was cheaply packaged, consumers would become confused. The reality would fail to meet their expectations about the brand and, rather than thinking 'What a bargain!', they would probably decide not to buy. Equally, while Chanel No. 5 is a strong brand name for an expensive perfume, it would not be a good name for a household cleaning product.

Brands enable *marketers* to build extra value into products and to differentiate them from competitors. Well-known brand names are a company's most valuable assets. They represent the accumulation of years of favourable consumer experiences and heavy investment in advertising, packaging and quality. A name like IBM is worth more than the gross national product of many countries.

● The Background to Branding

The mechanism of branding

A brand name's value lies inside the customer's mind. Its mechanism can be compared to a continuous production line. The company feeds in raw materials of product or service performance, pricing, advertising and so on. The customer reacts to and processes these into attitudes and image. The final result is a mental inventory. Then the process begins again, as illustrated in Figure 26. It can therefore be seen that a brand image is dynamic not static; it will strengthen or weaken in line with the company inputs.

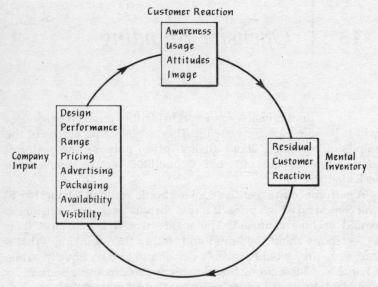

Figure 26. Mechanism of Branding – A Continuous Process

Types of branding

There are four main types of branding: corporate umbrella, family umbrella, range and individual brand names. Many brands are a mixture of two or three types.

Corporate-umbrella names are sometimes also used as brand umbrellas. They may be used as lead names, like McDonald's or American Express, or as supporting brand names, such as General Motors or United Biscuits. In the latter case, the names are better known to stock markets than to consumers and are typically shown only in small print on sales literature or packaging.

Family-umbrella names cover a range of products in a wide variety of markets. There will often be common links in packaging style, quality levels and even advertising between all the products carrying the umbrella name. The manufacturer assumes that good experience with one product within the family umbrella will encourage consumers to buy others.

Examples of family-umbrella names are Mercedes (the corporate name is Daimler-Benz) and St Michael. Mercedes competes in a wide variety of vehicle markets, from small vans to large trucks, from saloon cars to safari vehicles. All its products sport the familiar three-pointed star as a common branding device. St Michael products cover an ever-broadening range but have two factors in common: quality is high and the brand can be bought only in Marks & Spencer stores.

Range brands also comprise a range of products, but they differ from family-umbrella brands in having clearly linked benefits, in one major market. Mr Kipling Cakes is an example.

Individual brands comprise one product type in one market, but include different sizes, flavours, product/service options and packaging formats. Examples are Ribena, Ariel or Twix.

These different types of branding are illustrated in Table 51.

Brands may vary from being 100 per cent umbrella or range (e.g.

Table 51. *Examples of Brand Types in Practice*

	Corporate Umbrella	Family Umbrella	Range	Individual Brands
Mail on Sunday			●	
Twix				●
American Express Gold Card	●		●	●
Ford Sierra	●	●	●	●
McDonalds' Big Mac	●		●	●
McVitie's Digestive			●	
Apple Mackintosh	●		●	●

St Michael yoghurt) to being 100 per cent individual brand (e.g. Twix), but there are many gradations in between. For example, with McDonald's Big Mac, the range name – McDonald's – is the most important element, whereas with Rowntree's Kit Kat the individual brand name, Kit Kat, matters most.

Figure 27 illustrates different degrees of importance between the umbrella or range name and the individual brand name.

100 per cent UMBRELLA or RANGE BRAND

100 per cent INDIVIDUAL BRAND

| St Michael Yoghurt | McDonald's Big Mac | Ford Sierra | Johnson's Pledge | Rowntree's Kit Kat | Twix |

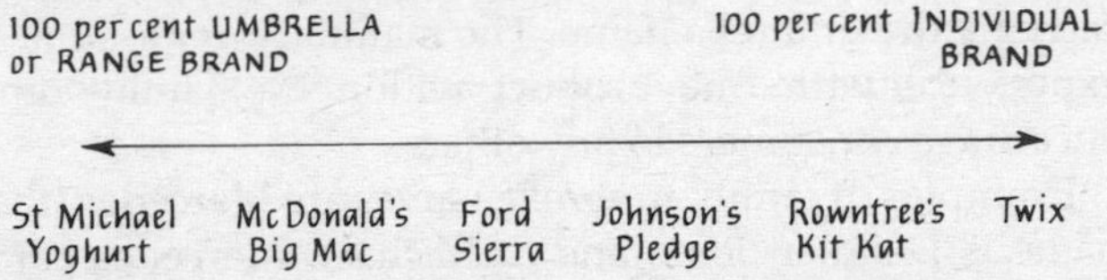

Figure 27. Scale of Umbrella or Range v. Individual Branding*

The inner and outer core of brands

Brands have an inner core and an outer core of qualities. The inner core is made up of intrinsic qualities, which, if tampered with, would change or damage the integrity of the brand. The outer core consists of optional qualities, which have elasticity and can be used to stretch the associations of a brand name.

Beyond the outer core are 'no-go' areas, where use of the brand name would not only be unproductive, but would also damage the core.

Figure 28 on p. 297 illustrates the brand profile for Ribena, a blackcurrant-drink brand owned by Beecham. For decades this product was a concentrated still drink, designed to be diluted in water, packaged in a glass bottle, and consumed mainly by children.

Its inner-core qualities were real blackcurrant flavour and health benefits. Elements in the outer core were glass-bottle packaging, concentrated product form and consumption in-home by children. These were successfully extended by Ribena's move into a diluted product packed in small cardboard tetra-paks with straw attached.

---

* Format for diagram originated by Saatchi & Saatchi, London office.

This extension did not detract from the inner core and was consistent with the consumer's understanding of the outer core. Further extensions have been made into a carbonated version in cans and into a blackcurrant/apple-flavoured drink.

What other moves could Ribena make? Could it move into blackcurrant jams with health benefits, or into sauces and condiments with a blackcurrant base? Could it go the same way as Ocean Spray in the USA, with its massive range of successful cranberry-based products?

Figure 28 illustrates the make-up of the Ribena brand.

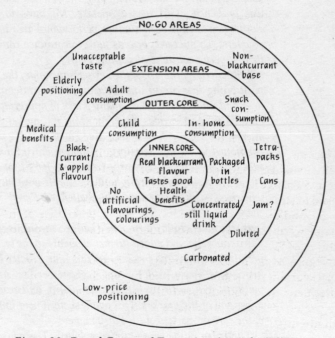

Figure 28. Brand Core and Extension Areas for Ribena

Ribena has been a well-handled brand. A less effectively exploited family-umbrella brand is Procter & Gamble's Fairy range, originating with Fairy Hard Soap and now comprising Fairy Liquid, Fairy Snow and Fairy Toilet Soap. Procter & Gamble is generally much better at marketing individual brands than umbrella ranges:

Offensive Branding

When Procter & Gamble started in the UK by acquiring Thomas Hedley in the mid-1930s, it held under 1 per cent of the cleaning market and most of this consisted of Fairy Hard Soap, used mainly for cleaning floors.

In the 1950s and 1960s Fairy continued as a strong brand, and was clear leader of the hard-soap market. Its core properties were mildness, association with cleaning, green colour and the baby symbol.

The Fairy name was excellently exploited with the launch of Fairy Liquid in 1959. All the core properties were effectively used. At about the same time, Fairy Snow, a new soap powder, was launched. This was a mistake. Mildness to hands or clothes has always been a minor performance area in washing powders. To succeed, brands have to convince consumers of their superior whiteness/cleaning ability.

Influenced by the use of the Fairy Snow name, the product's positioning was on an unsatisfactory twin strategy of whiteness and mildness. The company's lack of appreciation of the brand's properties was apparent from its market test of an alternative approach – 'Power Blue Fairy Snow' – which was positioned in 'no-go' territory. Although Fairy Snow was an excellent product – regularly trouncing Persil by 60:40 or 70:30 in blind tests throughout the 1960s with big wins for whiteness – it never seriously challenged Persil in market share.

By the mid-1960s Fairy Liquid had become the flagship of the Fairy umbrella and added further elements to the brand core – premium quality and pricing. At this time Procter & Gamble introduced Fairy Toilet Soap, a green bar, on a mildness platform, but with parity product quality and priced at the lower end of the market. This again showed poor appreciation of the core properties of the Fairy name.

The Fairy name seems underexploited. There is a growing market for mild and gentle hair shampoos, which Fairy's sister brand in the USA – Ivory – has recently entered with some success. Procter & Gamble has good technology in hand creams. The Fairy name would also seem ideal for a range of baby toiletries, to compete with Johnson & Johnson.

● **The Seven Principles of Offensive Brand Development**

Now that the groundwork of branding has been covered, we can move on to the seven principles of offensive brand development.

1. Understand your brands

First, fill in the chart shown in Table 51 (p. 295) with all your company's brands. Then, for each one develop a diagram of core, extension and no-go areas, as in Figure 28. This may be possible using only existing research and some judgement. However, the exercise may highlight the need for further research to clarify the nature of the brand's core and how far it may reasonably be extended.

A brand may have strong visual as well as verbal associations. For instance, part of the core of the Adidas brand is the three stripes and the trefoil symbol. An important element in the Rolls-Royce brand image is its distinctive radiator grille. Visual symbols need to be nurtured as carefully as brand names.

2. Determine how all your brand names fit

As already outlined, many brands consist of a combination of brand names, like the Ford Sierra Ghia. Ford is the umbrella name; Sierra is the model; Ghia is used across the Ford range and connotes luxury fittings/finish.

It is important to establish not only what individual names mean and how they can be extended, but also how they cross-relate. Which names can successfully be used in combination, why and with what relative emphasis?

Take United Biscuits' brand names as an example. This company has a clearly thought-out branding strategy:

> In the biscuit market, United Biscuits has two family-umbrella names – McVitie's and Crawford's – a number of individual brands and some combinations.
>
> In general, the Crawford's umbrella is used at a secondary level on a low-price range called Pennywise, on savoury products such as Tuc and on Tartan Shortbread.

299

> *The McVitie's brand umbrella is easily the strongest in the biscuit market. It is exploited as a brand name in most packaged sweet-biscuit markets, together with a generic description. Examples are McVitie's Digestive and McVitie's Rich Tea. The brand is McVitie's, since anyone can market Digestives and Rich Tea, but the McVitie's name has connotations of superior quality. McVitie's is also used at a secondary level to support distinctive products with an individual branded identity, like McVitie's Krackawheat or Hob-nobs.*
>
> *The name has also recently been extended to frozen foods, mainly pizza and desserts. The reasoning behind this move was no doubt more sophisticated than 'We've got a strong high-quality-food brand name in McVitie's, so let's use it to replace our collection of weak and little-known frozen brands.' However, results have not been impressive.*
>
> *Finally, United Biscuits has strong, individual branded chocolate biscuits like Penguin, United and Bandit. They stand alone, since testing showed that adding an umbrella name like McVitie's did not help and merely cluttered up a small pack-face.*

The same principles apply to brand symbols as to names. All Adidas sports shoes incorporate the three stripes. However, many of the Adidas fashion and leisure products use the trefoil brand mark instead, since this is often better suited to fashion wear.[1]

3. Decide which brand names can be stretched and how

Brand-name stretching is an aspect of asset-based marketing (see p. 32). The secret of success is not to stretch them so far as to weaken the core, and to extend only into markets which are commercially attractive. The two key questions to ask are:

1. Bearing in mind what we know about the core qualities of this brand, how far can it be stretched and in which directions? How stable and profitable are these directions likely to be?
2. These are the new markets into which we wish to extend. Looking at our stable of brand names, which

ones fit these markets or can be stretched to fit? Do we have the capability to develop a superior product?

Figure 29 illustrates the desired match between brand stretch and market attractiveness. The aim is to fill the three blocks in the top left-hand corner where brand names can be naturally stretched into attractive new markets.

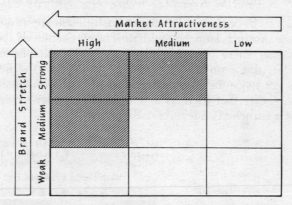

Figure 29. Brand Stretch vs. Market Attractiveness

Umbrella brands can often be stretched more widely than individual brands, since they are usually more broadly constructed in the first place.

4. Know when to develop new brand names

Everyone knows that new brands involve heavy marketing expenditure and have a high failure rate. For most new consumer brands, advertising expenditure of at least £1 million a year is necessary to achieve even minimum impact.

An advertised new brand in snacks, confectionery or chocolate-biscuit count lines typically needs to achieve at least £8–12 million in sales which are incremental to the company, in order to recover its costs in reasonable time. After allowing for cannibalization of existing company products, this can often amount to a gross sales target of £11–15 million, a formidable objective.

Because of the cost and the risks, new brand names should be launched only on an exception basis, where some or all of the following conditions apply:

- the new product is distinctive with a strong consumer benefit and superior acceptance.
- the use of an existing brand name would weaken the novelty impact of the new product.
- no existing brand or umbrella has a sufficiently good fit.

An analysis by Nielsen of 115 cases (illustrated in Figure 30) showed that new products launched with new names achieved about twice the market share of those introduced with established ones.[2] However, the main reason appeared to be that the new brand names got twice the advertising support of the established ones. This suggests that there is a tendency to under-advertise new products launched under an existing name.

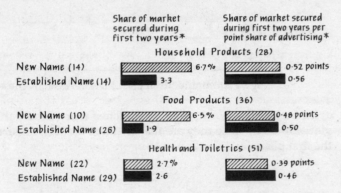

Figure 30. Comparative Sales Performance During First Two Years. 115 New Products: New Names versus Established Names

* All share figures are median values

5. Consider licensing your brand name

Licensing popular brands, logos and characters enables marketers not only to gain free media exposure, but also to generate considerable extra profits. Retail sales of licensed products have increased from $4 billion to $30 billion in the past seven years in the

USA. Kellogg's is estimated to generate profits of over $30 million a year from licensing of its cereal trademarks and characters.[3] However, in licensing brand names, companies need to establish detailed and watertight safeguards.

6. Cover your tracks

'Finding brand names . . . is one third strategy, one third creative and one third legal.'[4] The legal third may be the least exciting, but is by no means the least important. The list of horror stories of brands which have lost exclusive franchises by legal oversights does not need adding to. Equally, for those brands suffering from copyright infringements in the Far East and elsewhere, an offensive legal approach is essential.

7. Have a five-year brand development plan

Most companies would agree with the statements 'We believe in long-term plans' and 'Our brand names are our most important asset.' So why do companies virtually never include a section on brand-name development in their five-year plans?

A brand-development plan should analyse each brand name and describe how it is going to be used over the next five years. If it is seen as a name with unexploited potential, the development plan should be laid out by year, covering such questions as:

1. What is the meaning of the brand name today and what do we want it to mean in five years' time?
2. What line extensions and new products do we wish to develop under this brand name?
3. What changes in market needs and consumer demographics do we foresee that will require us to modify or change the brand meaning?
4. What are the detailed plans by year for achieving these changes in the next five years? What are the sales, spending and profit implications?
5. Bearing in mind the new markets we wish to enter in the next five years, which ones can be covered with existing brand names and which need new names?

● **Summary**

Brands enable consumers to identify products or services promising specific benefits. They enable marketers to build extra value into products or services and to differentiate them from competitors.

A brand is a constantly changing mental inventory inside the customer's mind. Its image is influenced by every facet of the marketing mix.

There are four types of branding: corporate-umbrella, family-umbrella, range and individual brand. Many brand names are a combination of two or more brand types. Each brand has an inner core, an outer core, extension areas, and no-go areas.

The seven principles of offensive brand development are as follows:

1. **Understand your brands.** Analyse all brands by type, then construct a diagram of core and extension areas for each one, using research as a guide.
2. **Determine how all your brand names fit.** Establish which names can be used in combination, why and with what relative emphasis.
3. **Decide which brand names can be stretched and how.** Stretch brands as widely as possible into commercially attractive new market sectors and usages, without weakening the brand core.
4. **Know when to develop new brand names.** To justify the costs and risks, new brand names should only be used for distinctive and superior new products, with which existing names do not fit well.
5. **Consider licensing your brand name.** This can be a profitable route for certain consumer products.
6. **Cover your tracks.** Strenuously protect your brand names and symbols.
7. **Have a five-year brand development plan.** This should analyse each brand name and describe its role over the next five years.

14 | *Offensive Trade-channel Marketing*

● **The Changing Face of Distribution**

Once upon a time retailers were passive middlemen who gratefully received goods from manufacturers at whatever terms they were offered and resold them to the public. The manufacturer was very much in control and the trade played second fiddle because private labelling was undeveloped and strong brands called the tune.

The concentration of retail power into few hands, increasing trade-marketing sophistication, and the growth of private labelling have changed all that. The division between manufacturer and retailers is becoming blurred. Retailers like Marks & Spencer, Habitat and MFI specify, brand and market their own products, using manufacturers as sub-contractors.

Now retailers regard the manufacturer's 'ultimate consumer' as their own customer. The perspective has changed. Retailers have become 'the customer's *buying* agent, not the manufacturer's selling agent'.[1] They are often offensive marketers in their own right, not passive 'channels', as detailed in the Sainsbury example in the Introduction.

However, this focus is not limited to the grocery trade, where the top five multiples account for over 50 per cent of packaged groceries. Consumer electronics, clothing, furniture and DIY manufacturers also face growing trade concentration.

Many wholesalers and industrial distributors have also reorganized into more powerful groupings and have used marketing effectively to strengthen their position.

Types of distribution channel

In today's context, 'distribution channel', with its passive connotations, is no longer an accurate description. The phrase will be used in this chapter only because it is so well understood.

Distribution channels vary greatly in complexity and efficiency. The channel for electricity is simple and almost ideal – the manufacturer has mass distribution and the consumer has instant availability, literally at the flick of a switch. By contrast, the channel for man-made fibres is extremely complex – the chain runs through spinners, dyers, weavers or knitters, garment manufacturers and retailers, until it finally reaches the consumer.

Most products reach the consumer by more than one type of distribution outlet:

1. Airline tickets can be bought direct from city ticket offices, from the internal travel departments of large companies, through travel agents or at the airport.
2. Consumers can purchase crisps from pubs, leisure centres, clubs, cafés, stations, vending machines, grocers, confectioners, newsagents and tobacconists. Over 300,000 outlets in the UK stock crisps.
3. Clothes are available from department stores, sports shops, boutiques, mail-order firms, specialist clothing shops, market stalls and variety stores.

For the majority of markets, however, one type of distribution outlet is predominant, even though others of less significance may exist. The main types of channel are direct selling, distributors, franchisees, sales brokers, tenants, wholesalers and retailers (see Figure 31).

In **direct selling**, the product is sold by the manufacturer straight to the consumer. Brushes, life assurance, encyclopaedias and certain toiletries are sold in this way. It is most suitable for products of high value which benefit by demonstration.

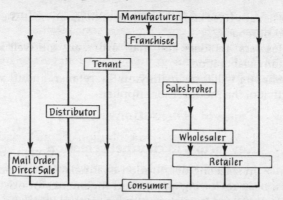

Figure 31. Common Types of Distribution Channel

Distributors usually act as the manufacturer's agent in selling its product, often on an exclusive basis. Most of the cars and petrol in the UK are sold through distributors. They normally own their premises and provide capital and labour. Manufacturers are responsible for the product and its advertising or promotion. They may also help with personnel training, technical advice or financial loans.

Franchising is common in soft drinks, launderettes, fast food and speciality retailing, e.g. Hallmark cards and Benetton. Coca-Cola is the most famous franchiser of all. It provides specially prepared syrup to the bottlers and is responsible for developing advertising, promotion and merchandising. The bottlers dilute and carbonate the syrup and distribute it throughout their franchised area. The advantage of franchising for a company is that widespread distribution can be achieved quickly and at low cost.

Sales brokers are independent sales companies which sell the products of a number of non-competing manufacturers and get a commission on sales in return. Their customers are either companies too small to have their own sales force, or larger ones who use brokers temporarily to meet a short-term situation like a distribution drive or the launch of a new brand. Sales brokers are common in the USA and are becoming more widely used in the UK.

The tenant is a feature of the licensed drink trade. Unlike the distributor, the lessee only rents his premises from the brewer.

Lessees usually have limited freedom of manoeuvre in the products they can purchase.

Wholesalers, retailers and mail order are too well known to require any elaboration.

This chapter will focus mainly on the retailer, and its viewpoint will be that of the producer, or supplier.

Key factors in channel selection

In selecting distribution channels for new products or services, or in reviewing channel arrangements for existing ones, six key factors need to be considered: exposure to target customers, performance requirements, influence, flexibility, producer profit and distributor needs. Each one is assessed below:

1. **Exposure to target consumers.** From the producer's angle, the primary purpose is to make its product or service available and visible to its target consumers. A good product may fail because it is in the wrong channel or not exposed to the people most likely to buy it.

2. **Performance requirements.** The supplier wants its products to reach the consumer in high-quality condition. Freshness is of particular importance to producers of chilled foods, newspapers, bread, meat and fruit.

   In addition, the producer may wish the channel to provide certain skills which are a necessary part of the sale (e.g. advising consumers on choice of cosmetic, servicing cars, computer education). Insurance companies operating through insurance brokers, banks or accountants will expect a high level of know-how about their products.

3. **Influence.** A supplier's influence over its channels depends upon degree of ownership, the number of links in the channel and the consumer appeal of its products. Large and powerful manufacturers like General Motors or Coca-Cola have a lot of influence over their independent distributors or franchisees, because their strong consumer appeal provides the channel with a large profit opportunity. At minimum, suppliers need enough bargaining power to achieve their aims of

exposure to the right consumers, maintenance of product quality and profitability.

4. **Flexibility.** Channel decisions are often long-term in effect, but even so it is desirable to retain maximum flexibility to alter channel emphasis.

5. **Manufacturer profit.** Offensive marketers will seek the type and mix of distribution channel that gives them maximum revenue at minimum cost in the long-term.

6. **Channel needs.** Owners of distribution channels usually have clear marketing and profit strategies. They will not bother with products which fail to fit.

The producer's dilemma

The dilemma confronting typical consumer-goods suppliers is simple. In order to sell their goods, they have to persuade the retailer not only to stock them, but to give them a fair share of shelf space. To carry out their marketing programmes they also need to get the retailer to feature their brands periodically.

Retailers, all too aware of these requirements, are thus in a strong position. Sitting across the table from a major supplier they know that the amount of shelf space and promotion allocated to a large brand in their stores will strongly affect their sales. This applies especially in markets like consumer durables or electronics, where floor and shelf space are both in very short supply.

With this substantial bargaining power behind them, and the skill to exploit it, retailers (and wholesale groups) have succeeded in squeezing extra volume discounts and larger promotion allowances out of producers. There is nothing vicious or unethical about this, since any organization is entitled to drive the hardest bargain it can.

Before examining how the marketer can remain on the offensive in this situation, let us just clarify a couple of points about the trade which are often misunderstood.

First, the interests of the producer and the retailer are very different and their supposed common objectives are a fiction. The producer's aim is to increase the sales and profits of particular brands. Retailers are concerned to raise the total turnover of their stores and they do not particularly care which brands they sell in doing so. Producers are also interested in furthering the image of their brands, while retailers think about the image of their stores.

Second, retailers see manufacturers' brands partly as resources which enable them to compete profitably with other retailers and partly as competitors to their own private-label brands.

● The Seven Principles of Offensive Trade-channel Marketing

There are seven principles of offensive trade-channel marketing which producers can use to develop their business and improve their long-term bargaining position.

1. Develop a trade-channel strategy

This requires the type of analysis outlined in Chapter 6, 'Grinding Out the Strategic Base'. It involves a review of the trade-channel environment, your own future plans, likely competitive moves and a SWOT analysis. This will relate your strengths to future distribution opportunities by trade channel and major account.

The result will be a strategy ranking existing and potential trade channels in order of importance and establishing your brand strategy by major account.

If you have a low share in a large fast-growing account, your strategy will probably be 'invest and build'. In the reverse situation, where you have a high share in a declining account which receives low priority from your competitors, likely strategy will be 'milk and maximize profitability'. In such accounts, you will take a hard line on discounts and only provide a level of service necessary to maintain your position.

Separate strategies will need to be developed for your branded and private-label products. For example, Safeway might be a 'cash cow' for your brands, but an 'invest and build' account for private-label offerings.

2. Structure your organization to reflect the strategy

The principles of organization structure and the need for close integration between marketing and sales departments, are covered in Chapter 5, 'Organization for Integrated Marketing'.

Structure will reflect your strategic decisions on channel priority. If you have decided to penetrate a new distribution channel, you will be wise to approach it like a new business. A new marketing proposition may be necessary, an investment mode possibly called for during the first year and many basic issues of trade terms and service levels will arise. A temporary or permanent task force with marketing, selling and financial expertise, with an agreed budget, is often the best structure for such a project.

A critical element in offensive trade marketing is the provision of fully allocated costs and profits by trade channel and major account, right down to the operating-profit level. Account managers can then be made responsible for volume growth, allocation of resources by account and profit. Trigger-happy, volume-driven account managers are a recipe for disaster in today's sophisticated and closely calibrated retail scene.

3. Get results from trade spending

Trade promotion is full of exceptions and its complexity makes generalization difficult. With that proviso, here are some common-sense suggestions:

- ensure that you fully understand the strategies and policies of each trade account in detail, not only for your product categories, but store-wide. What are the retailer's main problems and priorities, and how can your products help solve these?
- train your national account managers to manage the profitability of each account, including discounts, overriders, promotions, selling and distribution costs. They also need to have a thorough knowledge of sales promotion, since retailers have become expert promoters in their own right.
- relate promotion spending by account to profitability and effectiveness. If an account generates below-average profits and promotes your brands ineffectively, cut back on promotion spending. Conversely, increase promotion effort in profitable accounts which support your featured brands effectively.

To apply this approach, it is necessary to evaluate the

results of promotions by account. Extra sales, space, advertising features, displays and so on have to be monitored, and this requires disciplined reporting from sales representatives in the field as well as statistical analysis.

– keep control of the promotion budget, and spend it in the way that is best for you, but also acceptable to the trade.

Your worst enemy is often your own account manager. If he does not understand the promotion rules and the penalties for non-compliance, chaos will ensue.

– treat your major and minor brands differently. On major brands you may have a strong bargaining position, and in any case retailers are usually happy to promote such products. On minor brands your distribution may be patchy, and you can expect much less trade cooperation.

– avoid too much price promotion. Case allowances to the trade, to be used for price featuring, have their place, but they also appeal to lazy and unimaginative marketing people.

There is evidence from studies by A. C. Nielsen[2] that price reductions appeal mainly to regular users and may only bring forward purchases which would have been made later at regular prices.

The effort it takes to set up tailor-made promotions with major accounts, especially when they overlay a national offer, is often worthwhile. However, they are time-consuming and expensive, and should be avoided on small brands or in accounts which run so many promotions that they are weakly featured.

– do not allow retailers to 'bunce'. 'Buncing' occurs when a retailer buys eight weeks' supply of a promoted brand at reduced price, features it for two weeks and takes a profit on the remaining promoted stock. This is now much less prevalent than it was five years ago, but some multiples are known to 'bunce' while others are impeccable.

The volume of promoted stock should be carefully planned and ideally should not exceed two weeks' sell-out. The major benefit of a price-featured promotion is usually concentrated in the first two weeks, with severely diminishing returns thereafter.

Getting profitable results from trade promotion can be difficult for manufacturers. As so often in marketing, the key to success is to build strong consumer brands. For the majority, who do not have such brands, common sense, fair dealing and attention to detail are boring clichés, but essential selling aids.

The degree to which you can actually achieve your objectives with the trade will naturally depend on the size of your business: the small manufacturer will have less bargaining power than the large one. It is of course much easier to talk about principles than to apply them in action. But the trade has a ready eye for a 'softie' whom it can take for a ride, and it also quickly recognizes hard bargainers who know exactly what they want for their money.

4. Get the right balance between trade channels

As Peter Drucker points out: 'Many businessmen – especially makers of industrial products – are as unaware that they use distribution channels, let alone that they depend on them, as Molière's Monsieur Jourdain was of the fact that he spoke prose.'[3]

Distribution channels resemble the hour hand of a clock. They are always moving, but each individual movement is so small as to be invisible in isolation. The cumulative movement over a number of years can, however, be massive. New approaches to distribution are often easier to develop than superior products, yet they can lead to equally large breakthroughs in profit.

Often the key to success is to anticipate changes in trade channels and to capitalize on these ahead of your competitors, as Coloroll did. Coloroll has succeeded in the static wall-coverings and furnishing-fabrics markets by persistently asking itself the right basic questions:

> Coloroll's sales have increased from £6 million in 1977 to £37 million in 1985. In wall-coverings, it increased its share from around 3 per cent to 20 per cent over this period, and an important element in this was an offensive trade-channel strategy.
>
> Coloroll anticipated the growing strength of DIY multiples

and recognized their requirements for a limited number of quality suppliers, offering high service levels. It told retailers that to maximize stock return, while also offering broad range, all they needed was four suppliers, of which Coloroll should be one. Three-day delivery was guaranteed, a national accounts team was set up and stock control was taken away from production and handed over to marketing.

Distribution was heavily geared to multiples who were offered high service levels, and a strong position was built in accounts like Texas, B & Q, Do it All and Homebase.

As the Chief Executive said: 'Our business has been geared to asking the retailers what they want and then doing our damnedest to make sure they get it. That sounds extraordinarily basic, but it's amazing how many of our competitors still fail to do that.'

Coloroll applied a similar approach to furnishing fabrics, but used a separate distribution network. Delivery lead times were cut from weeks to days, and market share rose from zero to 14 per cent.[4]

By contrast, companies which were slow to respond to change include Tupperware and Avon:

Avon innovated direct-selling techniques in the cosmetic market and although it had many followers, none achieved the scale of success that made the company a superstar of the 1960s and early 1970s.

The basis of Avon's success was the greater security women felt about buying cosmetics in the privacy of their home, the availability of large numbers of part-time saleswomen and the ability to contact people at home.

All these factors have changed. Women have greater self-confidence in choosing cosmetics, and methods of retail selling have improved. The much wider range of employment opportunities open to women has made the role of 'Avon Lady' relatively less attractive. Finally, women spend less time at home during the day, as an increasing number have paid jobs.

Avon share price peaked at $140 in 1973 and hit a low of $18 in June 1985.

Tupperware, a division of Dart & Kraft, has also been faced by similar demographic changes, and operating profits have plunged from $229 million in 1981 to $139 million in 1984.

It is responding to the pressures on time created by today's lifestyles by using more flexible party formats – one-hour, lunch-time and rush-hour gatherings – and developing new incentives for its personnel.

Analysing profitability by trade channel is important for getting the right balance between profit levels and volume growth. All too often, the fastest-growing channels are the least profitable because they attract so much competition. A well-run company will review its profitability by channel at least every half-year and take decisions on future balance by channel as a result.

Table 52 is a real-life example of such an analysis, which has to remain anonymous. The allocation of selling and distribution costs was based partly on work study, partly on judgement.

Table 52. *Analysis of Profitability by Trade Channel*

	Distribution Channel			
	A	B	C	D
Channel volume trend	Flat	Down	Up	Up
Cases per delivery	203	175	1,125	37
Gross margin (%)	31·7	40·2	26·4	25·4
Operating expenses (%)	19·7	13·4	7·8	23·0
Operating profit (%)	12·0	26·8	18·6	2·4

Differences in margin by channel were very wide, and as a result of this analysis, a number of decisions were made:

- on Channel A, promotion spending was reduced as a percentage of sales, since it was expensive and not particularly effective.
- on Channel B, priority was increased, new account targets set and frequency of sales calls raised. Because of its declining trend, this channel had been somewhat neglected.
- on Channel D, delivery arrangements were renegotiated to achieve larger drops and a target was set to

expand product range stocked, and so increase cases per drop. A hard line was to be taken on discount arrangements, and selling costs were to be reduced by replacing sales representatives with order-taking merchandisers.

5. Investigate existing channels not used by your markets

A suitable new channel for your market may be lying unexploited, waiting to give an innovator's advantage to the first company to discover it. As observed earlier, there is an in-built status quo in distribution channels, and some channel arrangements are based more on tradition than on logic.

New entrants often make better use of new distribution opportunities than existing competitors, since they are not hampered by long-standing relationships or past practice and can view alternatives objectively.

In entering the US copier market, Japanese manufacturers used independent office-equipment dealers, rather than following the direct sales-force system of Xerox.[5] Apple tried a similar approach in successfully entering the personal computer market in the late 1970s:

> *Personal computers can be defined as desk-top machines, micro-processor based, with their own power supply.*
>
> *In 1977 usage of personal computers in the USA was segmented into three sectors, as shown in Table 53.*

Table 53. *Breakdown of PC Usage by Sector*

Sector	Percentage Unit Share	Price Range ($000)
Hobby	57·1	1–5
Home	28·6	Under 1
Professional/business	14·3	5–20
Total	100	—

> *Apple decided initially to target the home sector, since growth and margin prospects looked attractive and there was*

an opportunity for a more user-oriented machine at a lower price. However, Apple soon switched to professionals and small businesses as its main market, emphasizing software and ease of use.

The launch of the Apple II in 1977 became a business legend. At the time, however, Apple seemed to be attempting 'mission impossible'. One of the largest problems it faced was the lack of appropriate distribution systems offering customer exposure and service support at low cost.

By 1979 Apple was number two in the USA, despite being available in only 500 retailers. Its distribution system was via five independent distributors who sold on to dealers and other customers. Tandy was market leader, but sold through its own 8,000 Radio Shack outlets.

In 1980 Apple set up its own network of four regional replenishment centres and in 1981 it moved to a single-tier system by eliminating intermediaries. It now sold direct to 800 independent retail outlets such as Computerland Inc.

Apple provided toll-free software hotlines for users, a monthly newsletter and a magazine that focused on different applications in each issue. A cooperative advertising campaign reimbursed dealers for 3 per cent of their dollar purchases and direct training was given to dealers through sales seminars. Dealers were provided with structured presentations which they could use to educate end-users.

Apple also equipped dealers to do same-day walk-in repairs and replace equipment for free if needed. Apple thus overturned a key computer-industry marketing law established by IBM – that selling computers requires armies of direct sales people schooled in the hand-holding of the end-user.[6]

6. Create new channels

Companies entering a new market may find that existing channels do not adequately meet their needs. If they are particularly enterprising, they will pioneer new channels of their own making, like MFI and Habitat:

Mullard Furniture Industries, now MFI, was incorporated in 1964. It built up £1 million in furniture sales by direct mail. To reduce breakage, MFI decided to flat-pack furniture, but damages on road and rail persisted.

Consequently, MFI decided to develop its own retail outlets. It opened warehouses on edge-of-town sites. Low rents, plus the ability to offer manufacturers long production runs, enabled MFI to offer low prices, often half the high-street level for the equivalent product. This in turn encouraged customers to beat a path to MFI's distant doors.

Following subsequent expansion, and merger with ASDA, ASDA/MFI has become one of the country's leading retailers.

Habitat started life as a furniture manufacturer selling to retailers. But Terence Conran, the company's founder and Chairman, was dissatisfied with the retail environment. Stores were large and gloomy, poorly designed and with insufficient floor space to fully display merchandise. Conran decided to create his own retail environment and to integrate this with the products on sale. The first Habitat store opened in Fulham in May 1965.[7]

Like MFI, Habitat has also become a major influence in the UK retail scene. Together with Mothercare and British Home Stores, it is a part of the new Storehouse Group.

7. Tailor your products and services to channel needs

Some companies with a responsive approach to consumers apply quite different yardsticks to retailers. They still assume that they can create strong consumer demand by providing an appealing product backed by heavy advertising and that the trade has no choice but to stock it.

Companies recognizing that retailers are a customer, and searching for ways to fulfil their needs profitably, are likely to get the best out of their distribution channels. Some manufacturers have a number of distribution channels with different requirements and a distinctive trade-marketing package for each one, covering questions like these:

1. **Customer profile**. What type of customer shops in this trade channel? Which of your products make up the

range most likely to appeal? Are certain accounts trying to change their customer profile? What products can you offer which will help achieve this?

2. **Range.** What is the space and merchandising situation? Can the channel handle a wide range, or is it looking for a narrow selection of high-volume products? For example, department stores will accept quite large ranges, while discount stores prefer to feature a small number of fast movers.

3. **Price/quality strategy.** Is the outlet following an image of low price/reasonable quality, premium price and quality or somewhere in between? Which products in your range fit this strategy? Do you need to develop new products for this trade channel in order to make your range fully effective?

4. **Consumer service levels.** What level of service does the consumer require and how far does the retailer meet this? What service can the manufacturer offer, either incorporated in the product or as an add-on (e.g. Apple's toll-free software hotlines).

5. **Trade service levels.** How much stock can the trade channel handle? Are products packaged so as to fit the handling systems and space availability of the retailer? What frequency of delivery and sales call is required?

6. **Branding strategy.** What is the outlet's approach to branding and private labelling? Will it accept two major brands in each market or only one? What is its attitude to speciality or niche brands and which types does it favour? What are the private-label needs and opportunities?

7. **Margin needs.** How do the margin needs relate to what you can afford to offer? What is the best way to structure trade terms so as to have most appeal?

The varied channel requirements of greetings cards illustrate some of these points. There are at least eight distinct distribution channels with differing needs in price, types of product, ranges and delivery systems. Table 54 demonstrates this.

Compare the very different needs of specialist card shops and grocery multiples. Specialist card shops stock a wide range of

Table 54. *Greetings Cards: Characteristics of Differing Trade Channels*

Channel Type	Average Price	Main Type	Range	Source of Goods (Main)
Specialist Card	High	Everyday	Very wide	Direct
Newsagents	Medium	Everyday	Medium	Wholesale
Stationers	Medium	Everyday	Medium	Wholesale
Non-food multiples	Medium	Everyday	Medium	Direct
Department stores	High	Everyday	Wide	Direct
Grocery multiples	Low	Christmas	Narrow	Direct
Mail order	Low	Christmas	Medium	Catalogue
Other	Low	Christmas	Medium	Wholesale

over 2,000 cards, selling mainly 'everyday' cards (e.g. birth, marriage, sickness, anniversaries etc.) and they achieve an average retail price of 40p to 60p per card. They also require extensive merchandising and sophisticated stock-control systems from manufacturers.

Grocery multiples provide limited space and no ambience, have a range of under twenty card types, sell in multipacks and average under 15p per card. They need little servicing from manufacturers and usually get central warehouse deliveries. There is therefore great scope for segmentation by trade channel for the offensive marketer in greetings cards.

Trade channels offer outstanding opportunities for the offensive marketer who sets clear strategies, innovates in response to change and executes with strength and resolution.

● **Summary**

The face of distribution is changing rapidly and it will continue to do so in future, especially as the division between producers and retailers is becoming blurred. Many retailers are themselves offensive marketers, with clear strategies regarding type of customer, products and trading proposition.

Distribution channels vary greatly in efficiency and complexity. The main types are direct selling, distributors, franchisees, sales brokers, tenants, wholesalers and, most importantly for the consumer, retailers.

In selecting or balancing trade channels, six key factors need to be considered. They are exposure to target customers, performance requirements, influence, flexibility, profit and trade needs.

The balance of power between producer and retailer has changed sharply in the past twenty years. Concentration and success in offensive marketing have greatly strengthened the retailer's bargaining position.

There are seven principles of offensive trade-channel marketing which help producers to develop their business and improve their bargaining position:

1. **Develop a trade-channel strategy**. Decide which channels and accounts to concentrate on.
2. **Structure your organization to reflect the strategy**.
3. **Get results from trade spending**.
4. **Get the right balance between trade channels**. Anticipate changes and capitalize on them ahead of competitors. Regularly analyse your profit by trade channel and make the necessary adjustments in service levels and investment.
5. **Investigate existing channels not used by your markets**. A suitable new channel for your market may be lying unexploited, giving an innovator's advantage to the first company to discover it.
5. **Create new channels.** MFI and Habitat both created new channels for their products, since those existing at the time failed to meet their needs.
7. **Tailor your products and services to channel needs**. This applies to both branded and private-label products.

6 | *Offensive Marketing for the Future*

15 | *New Products: Success and Failure*

There is a mythical corporation known as Lip Service Inc. It does not manufacture pomades for chapped lips. Instead it manufactures executives who say, 'We're determined to mount an aggressive acquisition program' and 'Our company is dedicated to being in the forefront of key breakthroughs in the all important field of new products.'

Of course, all the key men thrusting forward and breaking through at Lip Service are only expected to talk about these things, not to do them. New-product development and marketing, especially, is the 'motherhood' of management. You never read a president's letter to stockholders that says, 'New products could cost this company its shirt and we're going to steer clear of them.' Just the opposite. New productry is a synonym for success and executives desperate to appear 'modern' make it the order of their day.

The doing, not the talking, is a traumatic experience for any company.[1]

● Chairmen Who Cheat

How often have you read statements like this in an annual report, especially in the USA?

325

> Chuck T. Bogus Jr II, Chairman of Dynamic Food Corporation Inc., reported to stockholders that '25 per cent of our sales volume this year has come from new products developed in the past five years.'

If Chuck could be persuaded to break down the 25 per cent, it could well look like Table 55.

Gross extra sales from new brands and products are 15 per cent, with a further 10 per cent coming from line extensions, which should not be counted as new products. After allowing for loss of sales on existing company brands directly related to new launches, the net gain in sales due to new products is only 5 per cent. This is very different from the 25 per cent claimed by Mr Bogus.

Table 55. *Breakdown of New-Product Sales Volume*

New brands	5%	⎱ 15%
New products under existing brand names	10%	⎰
Line extensions (new flavours, etc.)	10%	
Gross extra new brand/product sales	15%	
(Cannibalization of existing products)	(10%)	
Net extra sales from new products	5%	

New brands and products, line extensions and even, with no little deception, improvements to existing products are often confused – especially by companies wishing to appear innovative. The key to the correct definition of innovation is consumer perception, rather than degree of technical change. This is the approach taken in the next two chapters.

New brands use a name completely new to the consumer. **New products** use existing brand names applied to new or different market segments (e.g. a Halifax Building Society credit card would be a new product, not a new brand since the brand is Halifax Building Society). **Line extensions** refer to extensions of existing brands, usually new flavours, colours, varieties and so on. **Product improvements** replace an earlier product version with no change in brand name.

The first and the last are usually easy to identify. However, even for those genuinely striving to be objective, it can be difficult to differentiate between a new product and a line extension. Table 56 gives some examples from consumer products in the UK.

Table 56. *New Product or Line Extension*

New Brand	New Product	Line Extension	Product Improvement
Wispa	Chum Mixer	Chum Turkey Chum Lamb	New Persil

Chum Mixer, consisting of cereal pellets for dogs, is defined as a new product rather than a line extension, because it covers a market segment new to the Chum brand. Chum Turkey is obviously just a flavour extension of the main Chum brand.

These distinctions have practical importance, because companies which fail to distinguish between new products and line extensions, and lump them together under 'new-product activity', tend to overrate their level of innovation. This means that they may be too easily satisfied and not set their sights high enough.

While new brands and products are properly regarded as development activity, line extensions are usually no more than a maintenance obligation. Successful new brands and products improve a company's overall market position and move it forward in the long-term. Line extensions, however, are usually essential to hold a brand's standing.

Every brand is continually seeking flavour or size opportunities. Those with large lines like soups or baby food typically add a few new flavours every year and withdraw the weakest ones as a matter of good housekeeping. Unit trust groups regularly add new trusts to their portfolios, in response to market opportunities.

● Eight Conclusions About New-Product Development

Having established definitions, this chapter will draw eight conclusions about new-product development and end with a single question: are new products worth investing in? Many of these conclusions are disproportionately influenced by evidence about consumer products, because research data on these is the most extensive.

1. The product life cycle is alive and kills products and services which ignore it

The product life cycle is a truncated version of the seven ages of man and consists of growth, maturity, saturation and decline.

According to this concept, sales volume peaks soon after maturity, but is sustained during saturation by product or service improvements, line extensions and so on. Profits are meagre during the early stages, when heavy investment has to be made. But they are maintained even during decline, as additional operating efficiencies are achieved and marketing support reduces. In the end, though, the product, like man, dies. The Booz Allen chart given in Figure 32 illustrates this process.

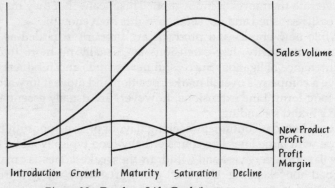

Figure 32. Product Life Cycle*

The product life cycle has been widely accepted partly because it is an elegant analogy, partly because it contains some truth. It is self-evident that products cannot stand still, and most leading products or services are frequently improved. Changing customer tastes, accelerating technology and competitor activity ensure this. Figure 33 illustrates the evolution of SR toothpaste over fifteen years.

Can products defy the ageing process by constantly updating and extending lines? In low-tech markets like food or cleaning

---

* Booz Allen & Hamilton, *New Product Management for the 1980s*, internal publication.

1966

ABRASIVE	HUMECTANT	DETERGENT (FOAMING AGENT)	TASTE	ACTIVE INGREDIENTS
Chalk (with a small amount of silica)	Glycerine	Sodium laurylsulphate	Flavouring oils Flavour enhancer	Sodium rincinoleate (SR)

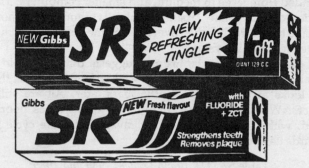

1981

ABRASIVE	HUMECTANT	DETERGENT (FOAMING AGENT)	TASTE	ACTIVE INGREDIENTS
Alumina trihydrate	Sorbitol	As above and sodium dodecylbenzene-sulphonate	Flavouring oils	Zinc citrate (ZCT)-anti-plaque benefits Sodium mono-fluorophosphate (fluoride)

Figure 33. How SR Toothpaste Has Changed over the Years
Source: Unilever house magazine, 1982.

products the answer is 'sometimes', as Fairy Liquid, Nescafé, Mars, Kit Kat, Chum and others have shown. In hi-tech categories, the answer is clearly no. The IBM 360, Xerox 914 and VW Beetle were great products in their day, but they would not find a market today.

2. New brand names should be used most selectively

Chapter 13, 'Branding', covers this under the heading 'Know When to Develop New Brand Names'.

While new products are necessary to defeat the product life cycle, they can often be introduced with at least partial support from existing brand names. The evidence for the existence of a product life cycle is strong. There is not a brand life cycle to the same degree, and well-marketed brands can continue to grow at least for the career span of most executives.

IBM has introduced many new products, but the IBM brand name has been the main brand platform. Over time, it has been extended from large to medium and smaller computers. The same applies to Xerox. Many Japanese umbrella brands like Canon, Sony or Seiko have strengthened over time. Some insurance brands have existed for over 100 years.

In consumer products, history suggests that many old brands remain strong. Table 57 lists some well-known brands of the 1930s and looks at their position fifty years later. All are still brand leaders. Weaker consumer brands, or strong ones poorly marketed, will suffer the unpleasant ravages of a life cycle moving towards its end.

Table 57. *UK Brand Leaders 1935 and 1985**

Category	1935 Leader	1985 Position
Custard	Bird's	No.1
Soup	Heinz	No.1
Margarine	Stork	No.1
Cornflakes	Kellogg's	No.1
Digestive biscuits	McVitie's	No.1
Chocolate bars	Cadbury	No.1
Mixer drinks	Schweppes	No.1
Fruit pastilles	Rowntree's	No.1
Toothpaste	Colgate	No.1
Film	Kodak	No.1
Razors	Gillette	No.1
Tea	Brooke Bond	No.1
Vacuum cleaners	Hoover	No.1
Floor polish	Johnson's	No.1

*Sources: Saatchi & Saatchi and A. C. Nielsen.

Strong old brands can be dramatically developed and Table 58 illustrates how many lively old-stagers are lasting the pace. It also demonstrates that successful new brands can be created. As indicated in Chapter 13, new brands are necessary, but on a very selective basis, where existing brands do not fit. To justify the high cost and risk of launching a new consumer brand, it is essential to have a distinctive and superior product.

Table 58. *Consumer Products: Strong Brands 1965–85*

Strong Old Brands (40)	Strong New Brands (40)
Nescafé	Flora
Shell	Ariel
Burtons	Canon
Wedgwood	Sony
Equitable	Heineken
Cadbury's Dairy Milk	Krona
Quality Street	Bejam
Kit Kat	Amstrad
Norwich Union	Racal
Bisto	Toyota
Gillette	Ski
Schweppes	Dixon
Bell's	Walkers Crisps
Persil	Hula Hoops
Dettol	Coloroll
Ford	Laura Ashley
The Times	McCains
Jaguar	MFI
Rolls-Royce	Bic Razors
Kodak	St Ivel Gold
Lux	Bailey's Irish Cream
Waterford Glass	Perrier
Oxo	Nike
Heinz	Adidas
Ribena	Head & Shoulders
W. H. Smith	Harris-Queensway
Whitbread	Sara Lee
Maclean	Zanussi
Stork	Mothercare
Boots	Apple
Imperial Leather	Mr Kipling
Trust House	Twix
Lucozade	Habitat
Horlicks	Angel Delight
Kellogg's	B & Q
McVitie	Comfort's
Sainsbury	Duracell
Elastoplast	*The Sun*
Marks & Spencer	Seiko
Prudential	Cup-a-Soup

For industrial brands, there does appear to be more of a brand life cycle. The survival rate of leading industrial brands of the 1930s is relatively low. So why do leading industrial brands seem to have a much higher mortality rate than consumer brands? The main reasons probably include:

- weaker customer franchise of industrial brands.
- greater ease of entry to industrial markets. Heavy advertising thresholds and concentrated distribution channels are barriers to entry to consumer markets.
- higher rate of technological change in industrial markets.

The survival rate of industrial brands is likely to be much higher in the future, with stronger marketing and greater focus on umbrella branding.

3. Old-brand development is as important as new brand development

This follows logically on from conclusions 1 and 2. Much depends on how strong and extendable your old brands are.

4. New products launched in the past five years account for perhaps 10 per cent to 20 per cent of today's profits

A survey of 700 US manufacturers and 13,000 new products indicated that products introduced in the past five years contributed 21 per cent of 1981 profits. The picture varied somewhat by industry, from a low of 16 per cent for consumer nondurables, to a high of 32 per cent for information processing, as shown in Figure 34.

However, Booz Allen used a broader definition of new products than that applied here. Of its 'new products', 44 per cent were line extensions, product improvements or cost reductions.

Taking the stricter definition of new products outlined earlier in the chapter, and allowing for cannibalization of existing products, it would be surprising if new products contributed as much as 21 per cent of today's profits. A guesstimate could be 10 per cent to 20 per cent.

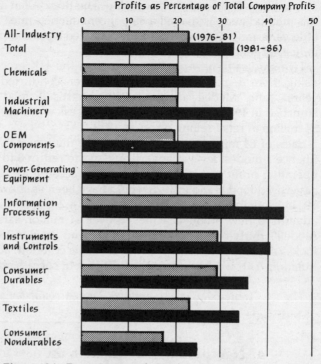

Figure 34. Percentage of Profits Derived from New Products
Source: Booz Allen & Hamilton, *New Product Management for the 1980s*, internal publication.

5. Over 90 per cent of new consumer products fail

Now we come to the biggest dogma of all: failure rates. Clear definitions are again essential. What is a success?

One criterion is survival for five years, but survival does not mean success. A study of almost 500 new *advertised* food products in 1974–8 showed that 63 per cent had survived.[2] A similar survey of *all* new grocery products indicated a survival rate of only 15 per cent after five years, establishing the obvious point that *advertised* new products are more likely to survive.[3]

Another criterion is the manufacturer's stated view of success.

This is likely to be unduly favourable. The Booz Allen study used this method and discovered a 65 per cent success rate. There was little variance between grocery products, consumer durables and industrial goods.[4]

Two studies of new-product success in the UK grocery trade, using more demanding criteria, have been conducted in recent years. John Modell analysed 730 advertised food products launched in 1969–78. His criterion for success was sales of at least £4 million at retail-selling prices in 1978.

Sales of £4 million were considered the minimum necessary to finance a modest level of advertising and to return 8 to 9 per cent operating profit. A typical profit and loss account for a £4 million advertised food brand in 1978 would have been as shown in Table 59. In Modell's study, only thirty-one, or 4·2 per cent, of the 730 advertised new products achieved over £4 million sales in 1978. Modell's thirty-one successes were reviewed again in 1985. It now looks as if only twenty-four would meet his criterion, adjusted for inflation. This would convert to a 3·2 per cent success rate.

Table 59. *Typical Profit & Loss Account for an Advertised Food Brand in 1978*

	£000	Comments
Retail sales	4·0	
Net sales to trade	3·4	Assumes 15 per cent trade margin
Gross profit	1·4	41 per cent of net sales
Advertising	0·5	Minimum effective level
Sales promotion	0·2	
Other expenses	0·4	Selling, distribution, administration
Total expenses	1·1	
Operating profit	0·3	8·8 per cent of net sales

Another series of studies of new grocery product success by Bill Ramsey, conducted in both the UK and the USA, reached a similar conclusion: 3 per cent success rate.[5] The period covered was 1971–80, and the criterion for success was £4 million sales in the UK, $30 million in the USA. Ramsey examined eighty-four product classes in the UK, and fifty-eight of these did not have a single new-product success in the ten-year period.

On this basis, it looks as if over 90 per cent of new consumer products fail to reach a sales level likely to ensure long-term profitability. The failure rate may be lower for consumer durables and industrial products.

Finally, retailers have a much higher success rate than manufacturers, since they do not face the two main barriers to entry for new products: heavy advertising support and trade distribution. Many have also become quite innovative in their new products, especially Marks & Spencer in food.

6. Successful new products are distinctive and offer better value

The few pieces of authoritative data on why new products fail are rather general in scope. In the hope of delving more deeply into this question, fifty new-product successes and fifty failures, introduced in the UK between 1960 and 1970, were analysed. They cover thirty-eight product categories, mainly in the grocery trade.

In order to ensure accuracy, each case study was discussed with someone having first-hand knowledge – often the brand manager or assistant at the time, or the marketing manager. The analysis does not pretend to be comprehensive, but it is sufficiently representative to support the points made.

This study has not been updated, since results are not likely to be much different today. The failure rate of new grocery products appears to have been broadly the same in the 1970s as it was in the 1960s.[6]

Table 60. *Successes v. Failures*

Successful Products	Failures
Significant price or performance advantage	Marginal advantage, if any
Significant difference from existing brands	Marginally different or similar
First in with new idea	Follower

New Products: Success and Failure

There are exceptions to every rule about new products, but, in general, successful new products tend to differ from failures on the three scores shown in Table 60. Let us look at these in more detail.

(a) Significant Price or Performance Advantage

Of the successful products, 74 per cent offered better performance than existing brands, though usually at higher prices. The corresponding figure for failed brands was 20 per cent. Only a minority of successful products (18 per cent; these were mainly cigarettes and snack brands, for which packaging and product positioning are particularly influential) were of parity or inferior value, whereas 80 per cent of failures were in this category. This can be seen more clearly in Table 61. Level of performance was based as far as possible on blind product tests among target consumer groups where the benefit was a product one, and it was based on judgement in some other cases.

Table 61. *Differences in Value between Successful and Unsuccessful New Products (%)**

Difference	Fifty Successes		Fifty Failures	
Significantly better performance, higher price	44		8	
Marginally better performance, higher price	6	74%	12	20%
Better performance, same price	24		0	
Same performance, lower price	8		0	
Same performance, same price	16		30	
Same performance, higher price	2	18%	30	80%
Worse performance, same or higher price	0		20	
Total	100		100	

*The key figures in this table are indicated by bold type.

336

As many as 20 per cent of failed products had better performance at a higher price, which on the face of it is surprising. However, they failed either because their price was too high or because they did not communicate their advantage clearly to consumers. Quite a few products in this category failed because, although they offered a superior performance to their target segment of consumers, this segment proved too small to support a profitable business.

One very clear pointer which emerges from this analysis is that the successful products more often had advantages in areas that mattered to consumers, whereas the point of difference among the failures tended to be in a fringe area.

(b) Significant Difference from Existing Products

The previous section viewed new products from the standpoint of product performance related to pricing. This one concentrates on the extent of differences between new products and existing offerings, and the purpose is to check whether there was any correlation between new-product success and degree of innovation.

All new products were divided into three categories: dramatically different, very different, and marginally different or similar. The judgement was inevitably subjective, but certain yardsticks were used consistently. Each new product was compared with the brand on the market nearest to it and the criterion was how the consumer would view it.

The 'dramatically different' class was made up of those products which had a radically new appearance or performance that would be immediately apparent to the consumer even before using the product. The 'very different' group was composed of those with differences not fully apparent until after usage. The third group comprised products that were different in unimportant ways or straight 'me toos'.

Based on this analysis, it was found that 68 per cent of the successful products were dramatically or significantly different, compared with 30 per cent of the failures (see Table 62). The 'dramatically different' or 'very different' new-product failures are worth further examination, and they seem to fall into three major groups.

The first group consists of those which had major performance

Table 62. *Relative Distinctiveness of Successful and Unsuccessful New Products (%)**

	Fifty Successes		Fifty Failures	
Dramatically different	20	68	8	30
Very different	48		22	
Marginally different	12		38	
Similar	20		32	
Total	100		100	

*The key figures in this table are indicated by bold type.

weaknesses. The second is made up of products whose benefits were insufficient to justify their premium price. The third group comprises new products which unsuccessfully attempted to change established consumer usage habits.

It is possible to alter existing usage habits, but this requires a product improvement of a high order, allied to very skilful marketing.

(c) The Early Bird Catches the Worm

While examples can always be given of companies which have succeeded despite late entry to a market – like Toyota in the American car market, Seiko in watches and Honda in motor cycles – it is almost always better to be first.

There is inevitably a risk with a pioneer product that competitors will improve on the original technology and bring out something better. This risk is usually worth taking because the news value of an innovation is always at a peak in the early stages, and this enables the pioneer brand to obtain widespread consumer trial. The fact that the originator gains initial possession of the consumer's usage means that the follower has to produce a better or less expensive product to make consumers switch.

Certainly in grocery markets, the dictum that 'first is best' is borne out by results in a selection of categories developed since the Second World War. In the twenty-one markets shown in Table 63 the original pioneer has been overtaken by a competitor from another company in only seven cases. In almost every case, the overtaking brand (italicized) succeeded because it had a superior product or better market positioning.

Table 63. *Twenty-one UK Grocery Markets – Innovators versus Challengers*

Market	First major brand pioneer	Overtaker 1970	1985
Washing-up liquid	Quix (Unilever)	*Fairy Liquid (Procter & Gamble)*	—
Dog food	Chappie (Petfoods)	Chum (Petfoods)	—
Cat food	Kitekat (Petfoods)	Whiskas (Petfoods)	—
Hair sprays	Supersoft (Reckitt & Colman)	*Sunsilk (Gibbs)*	—
Stainless Steel razor blades	Wilkinson	*Gillette*	—
Mashed potato	Yeoman (Dornay)	*Smash (Cadbury)*	—
Crisps	Smiths	*Golden Wonder*	*Walkers*
Frozen foods	Birds Eye (Unilever)	—	—
Cakes	Lyons	—	*Mr Kipling*
Canned desserts	Ambrosia (Bovril)	—	—
Packet desserts	Instant Whip (General foods)	Angel Delight (General foods)	—
Household floor cleaners	Flash (Procter & Gamble)	—	—
Nuts	KP (United Biscuits)	—	—
Hair Colourants	Color Glo (L'Oréal)	*Harmony (Gibbs)*	*Recital (L'Oréal)*
After-shave lotions	Old Spice (Shulton)	—	—
Tampons	Tampax	—	—
Yoghurt	—	Ski	—
Instant coffee	Nescafé	—	—
Muesli	—	Alpen	—
Fabric softener	—	Comfort	—
Automatic powders	—	Persil	—

7. Losers lack objectivity[7]

Since the vast majority of marketers responsible for new products probably accept the validity of these rules for success, why do they regularly break them by launching undistinctive 'me toos' with a very low chance of success?

Simply put, the answer is that they lack objectivity. Time and again, they swallow a whole bevy of internally generated prejudices which pollute their perspective.

What are the deadly enemies of objectivity?

Enemy No. 1: Unrealistic Time Schedules

Consider this typical scenario. A competitor launches a genuinely new product that may seriously damage your own company's franchise. It also offers a clear improvement to the consumer and one your company has not thought of.

First reactions among top management are usually well-disguised panic and embarrassment, quickly followed by aggressive talk and resounding phrases ranging from 'We can't let them steal our market' to 'We're certainly not going to abandon this business to our competitors.'

Urgent messages now start to fly from the managing director to the directors of marketing and R & D. The latter in turn confer until late at night with their subordinates and two days later they ask the brand manager to work out a 'crash-action timetable' for the introduction of a new product to take up the competitor's challenge.

The plan reduces a normal lead time of eighteen months to the unreasonable length of four. There is no time to test the brand among consumers or to run a test market.

Predictably, six months later, the company unveils yet another copycat with much trumpeting, great expense and no success. It would have done much better to apply some basic strategic thinking and launch a superior item in eighteen months' time.

Enemy No. 2: Frozen Targets

If a new-products group is committed to a certain number of new products per year, it will often produce those numbers while sacrificing quality.

Suppose that your group is targeted to introduce two new products nationally every year. There may be two possibilities already in the test market – one a proven winner and one very marginal. The temptation to push the marginal one ahead, just to hit your objective of two per year, will be strong.

While it often makes sense to give the new-products group clear targets, management should beware of any inclination to give too many targets and thus sacrifice quality in achieving them. Even if word happens to be in the air that 'the Chairman wants more new brands this year', the quest for sheer numbers is unwise and doomed to failure.

Enemy No. 3: Lack of Courage

Executives associated with new products may feel that a particular venture or project has little chance of success, but be afraid to say so. Internal company pressures to remain silent can be powerful. No one becomes a hero by stopping a project.

However, despite these internal constraints, a strong and professional executive will resist any new-product idea that fails to answer two simple questions:

1. Is there a sound reason for consumers to buy the new product rather than the one they are already using?
2. Will the new product make money for the company?

While saying no often takes courage, saying yes also requires a cool nerve, especially when the project is unusual, innovative and high-risk.

Enemy No. 4: Vested Interest

Any new project will rapidly acquire a momentum of its own, but it may be a momentum unrelated to market potential. The people who had the idea in the first place, and those who have invested time in it since, all become its natural supporters. And the more money that is spent, the harder it becomes to draw back. Few people will say, 'We've already wasted £500,000. Let's stop here.' A much likelier tack is, 'We've already spent £500,000. It'll be wasted if we stop now.'

Here is an example of an unstoppable American military project, but it could just as easily have applied to a new product:

> *The Sontay prison raid of 1970 was brilliantly planned . . .*
>
> *Ninety-seven army volunteers were flown into North Vietnam by helicopter to rescue seventy American prisoners of war.*
>
> *The operation was textbook-perfect – not one American was killed or wounded, and some 400 enemy soldiers and Russian and Chinese advisers lay dead.*
>
> *There was only one snag. The POWs had been moved out four months earlier. The fault lay not with intelligence experts. They knew the camp was a dry hole. It was the commanders in Washington who blew it. They were so wrapped up in the momentum of planning that they ignored the intelligence reports.[8]*

Enemy No. 5: Arrogance

Just because you are bigger than your competitors, or have stronger brands, you still cannot afford to break the basic rules for new-product success. A new product which offers the consumer parity value will fail even if it achieves wide distribution and is backed by a strong brand name.

Enemy No. 6: Absorption in the Process

The amount of energy, planning and plain hard work required to get a new product into even a test market is immense. It is very easy to get so immersed in the process that you miss the forest for the trees.

It is important for management to keep the three criteria for a successful new product – significant price or performance advantage, some significant difference from existing brands and a new untried idea – always in the front of their minds. And it is crucial to remember that any one of the six enemies can jinx a good idea. No company or individual is immune to attack. It can happen any time, anywhere. And when it does, management needs to struggle harder against the presumption that everything will turn out right in the end.

8. A handful of companies do it right

The skills of certain companies in new-product development ment are well known. Companies like 3M, Canon, Sony, Johnson & Johnson, IBM, Marks & Spencer, Procter & Gamble, Merck and General Electric come to mind. There is a suspicion, but no proof, that a high proportion of all successful new products is developed by a relatively small number of companies who 'do it right'.

This was certainly the case with grocery products in the 1970s. In their studies of successful new grocery products in the UK – where only 3 per cent of launches met the success criterion of £4 million annual sales – both Ramsey and Modell found that at least half the successes were achieved by only four to five manufacturers, as shown in Table 64. Ramsey also found that in the USA the situation was similar, with seven major grocery manufacturers achieving 69 per cent of new-product successes.

Table 64. *Percentage of all New-Product Successes Achieved by Four to Five Grocery Manufacturers*

Survey	Product Classes	Period Covered	Successful Products	Percentage of All Successes by four to five Manufacturers
Ramsey	84	1971–80	43	50
Modell	30	1969–78	31	61

In its survey of 700 US manufacturers, Booz Allen took this issue further.[9] It compared new-product practice in companies with a high success rate versus those with a low success rate. There were many similarities, but the main factors differentiating successful companies were:

- **operating philosophy**. Stronger commitment to internal growth through new products, and a clear new-product strategy integrated with the total company plan.
- **organization structures**. More marketing and R & D involvement in new products. Senior executive for new products in place longer.

- **experience effect**. Greater experience in developing new products increases success rates.
- **management styles**. Flexibility in tailoring structure and style to changing new-product opportunities. For example, an autonomous venture group approach may be suitable to 'new-to-the-world' products, whereas a more controlled style with strong top-management involvement may be appropriate for major new products close to the existing business.

We shall look at the requirements for success in new products more comprehensively in the next chapter.

 Are New Products Worth Investing In?

Anyone wishing to make a case against new-product investment would probably come up with the following arguments:

- the success rate of new products is under 10 per cent. Acquisitions are a better route because the success rate is much higher, at least 30 per cent.
- new-product investment is very expensive and affects this year's bottom line. Acquisitions can be made without having an impact on the profit/loss of a company's existing business.
- new products are a long-term investment which may never pay out. Stockholder and management pressure for short-term results are such that new products are just not a practical proposition.
- new products absorb a great deal of management time at all levels. This would be better spent on building and improving existing products.

These arguments could be rounded off by saying: 'We'll develop, improve and line-extend our existing products, enter new businesses by acquisition, but avoid investment in new products because the reward/risk ratio is poor.'

One of the reasons for the recent spate of acquisitions in the USA and the UK is the difficulty of developing strong new brands, especially in fast-moving consumer markets. The response to these arguments and the case for new products goes something like this:

- in the many markets where technology is changing, investment in R & D and new products is essential for survival. Failure to invest will result in an ageing, and ultimately obsolete, product line.

   In low-tech markets like food, new-product investment is less important in the short-term, but, over time, its absence will cause a company to lose the initiative and become a follower.
- with growing retail powers, new-product development is essential to retain a distinctive edge for branded products which justifies their premium price over private labels.
- new products are necessary for growth. Only a limited number of companies have strong existing products like Ribena, or Mars Bar, with unrealized potential for further growth. This growth will not continue for ever. For the majority, the hard road of new-product development has to be followed.
- worthwhile acquisitions have become very expensive and the ones you would like may not be available.
- companies which are strongly committed to new products, and treat them as essential, have a success rate way above the average.

New-product investment has appeal only to companies prepared to take a long-term outlook (see Chapter 3, 'Offensive Attitudes').

Reviewing the competing arguments, the following conclusions could be drawn:

- new-product investment is essential for all companies in their existing markets, where they have skills and strengths. It is necessary both to secure their existing position and to achieve new competitive advantages as a basis for further growth. The costs and risks in driving to success are high. But the penalty for not taking part in the race will be eventual extinction.

   Provided that a company operates the principles of offensive new-product development (see the next chapter), it can gain a good return on new-product investment.

- in developing global products, large multinational companies have a competitive advantage in their ability to set off R & D costs against volume in many countries, as well as the opportunity to learn from experience as products are rolled out. Many of the forty strong new brands listed in Table 58 (p. 331) come from multinationals.
- small- or medium-sized local companies should focus their new-product effort and supplement it by seeking licences from overseas companies not operating in their market.
- for new products in new markets outside your area of expertise, acquisition is the best route, if the right candidate can be found and purchased. If not, outside executive experience may have to be brought in and new-product development set up on a project basis.
- in the future, retailers with their own brand names will play an increasingly active part in innovating new products, using manufacturers as sub-contractors, and exploiting their captive distribution and competitive cost structure.

In the next chapter, we shall look at ways to increase the chance of success in new products for those with a strong commitment to them.

● **Summary**

It is important to define the various types of new-product activity correctly. Failure to do so may cause a company to overestimate its rate of innovation.

New brands are products which use a name completely new to the consumer. New products use existing brand names but take them into new territory. Line extensions typically consist of new flavours, colours or varieties added to an existing brand. Product improvements replace an earlier version of the product with no change in brand name.

346

Summary

Eight conclusions are drawn about new-product development, as follows:

1. **The product life cycle is alive and kills products and services which ignore it**. It is self-evident that products cannot stand still. In low-tech markets, the ageing process can be defied by constant product improvement and line extension.

2. **New brand names should be used most selectively**. The brand life cycle is more generous to the old than the product life cycle. Strong brands can be developed over time if the products they represent are carefully improved and updated. New brand names should be developed only when absolutely essential.

3. **Old-brand development is therefore as important as new-brand development**.

4. **New products launched in the past five years account for perhaps 10 to 20 per cent of today's profits**. The figure is approximate, but represents a reasonable target for most companies.

5. **Over 90 per cent of new consumer products fail**. The failure rate is certainly lower among retailers and may also be lower for consumer durables and industrial products.

6. **Successful new products are distinctive and offer better value**. In addition, the early bird usually catches the worm.

7. **Losers lack objectivity**. The six enemies of objectivity are unrealistic time schedules, frozen targets, lack of courage, vested interest, arrogance and absorption in the process.

8. **A handful of companies do it right**. For these companies, success rate on new products is far above average.

Overall, therefore, new-product investment by companies in their existing markets is essential both to secure their position and to provide a competitive edge for the future.

16 | New Products: Offensive Principles

● **The Eight Principles of Offensive New-Product Marketing**

As the statement at the beginning of the previous chapter emphasizes, 'the doing, not the talking, is a traumatic experience for any company'. This chapter concentrates on 'the doing' and outlines eight principles for offensive new-product marketing.

1. Establish a clear new-product strategy

A business strategy for the total company is the rock from which a new-product strategy is hewn. The strategy will identify which markets the company competes in now and which ones it wants to be in five years hence. If you do not like the prospects in your present markets, you will have an added stimulus to look at new ones.

For example, a company strongly committed to the manufacture of commercial vehicles or glassware in the UK would be wise to consider new markets for the future, since 1981–4 profit margins in these industries were −7 per cent and −3 per cent respectively.[1]

For each target market, a winning strategy needs to be developed. The way to do this, and the strategic groundwork required, is covered in Chapters 6 and 7. In each market, the role of existing products, new products and new brands will require careful thought and planning. In particular, it is worthwhile setting minimum volume and financial criteria for the main types of innovation. A typical list of criteria for a consumer products company could be that shown in Table 64. In this example, the company is on average achieving 8 per cent return on sales and 20 per cent return on investment (ROI) in operating profit.

Table 65. *Minimum Criteria for Innovation*

Type of Innovation	Incremental Sales (£ m)	Minimum Year 1 Advertising (£ m)	Year 3 Incremental Profit		Payback (years)
			% of Sales	% ROI	
New brand, new market to company	10	2·5	10	25	4
New brand, existing market	8	1·5	9	22	3
New product, existing market	5	0·5	11	28	2
Line extension, existing brand	2	—	12	30	0·5
Company average per existing brand	9	0·7	8	20	—

A new brand in a new market has above-average profit objectives, since both risk and initial investment are high. A four-year payback is acceptable, since the investment necessary to establish the brand will be heavy. In Year 1 this type of new brand is likely to make a heavy loss, which will be recouped only in later years.

A new brand in a market with which the company is familiar involves less risk of failure and a lower level of marketing support, while a new product in an existing market, utilizing an existing brand name, would require very limited initial investment.

Finally, incremental sales on a line extension are usually very profitable, since they utilize existing plant and do not normally require long-term advertising support.

Table 65 illustrates why different financial criteria should be applied to different types of innovation. Among the principles applied are these:

- high-risk projects should yield high profit margins, to compensate for the risk.
- low-investment/low-volume projects should also generate high returns.
- volume should be the minimum necessary to give retailers or distributors a satisfactory return on space, and to produce an acceptable operating profit for the manufacturer.

2. Plan the innovatory output required

First estimate sales and profits expected from existing products and brands over the next five years, assuming no innovation on your part. Whatever your markets, this line is likely to

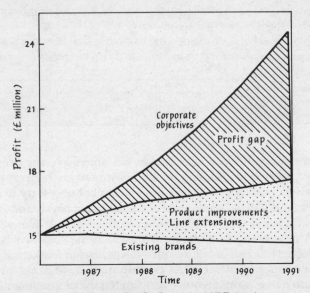

Figure 35. Five-year Profit Gap (at 1987 Prices)

350

point downwards, since competition will undoubtedly improve its customer proposition and no change on your part will lead to decline.

Next, allow for specific product improvements, line extensions, and brand repositionings planned, and add on their incremental effect. Compare this adjusted line with corporate objectives and you have the profit gap to be filled by new brands, new products and acquisitions, as shown in Figure 35.

The profit objectives in this example are ambitious. A gain of 60 per cent in real terms in five years is called for, from £15 million to £24 million. Of this £9 million gain to be achieved by 1991, only £2 million is expected to come from existing brands. Therefore, £7 million has to be generated from new products (for the purpose of this chapter, we are ignoring acquisitions).

If this particular company were starting from scratch, with a bare cupboard on new products, the objective would be unrealistic. However, it has two modest successes already fully tested and a large success recently launched nationally. The make-up of the profit gap by year would look rather like Table 66. The new-product plan depends entirely on New Products A, B and C. But New Product D and New Brands A and B are also important to the longer-term future of the company.

What kind of action is needed to ensure that the plan is achieved? Let us suppose that you have just been made New-Products

Table 66. *Incremental Operating Profit from New Brands/Products (£ million)*

	1987	1988	1989	1990	1991	1987–91 (cumulative)
New Product						
A	(0·8)	1·0	2·0	2·7	3·0	7·9
B	0·5	0·7	0·9	1·0	1·1	4·2
C	0·6	0·8	1·0	1·2	1·4	5·0
D	—	—	(0·5)	0·3	0·6	0·4
New Brand						
A	—	(1·0)	(0·4)	1·0	1·2	0·8
B	—	—	—	(0·7)	(0·3)	(1·0)
Total Profit	0·3	1·5	3·0	5·5	7·0	17·3

Manager of this company. The first thing you will want to know is the mortality rate of new ideas. How many R & D projects has it taken in the past to yield both medium and big ideas? Past performance is only a partial guide to the future and perhaps you can improve on it. You conduct an analysis of past performance which tells you that you need at least 100 well-constructed R & D projects in order to achieve four national successes. It also shows that the success rate is higher on projects using existing technology. But the one highly innovative success generated the most profit (see Table 67).

Table 67. *R & D New-product Development Projects 1982–6**

Development Stages	Existing Technology	Highly Innovative	Total
Number of projects	70	30	100
Discontinued	30	20	50
Market-researched (e.g. product tested)	40	10	50
Test marketed	10	4	14
Expanded nationally	3	2	5
Successful	3	1	4
Annual Profit from Successes (£ million)	3·0	2·5	5·5

*The key figures in this table are indicated by bold type.

If you apply the results of this analysis to your 1987–91 plan, you will need to have three new national successes in the market-place by 1990. On a purely mathematical basis, this would require seventy-five new-product projects. To be on the safe side, then, you might plan 100 projects and aim to beat the historical success rate, so as to comfortably exceed your five-year objectives.

A planned approach of this kind should not in any way inhibit creativity in execution. However, at least one very successful new-products manager rejects it as being too mechanical. As long as her success continues, no one will complain.

3. Operate from strength

Asset-based marketing (Chapter 1) and capitalizing on strengths (Chapters 6 and 7) apply as much to new as to existing products. A ten-year analysis of new consumer products (1971–81)[2] indicated that the most successful practitioners:

- leaned most heavily on previous experience, equipment and franchise.
- exploited what they could do uniquely well.
- discovered and exploited market areas where they could exercise dominance.

This mirrors the results of John Modell's study of 730 new consumer products launched in 1969–78. Twenty-seven out of the thirty-one successes were within existing areas of company competence and reputation.[3]

It would obviously be wrong to conclude from this that companies should not diversify outside their existing areas of competence or consumer franchise. However, the lower success rate of new products when diversifying should be recognized.

4. Get the right organization and attitudes

As outlined in Chapter 5, 'Organization for Integrated Marketing', organization structure must stimulate innovation. For most situations, a new-products department, responsible for new products, new businesses and new acquisitions, probably works best. However, the organization of innovation needs to be flexible and structures may need to be changed to meet changing company needs and strategies.

A study by Booz Allen & Hamilton splits innovation into three structural categories – established products, new products in established markets, and new businesses – and highlights the different focus on each one (see Table 68). In a structure of this kind, the new-products department would handle the middle category, and multi-discipline venture groups might develop totally new businesses. This would be possible in large companies. In medium-size and smaller ones, the new-products group might well manage both functions and be responsible for acquisitions as well.

Table 68. *The Management of Innovation*

	Managing Established Products	Managing Established Markets	Managing New Businesses
Focus	Cost reductions Product improvements Line extensions Flankers	New brands New positions Expanded	New to company New to world
Issue	Product management	Market management	Business management
Responsibility	Line management	Shared	Chief Executive

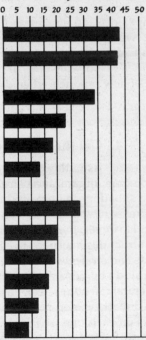

Figure 36. Internal Obstacles to Successful New-Product Introductions

While the right organization is important, the right attitudes are even more critical to successful innovation. This issue was covered at length in Chapter 3, 'Offensive Attitudes'.

The Booz Allen new-products study[4] showed that lack of top-management commitment was the greatest internal obstacle to innovation, and this is shown in diagram form in Figure 36.

To succeed in the battle for internal resources, a new-products group needs positive discrimination in its favour. 'New products' may have a manager, but it is rarely a function. For most people in a company, it is a by-product, to be fitted in when their main tasks allow.

What is commitment? It is a conviction by senior management following thorough analysis, that a new project can be successfully accomplished, the willingness to pursue it without reservation and the determination to ride out obstacles when they occur.

Commitment to new products is unfortunately rare. More common is half-hearted attachment, allied to plans to bale out if the going gets tough. Management continually looks over its shoulder, asking, 'Should we really be entering this business?' The willingness to consider getting out is too high. This usually results in compromise, retreat and failure.

Commitment is a combination of business logic and gut feeling, but it is the latter which sees companies through in hard times, when things are looking sour. In the 1950s Procter & Gamble committed itself to entering the paper market, but success did not come through until the 1970s. When it came, it was worth waiting for:

> In the 1950s Procter & Gamble investigated the market for consumer paper products (toilet and facial tissues, largely) and liked what it saw. The market had reached a good size, was expanding fast and offered sufficient margins to permit heavy advertising and promotion spending.
>
> What is more, the criteria by which consumers judged the performance of paper products – notably softness, absorbency and wet strength – could be assessed objectively, just like the whiteness result of a washing powder.
>
> There were only two snags – Procter & Gamble knew nothing about paper technology, and the two entrenched competitors, Scott Paper and Kimberley-Clark (Kleenex), were well-managed companies.

Procter & Gamble bought a small regional paper firm called the Charmin Company, and used that as a base for learning about the business. It spent some years developing a better tissue. Eventually, a method of adding perfume was worked out and on blind test Procter & Gamble's perfumed product beat the competition by 2:1.

A test market was opened, supported by heavy advertising and full-size free samples delivered to consumers' homes. The brand quickly gained a high share. However, when the launch activity was over, market share plummeted. The perfume had novelty appeal, but when this wore off, consumers went back to their regular brand.

Procter & Gamble did not give up. Senior management continued to feel that the company had the technical and marketing skills to succeed in paper.

More R & D work was done and eventually a product was developed with superior softness and wet strength. This was tested and launched nationally. It ultimately achieved brand leadership in toilet paper and paper tissues.

A spin-off of Procter & Gamble's move into paper was the development of Pampers disposable nappies (diapers) now the company's biggest brand, with retail sales of over $1 billion.

Japanese international marketers are also well known for their willingness to soldier on through adversity, in pursuit of an opportunity they feel is within their grasp. The establishment of Toyota as the number one American import brand is an example:

Toyota first started to export to the USA in 1957. A few hundred Crown models were sold. But their owners were not pleased. The cars had been designed for the narrow-road low-speed driving of contemporary Japan. At 80 m.p.h., loud noises soon erupted and power dropped sharply. The first beachhead had proved a disaster.

Toyota did not give up. The US Manager, Seisi Kato, at one time recommended throwing in the towel, but Tokyo refused to do so. Kato recalls that the failure 'served as a burning stimulus to develop better products'.

The next ten years were very tough. In Kato's words: 'The reality was that the first ten years of Toyota's export efforts to the USA had been nothing but a series of humiliations and

> *frustrations, with little to sustain us but a burning ambition to realize this dream of dreams . . . we had kept on trying, determined that we would take two steps forward for every step backward.'*
>
> *Nineteen years after its first disastrous entry, Toyota overtook the Volkswagen company in U S sales. Toyota remains the leading foreign automobile manufacturer in the U S A and is now planning to open its own plants in the U S A and Canada.*[5]

As Robert Heller observes, 'Persistence can turn a losing cause into a victory, provided that the essential resources are available', and provided that the initial judgement was right.

5. Invest consistently in new-product development

This principle has been sufficiently emphasized in Chapter 8 but is worth a reminder. The experience curve can operate strongly in your favour on new products.

6. Place at least one third of R & D new-product effort on breakthrough opportunities

The setting of R & D priorities is covered in Chapter 8, 'Offensive Product and Packaging Development'. While the big ideas involve greater risk of failure, they can also produce success on a large scale. The idea may be 'big' in terms of technological challenge or market opportunity.

7. Develop a new-ideas system

There are numerous ways to develop new-product ideas, but it is difficult to forecast in advance which ones will produce the best results for a given company. The secret is to start by using them all and then to drop the ones which are least fruitful. Some of the main sources of new ideas are listed below.

Internal sources

Every employee should be regarded as a potential source of new ideas, but any company wishing to draw them out has to graduate beyond the hackneyed suggestion box, which is more often a repository for obscene suggestions than good ideas.

The trick is to tell all employees which markets the company is interested in, to have the resulting ideas passed to one person, probably the new-products manager, and to acknowledge all suggestions, giving clear reasons for rejection where ideas are deemed to be unusable. Most important of all, people making suggestions which are developed should be given credit and rewarded.

On balance, it is probably worthwhile offering substantial rewards to employee inventors of successful new products. The three countries with the greatest number of patent applications – Switzerland, Sweden and West Germany – all have laws requiring royalties to be paid to employee inventors. However, any incentive system must be handled with extraordinary skill to minimize piracy, undue secrecy and bad blood between employees.

Finally, in the course of normal development work, technologists often produce 'spin-off' ideas. The 3M 'Post-It' notes, described in Chapter 8, derived from this source. 'Spin-off' ideas should be encouraged and harvested by the new-products group.[6]

External sources

Advertising agencies, suppliers specializing in new consumer products (e.g. Monsanto) and banks should be acquainted with the company's new-product requirements. Banks sometimes know of small organizations with a number of new ideas which they wish either to sell or to develop jointly, because they lack the capital to go it alone.

For security reasons, some companies may feel hesitant about making their new-product interests too widely known. But it is difficult to see what action potential competitors could take, based only on the information that you have an interest in several markets. You may in fact never enter many of the categories listed on your new-idea requests, and the very act of making your interest known could result in an approach from possible acquisition prospects.

For many companies, the biggest source of new ideas is their own customers. But customers will usually respond only if they feel their ideas will be taken seriously by someone who is really listening.

Overseas sources

New ideas can be gained from overseas by subscribing to some of the many information bulletins or by personal visits. At minimum, it is worthwhile examining existing products in your present or future fields of interest in the USA, leading European countries and Japan.

Licences for sales rights of foreign products in the UK are also a worthwhile source of new products. Companies abroad may prefer to license a UK company rather than set up their own organization.

However, foreign countries, and America in particular, should be regarded as a source of ideas rather than ready-made products. Strong overseas brands should not be transplanted to the UK in their original form unless it is clear from consumer testing that they require no modification.

Patents

Patent information is easily available at little or no cost. There are many thousands of patents and the problem is to pinpoint those of possible relevance. A good approach is to limit your search to recently registered and expiring patents, in your areas of interest. This will enable you to exploit ideas previously covered by patents which have now expired, and to spark off fresh concepts arising from new patents but not covered by them.

Previous new ideas on file

Rejected ideas can often be a source of new ones. The old ideas may have been wrongly assessed, or circumstances may have changed since they were last evaluated.

The universities

Arrangements with universities can vary from large-scale sponsored research financed by a company, to the use of individual professors on a consulting basis, to informal discussions with university staff or students.

Procter & Gamble's successful toothpaste Crest was the result of years of sponsored research on stannous fluoride at Columbia

University, New York. The first electronic computer – the ENLAC – was designed by J. Mauchly and W. Eckert at the University of Pennsylvania, with money provided by the US Army.[7]

Group thinking[8]

There are many techniques for generating new ideas from groups of people. The best-known is the brainstorming or idea-generation group. Typical size is from three to twelve people, usually from varied backgrounds. Possible members are a consumer, a sales representative, a technologist from a different product field, a marketing person and a packaging expert. The focus is on generating as many ideas as possible. No evaluation of quality occurs during the group session because this would inhibit the flow of creativity.

The leader of the group is usually the key to its success, and he or she needs to be well prepared. It is little use standing in front of a blackboard and saying, 'Now let's have some new-product ideas in the market for "X".'

A number of stimulants can be used to create a flow and 'prompts' to overcome blockages or dead ends. These include:

- point of entry questions to switch the line of thought. If a group were considering a new type of car brake, the leader might ask: 'How can you stop a car that has no brakes?' or 'Why doesn't a ship have brakes?'
- analogies. These stop the brain moving along familiar lines.
- attribute mixing. The group would be asked to list the elements most important in structuring a new product, such as image, ingredients or types of consumer. For the most important elements a series of attributes is developed. For example, types of consumer might include commuters, tourists, teenagers, etc. A limited number of attributes would be selected by the group and written on coloured cards. These cards could then be mixed to stimulate discussion and ideas.
- lateral thinking.

Other methods

For every major product category, there will be other more specific sources of new-product ideas. Let us take food as an example. Restaurant menus can be a good guide on changes in eating habits and are a way of identifying popular dishes not yet covered by branded products. Leading printers of restaurant menus may cover as many as 500 different locations and will usually supply copies of these for a small charge. New ideas for food products can also be found in the more popular recipe books, or in recipes included in magazines.

New-product or design agencies

There are an increasing number of highly skilled new-product development agencies, capable of contributing to a company's new-product strategy, and developing ideas and positionings from scratch into the market-place. Design agencies can also add greatly to the success of new-product programmes.

8. Build objective filters

It is not much use generating hundreds of new ideas unless there is some system for assessing them and for separating those with promise from the non-runners. Most companies have good ideas bobbing around the place, but they often fail to spot the ones with the most potential. Conversely, as we have seen in the previous chapter, many poor ideas reach the market-place when in fact they should have been screened out at a very early stage.

Before proposing methods for screening ideas and projects, consider the four stages in the hatching of new products which precede national expansion. They are raw ideas, business analysis, R & D and test marketing.

The starting point is the generation of many unpolished ideas. Some of these can be quickly eliminated, but the more viable-looking ones will be subjected to preliminary business analysis, whose purpose is to check whether the idea holds together commercially.

The business analysis need be no more than a page long and will estimate total market size, brand share, pricing, chance of R & D success, marketing spending and profit. It is usually a fairly rough-cut affair, but sufficient for the purpose of eliminating commercial lame ducks at an early stage.

Using the development priority table (see p. 192), a decision will then be made whether to undertake laboratory development of the new idea. Many R & D projects will be discontinued. For those which survive and perform well in consumer tests, a full test-marketing plan will be drawn up and the company will be able to determine whether or not to move into a test market.

Even the most effective organizations do not find screening an easy process. Every successful new product requires a combination of objectivity in assessing its chances and enthusiasm in overcoming all the roadblocks implicit in the development of any new idea. There is always a danger that the enthusiasm necessary to bring an idea to fruition will cause a lack of objectivity in judging it.

The ideal screening system would seem to have three elements: continuity, clear yardsticks and top-management involvement. Continuous assessment of a new idea is essential, because as it moves through the four stages of product evolution, more becomes known about it. A project which looked very promising at the business-analysis stage may be a lot less attractive by the time development of the product has been completed. New data on the market, raw material price increases, fresh legislation or the entry of additional competitors may reduce the appeal of the project to the point where it should be discontinued.

It makes sense to evaluate each project on at least four occasions and a possible schedule for this is outlined in Table 69.

Table 69. *Schedule for Evaluating New Products*

Check Points	Data	Assessor
1. Raw ideas	Short verbal statements	New-Products Manager
2. Prior to R & D Development	One-page business analysis	New-Products Manager
3. Prior to test market	Full recommendation	Marketing Director
4. Prior to national expansion	Full recommendation	Managing Director

At the third check point, prior to entry into the test market, the Marketing Director should question the strength of the basic marketing concept. If he thinks that it fails to hold water, he should reject the test recommendation.

Although, in the difficult area of new products, there is no system which will guarantee success, any project which passes these tests at each check point is more likely to succeed.

● **Summary**

There are eight principles for offensive new-product marketing, as follows:

1. **Establish a clear new-product strategy.** This will emanate from the total company strategy. It should specify the role of innovation in achieving this and set minimum volume and financial criteria for each type of innovation.
2. **Plan the innovatory output required.** The gap between corporate profit objectives and likely future contribution by existing products has to be filled by new products. These need to be individually planned. To guide on what is needed to achieve future plans, the historical yield rate of R & D projects should be analysed. Lessons learned can then be incorporated in future plans.
3. **Operate from strength.** Play to your strengths and capitalize on what you do uniquely well.
4. **Get the right organization and attitudes.** Structure should encourage innovation and respond flexibly to changing conditions. Lack of top-management commitment is the greatest internal obstacle to innovation.
5. **Invest consistently in new-product development.** The experience curve can operate strongly in your favour on new products.
6. **Allocate at least one third of R & D effort to breakthrough opportunities.** The big ideas carry the greatest risk of failure, but also the largest potential pay-off.
7. **Develop a new-ideas system.** The main sources are internal, external, overseas, patents, 'old' new ideas, universities, group-thinking and outside agencies.
8. **Build objective filters.** The enthusiasm necessary to

bring an idea to fruition may cause a lack of impartiality in judging it. The ideal screening system has three elements: continuity of assessment, clear yardsticks and top-management involvement.

17 | *The Marketing Approach to Acquisitions*

> Too many acquisitions are based on an attractive-looking balance sheet and earnings statement plus a quick trip to the plant. The buyer is impatient to act quickly, lest somebody else grab up the prize, and he makes the deal with 'details to be ironed out later'. Later, unfortunately, may be too late.[1]

Of all the activities in which a company is concerned, acquisitions involve the highest risks, the least accountability and the greatest glamour. They are the one aspect of business that excites popular interest, and the winners of strongly contested acquisitions have become almost as well known as leading show-business people.

However, despite the aura of secrecy and excitement that surrounds them, acquisitions are also an alternative to new-product development and should always be seen as such.

Although financial and legal issues are important in most acquisitions, many of the major questions are marketing ones – the strength of a company's consumer franchise is at least as relevant as its past balance-sheet performance. This chapter takes a look at the current acquisition scene, and then outlines how the offensive marketing approach can best be applied to the business of buying and selling companies.

● Acquisitions: The Fun Side of Business – for a While

Peaks and troughs

In the past forty years there have been three waves of acquisitions in the UK. The first was in the 1950s, led by people like Charles Clore and Isaac Wolfson searching for undervalued post-war assets. The second was the late 1960s and early 1970s, with Jim Slater as a visible participant. The third has surged in the mid-1980s, as Figure 37 shows, and the USA is also in the middle of a massive acquisitions binge.

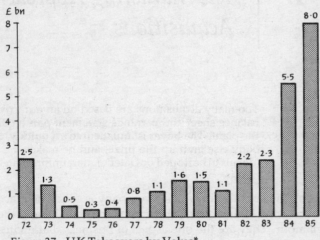

Figure 37. UK Takeovers by Value*

The main reasons for the dramatic increase in the volume of UK acquisitions include:

- increasing importance of pension-fund managers, under pressure for short-term performance, and therefore liable to be attracted by the share-price gains generated or promised by bids.
- the desire of American banks to strengthen their position in the London market, and their willingness to

* Source: *Financial Weekly*, 1986.

lend cash for acquisitions as an entry point to corporate clients.

- recognition by the City of the importance of brand names, and of how difficult and expensive it is to establish new ones. Understanding of the concept of asset-based marketing is spreading.
- a more deregulated environment and the growing influence of arbitrageurs.
- greater competition among merchant banks.
- opportunities for senior managers of acquiring companies to achieve visibility and increase earnings, both salary and stock options. Committing a murder or making a large, contested acquisition are two of the quickest routes to fame.
- the flock factor: 'Everyone else is doing it, so we'd better join in.'

The belated recognition of the financial value of brands is encouraging, but many of the other reasons for the surge in acquisitions are not relevant to the needs of consumers, the economy or the competitive environment. The rapid rise in acquisitions is to some degree a demonstration of failure by companies to generate sufficient internal growth.

Types of acquisition

The five main types seem to be:

1. Intended to spread risk/enter new markets. A good example is IBM and Rohm. The buy-out of Rohm will help IBM to move into the telecommunications market, dominated by AT&T, and to take advantage of the convergence between telecommunications and computers. IBM had twice tried to develop its own digital PBX switchboard. Rohm gave it a market position in telecommunications, plus the benefit of the excellent engineering for which it is well known.

   The R. J. Reynolds-Nabisco merger enabled Reynolds to spread its risk more widely away from tobacco into food.

2. Intended to achieve a better return on financial assets.

Many of the BTR and Hanson acquisitions have been of this type. Operations, controls and return on assets were strengthened following acquisition.

3. Intended to achieve a better return on marketing assets. Beecham has for decades been a classic exponent of this approach, with Horlicks, Bovril and many others. The Philip Morris acquisition of Miller Breweries was another example. Despite recent difficulties, Miller was propelled from seventh to second brewer in the USA.

4. Intended to be defensive. Many acquisitions by tobacco companies are at least partly defensive, covering the risk of sharp market decline in tobacco. Acquisitions by large companies of smaller, troublesome competitors are also defensive.

5. Intended to be synergistic. The rationale is that the combination of two companies creates economies by eliminating duplication of facilities and increasing bargaining power in the market. The Dee-International Stores and Habitat-Mothercare mergers both appeared to be synergistic.

Most acquisitions contain a number of these elements, although one is often predominant. See Appendix 5 for some examples.

A sale or a marriage?

In cold blood, buying a company is not very different from buying a suit. You see one you like and, if the price seems right, you purchase it. But many of the best write-ups on the subject see acquisitions and mergers more as marriages than as straightforward commercial transactions. They are replete with phrases like 'the courtship', 'the wedding' and 'the adaptations necessary to a new relationship'. The analogy is coy but true, because when you acquire a company, you are taking over people and your action affects their prestige, security and careers.

Many non-commercial factors enter into an acquisition and it is especially important to understand these if you wish to retain the existing management of an acquired company. Understanding the needs and motivations of the key personnel is as essential to a successful acquisition as a firm grasp of consumer needs is to an effective new-product development programme.

The high failure rate of acquisitions

Most studies indicate that less than 50 per cent of acquisitions succeed in increasing real earnings per share. At least half appear to be failures.

A recent study by Booz Allen & Hamilton is the most favourable we have seen for acquirers. It estimates, on a sample of all industries, that 49 per cent are winners, 39 per cent losers and the rest in-between. The important point it makes is that most acquisitions are either *big* winners or *big* losers, as Figure 38 shows.

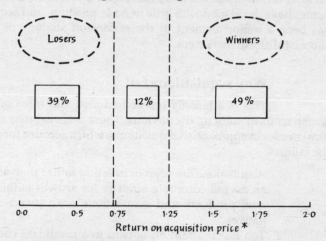

Figure 38. Most Acquisitions are Clear Winners or Clear Losers

High though the failure rate of acquisitions is, it is much lower than for new products. Contrast the fun and glamour of acquisitions with the grind and hard work of new-product development, as shown in Table 70, and you can see why acquisitions are such a popular route.

* Sample of acquisitions on all industries, net present value of ten years post-acquisition cash flow (including terminal value) divided by acquisition price. Source: Booz Allen & Hamilton.

Table 70. *Acquisitions vs. New Products*

	Acquisitions	New Products
Failure rate	50 to 60 per cent	90 per cent
Style	Glamorous	Grunt Work
Lead time	Short	Three to five years
Funding	Borrowings	This year's budget
Power	More	Little effect
Status	Yes	Little effect
Visibility	Big increase	Some increase

In the UK acquirers appear to be more highly regarded than innovators, whereas in the USA the reverse is probably true.[2]

However, many of the most successful UK and American companies have developed with little or no acquisition, and acquisition has been a minor element in the expansion strategy of Japan's successful global marketers.

Why acquisitions fail

This is a heavily researched area and most of the research tends to point up the obvious. There seem to be six common weaknesses in approach to acquisitions, which account for many of the failures:

1. Acquisitions are seen in isolation rather than as part of an overall corporate strategy for growth within which new products and acquisitions are viewed as alternatives.

2. Too much attention is paid to a candidate company's past record and present value, while much less thought is given to its future potential.

3. The motivations of the seller are not fully understood.

4. There is insufficient prior discussion and agreement as to how the acquired company will be operated after the acquisition is completed.

5. Companies pay too much for acquisitions. They overestimate the synergistic effect and base the price on optimistic assumptions about future developments.

6. Acquirers buy into markets they do not know and to which they bring few skills or relevant resources.

On the whole, the closer an acquisition is to the acquirer's base business, the more successful it is likely to be.

Why is there so little involvement by marketing people in acquisitions?

It is clear that marketing skills are highly relevant to acquisitions. Yet marketing people are rarely consulted. Acquisitions are just not regarded as traditional territory for marketing people, even by themselves. How many books on marketing have a chapter, or even a section, on acquisitions?

The reasons for the rare involvement of marketers in acquisitions include:

- the managing director's and chairman's view that acquisitions are their prerogative. They usually involve the financial director to run numbers and assist in contact with merchant banks.
- too much focus on the mechanics of the deal, which require financial expertise, and too little on the substance, which demands marketing skill. The emphasis is all on 'doing the deal'.
- there is often little regard for non-financial data. A major assumption in many acquisitions is that the future will mirror the past. The fact that the candidate may be on a cliff edge, facing a new competitor in a test market with a superior product or dominating an outmoded distribution channel, may be given little weight.
- lip-service is sometimes paid to five-year projections of the combined companies. The merchant bank may ask the acquiring company's sales or marketing director to produce five-year sales projections. These may be run up with little thought and no probing. Synergies are often 'plug numbers', over-optimistic estimates which justify the deal.

There are clear signs that all this is changing. Companies like Guinness and Pepsico understand the marketing approach to acquisitions very well and they apply it skilfully. Marketing people will become more involved in acquisitions in future, but need to push their way in rather than stand back in the shadows.

● **The Offensive Marketing Approach to Acquisitions**

The five elements of the offensive approach, outlined below, are marketing common sense, and it is surprising that they are not more widely applied. (Appendix 6 outlines the key factors for success (KFS) in acquisition programmes.)

1. The right organization

Organization for new-business development is covered in Chapter 16. There are many advantages in giving the new-products manager responsibility for acquisitions. The main one is that internal new-product development and acquisition will be viewed as alternative routes to growth and the merits of each will be regularly compared.

The close involvement of the chief executive in acquisitions is essential. Without high-level support and encouragement, little is likely to happen on the acquisition front.

If it is proposed to integrate the acquired company into the parent company organization, another golden rule is to involve the people who will be responsible for running the subsidiary company in the acquisition negotiations and to give them a major say in the final decision. This will pay dividends later because the executives' agreement to the acquisition decision will give them a greater stimulus to run it effectively (and no excuses for not doing so).

2. Develop an acquisition strategy

The second requirement in a successful acquisition programme is to have a clear acquisition strategy. This will stem from the total corporate strategy and plan.

It is important to specify a minimum sales turnover, because the problems of a small subsidiary can absorb just as much of the parent company's time as those of a large one. An American study showed that a high proportion of failed acquisitions accounted for less than 2 per cent of the parent company's turnover – they were not important enough to gain the share of the parent company's time which their problems required.[3]

The strategy should specify the markets in which you are in-

372

terested and the things you want to buy in making an acquisition. Do you want to buy a strong existing market position? Are you seeking a ready-made low-cost operator? Do you have the marketing skills, but wish to buy R & D know-how, or enter new distribution channels?

Appendix 7 contains a check-list of points to be covered in drawing up an acquisition strategy.

3. Do not waste time on non-runners

Some companies identify an acquisition candidate, spend months studying it, and then make an approach which is flatly rejected. This is quite acceptable for those prepared to bite the bullet and set up a contested bid. For the many companies reluctant to do this, it is much better to check the interest of the candidate before you spend much time looking at it.

The way to do this is to construct a long list of possible candidates, stemming from the acquisition strategy. This laundry list can then be quickly examined and obviously unsuitable candidates screened out. Depending on your strategy, you may, for instance, wish to scratch out companies with:

– long-term losses.
– none of the key benefits staked out in your acquisition
  strategy.
– a history of major industrial-relations problems.

The remaining names on the laundry list can then be briefly examined and a one-page summary prepared on each. This might contain basic facts like:

– market size and share of main markets.
– sales and profit history.
– statement of business, brands, products, distribution
  channels.
– ownership and key people.
– sites of factories and offices.
– balance-sheet summary.

Based on this brief screening, further candidates can be dumped and a short-list drawn up.

The next step is to establish whether there is the faintest chance of buying each candidate. This can often be ascertained by means of third-party soundings – banks, suppliers, retailers, etc. Otherwise a direct approach, asking for a meeting to discuss topics of mutual interest, needs to be made.

The result of this exercise will be that, with a minimum of time investment, you have developed a short-list of *qualified candidates*, i.e. companies which you may be interested in buying and which are not strongly opposed to selling. It is amazing how much time is still wasted on lengthy and expensive analyses of candidates which turn out, much later, to be *unqualified*.

4. Evaluate swiftly but in depth

When you acquire a company, you are buying a long-term commitment which will haunt or delight your shareholders ten years ahead. If you pay too much for it, your chances of making it viable are much reduced. So how does the offensive marketing company following the offensive marketing approach work out the value of an acquisition?

For a start, it looks beyond the balance sheet, which is a useful (though often misleading) recorder of history, and focuses on future potential rather than past performance. Secondly, it recognizes that any acquisition has a different value to any other company, depending on the synergetic effect expected.

Applying this marketing/financial approach, the evaluation of an acquisition prospect can be divided into three steps. First of all, an estimate of sales and profits of the prospect company for the next ten years should be made – and this is where the marketing people come in, because you can't make a ten-year forecast by looking at balance sheets and plant. Then the synergetic effects stemming from the acquisition should be worked out and an estimate made as to their financial effect. Finally, based on these estimates, the financial group should work out the maximum price worth paying for the acquisition prospect. (The financial group would take the final ten-year sales figures, profit and capital expenditure forecast, and translate it into a cash-flow plan, discounted at the acquiring firm's cost of capital. This final figure would represent the fundamental worth of the acquisition to the acquiring company over the next ten years.)

The main contribution of marketing people to this process would be the ten-year forecast and the example below shows the type of questions which would be examined:

Examination of Prospect's Market Strengths
All questions should be applied to prospective acquisition:

1. What are the growth prospects of the markets the company is operating in? Is the company well represented in the fastest-growing segments? For example, one would like a brewery acquisition to be particularly strong in lager.

2. What is the strength of the company's brands in the market? Did they gain or lose share in the past five years? How far will the factors influencing their success or failure in the past five years be repeated in the next ten? How far did the company's performance over the past five years deviate from its own forecasts and why?

3. What are the critical skills required for success in these markets and how far does this company possess them? What are the key company strengths and how effectively has it been exploiting them? Does it have any unique strengths or weaknesses compared with the competition in product or service performance, packaging, advertising, promotions, operating costs, selling or distribution, or R & D? How long are the strengths likely to remain unique and how easily can the weaknesses be eliminated?

4. What is the company's record of innovation? How well are its current test-market products doing, how likely are they to go national and when will they start to contribute to profit?

5. What is the likelihood of a major new competitive entry to this market? What is the trend of private labelling?

6. What is the price elasticity of the company's major products?

7. How far does it rely on raw materials with a history of volatile and unpredictable pricing?

8. What is the estimated gross and net margin for the company's major products?

Even where there is no access to the acquisition prospect's books, an experienced marketing executive or consultant could usually put together a workable ten-year forecast in three to six weeks based on interviews, published sources and personal contacts.

5. Treat the vendor like a consumer

Once a company has decided to make a formal approach to an acquisition prospect, a marketing job should be done on the vendors, to enhance their willingness to sell and to ensure that they are well motivated to continue in management after the acquisition.

The first task is to identify the key individual or individuals in the prospect company, and to approach them either directly or through a trusted intermediary.

One person, perhaps the chairman or the major stock-holder, is often the prime influence on whether the prospect will sell. If they wish to sell, one should try to understand their motivations and tailor the offer to meet these. They may be selling because their company lacks sufficient capital for expansion. They may be worried about the success of a major new competitor, or they may have lost interest in the business and want to retire. What are their worries about an acquisition? They may be concerned at loss of prestige or autonomy, about the future of the employees or about the way the business will be run.

All these are clear needs which the acquiring company should explore before making a formal offer. If it wishes to retain the services of the prospect company's top management after acquisition, it should also investigate their needs, and discuss how the company will be run after acquisition – covering reporting relationships, control systems, degree of integration with the parent company, management incentives and future profit objectives.

It all comes back to the boomerang sequence of investigation, design and sale, though in a new context. An acquiring company following these steps improves its chance of persuading the prospect to sell at a fair price and increases the likelihood that it will be run effectively by a well-motivated management after the acquisition is completed.

● Summary

Acquisitions have peaked three times in the past forty years, and the latest peak is with us today.

There appear to be five major types of acquisitions intended to:

- spread risk/enter new markets.
- achieve a better return on financial assets.
- achieve a better return on marketing assets.
- be defensive.
- be synergistic.

Most acquisitions include a mixture of factors.

The failure rate of acquisitions is high, probably 50 to 60 per cent, but not as high as the failure rate for new products.

Marketing people are rarely consulted closely on acquisitions, but this situation is changing and they are likely to be much more closely involved in future.

There are five elements in the offensive marketing approach to acquisitions, as follows:

1. **The right organization**. It is usually best to give the new-products manager responsibility for acquisitions. The chief executive needs to be closely involved.
2. **Develop an acquisition strategy**. This should specify the markets in which you are interested and spell out the things you want to get out of any acquisition.
3. **Do not waste time on non-runners**. Screen out the laggards at an early stage and concentrate on qualified candidates – companies you might wish to buy and which are not strongly opposed to selling.
4. **Evaluate swiftly but in depth**. Time is often of the essence in an acquisition, but so is thoroughness. Sensible short-cuts can be made to balance the two.
5. **Treat the vendors like consumers**. Use your marketing skills to analyse their needs and structure a package which meets them at minimum cost to your company. If that sounds like marketing, it is no coincidence.

Appendix 1:
Selective Check-list:
The Outside Business
Environment

1. Macro Factors

General economic:
- price inflation
- cost inflation (e.g. energy, commodities, labour)
- unemployment
- consumer spending
- exchange rate
- interest rates

Attitudinal:
- consumer attitudes
- industrial-relations climate

Competitive thrusts:
- UK
- other Western countries
- newly industrialized countries (NICs)

Management attitudes:
- acquisitions
- new products
- organization structure
- growth
- investment
- marketing
- quality
- risk

Government policies:
- regulation v. deregulation
- direct v. indirect tax

379

– attitude towards business
– free trade vs. protection

Technological developments:
– home technology (PCs, VCR, etc.)
– office technology (work stations, office of the future, etc.)
– retail store scanning
– speed of technological change

Regional:
– population changes
– unemployment
– consumer attitudes

Demographic:
– age profile, size of household unit, etc.

Advertising:
– changes in type of media
– media cost increases
– proliferation of TV channels

Transportation/distribution:
– major road improvements (e.g. M25)

2. Indirect Factors

Performance of related products/services:
– growth trend of related products/services
– changes in type of related products/services

Developments in related markets:
– performance improvements
– relative price changes
– past or upcoming changes in regulations
– changes in presentation/packaging
– changes in fashion

Distribution channels:
– new channels
– changes in relative importance of existing channels
– changes in distributor strategy
– changes in concentration/bargaining power
– acquisitions (e.g. ASDA-MFI)

3. Direct Factors

Consumers:
– total market and segment trends
– factors driving market
– changes in customer performance needs

- changes in packaging needs
- changes in service needs
- attitudes to price/quality alternatives
- attitudes to new products/innovation

Buyers/distribution channels:
- changes in strategies, needs, structure, criterion for purchase (e.g. private label, warehouse delivery)
- changes in personnel
- effect of new entrants or acquisitions among buyers
- attitudes to price/quality/service alternatives
- attitudes to new products/innovation

Bought-in products/services:
- raw material and energy price trends and availability
- transportation price trends
- advertising cost trends
- quality/performance levels

Government policy:
- changes in tax (e.g. higher National Insurance for higher-paid employees)
- changes in VAT
- new regulations (e.g. NHS drugs, deregulation policies)

Technology:
- UK or worldwide

Competitors:
- capacity situation
- pricing strategy
- new products/acquisitions
- cost structure/competitiveness
- marketing strategy
- investment levels
- new competitors

Appendix 2: Framework for Annual Brand/Company Health-check

1. The Market

Market performance overall:
- value
- volume
- real value

Market performance by segment:
- physical product type
- trade channel and major account
- sizing
- packaging type
- consumer benefit
- occasion of usage
- geographic
- price
- user type (demographic)
- branded vs. private label
- method of payment (e.g. cash or credit card)

Factors driving the market and individual segments:
- consumer habits
- trends in related markets
- changes in distribution channels
- distributor attitudes
- innovation and technology
- advertising and marketing spending levels
- pricing
- new entrants to market

382

2. The Company or Product/Service

Sales trends (real value):
- overall
- by market segment
- by trade channel
- existing and new accounts
- existing and new products/line extensions
- as for sales

Market-share trends:
- relative market position
- share mix
- reasons for changes

Trade distribution and space trends:
- by channel and major account
- sales per account stocking
- account gains/losses

Pricing:
- overall real value per unit
- changes in mix
- trend in relative price vs. competition
- volume vs. price-elasticity graph
- inflation recovery index

Buyers/distributors/retailers:
- percentage of sales by top ten accounts
- trends in sales and share
- discount trends
- relative bargaining power

Operations:
- real-cost trends per unit
- industry capacity utilization
- brand/company capacity utilization

Product/service performance:
- relative customer acceptance
- trial/loyalty levels
- awareness/image trends

Innovation audit:
- existing product or service development
- line extension or reduction
- new developments
- new distribution channels
- extension of usage
- new packaging/design
- new market segmentation
- merchandising

Profit analysis:
- by product

– by size
– by trade channel and major account

3. Allocation of Resources Audit: Questions to Ask

Trade discounts:
– how do we stop the increase?
– what are *we* getting?
– can we monitor performance of promises?
– do we have profit and loss figures by major account?

Gross profit:
– what is the mix by growth and declining products or services?
– is there an active value analysis programme? What are the results?
– contact between marketing and operations?

Advertising:
– is the consumer promise right?
– does the execution work? How do you know?
– absolute weight. Gross TV rating points per case
– percentage of market spending
– allocation of funds vs. opportunities

Sales promotion:
– is it offensive rather than defensive?
– is there a proper system of promotion analysis?
– do we know profitability by type of promotion?

Appendix 3:
Types of Competitive Advantage

Superior product benefit:
- better end result
- greater convenience
- superior service
- longer lasting
- more features
- superior product design
- better in-use characteristics

Focus or niche positioning:
- strong appeal to minority segment

Perceived customer advantage:
- built on imagery rather than function

Lower-cost operator:
- low-cost operations
- low-cost distribution
- low-cost overheads

Superior knowledge:
- segmentation, processes, systems, R & D
- superior allocation of resources

Stronger contacts:
- key customers
- innovative licensors/licensees
- joint venture partners

Scale advantages:
- market position
- branding strength
- product range

- advertising spend
- sales force/distribution muscle
- raw material sourcing/control
- financial muscle
- operations/processing

Legal advantages:
- patent protection
- exclusive/protected rights
- protective legislation/practices
- copyright

Company attitudes:
- e.g. long-term orientation.

Appendix 4:
Common Techniques for
Setting Advertising Budgets

1. **The task approach.** This method involves setting certain marketing objectives, deriving from these the task advertising has to fulfil and allocating an advertising budget accordingly. The objectives may be set in terms of revenue and profit, in which case the translation to an advertising budget is necessarily rather vague. Or they may be more sophisticated and spelt out in terms of the number of advertising messages necessary to achieve desired levels of awareness or changes in attitude.

The task method can be useful if it is based on detailed analysis of past results, but should not be used in isolation from the other methods.

2. **The historical approach.** Some companies base their determination of advertising budgets on the level spent in the previous year.

3. **The percentage-of-turnover (or 'case-rate') approach.** This consists of allocating a fixed percentage of a product's turnover to advertising. When the brand's volume grows, spending will increase; while if it falls, spending will decline.

Opponents of this approach claim that it favours brands which are growing and, cumulatively, kills those which are declining. This is one of its major strengths, since it tends to feed potential successes and starve problem areas. The method has to be used with discretion, and exceptions should be recognized, since there can sometimes be justification for pouring more money into a declining brand (e.g. it may be relaunched with a major performance improvement).

However, the big weakness of this approach is that the percentage to

387

be allocated to advertising is usually arrived at arbitrarily – why should the figure be 2 per cent rather than 1 per cent or 5 per cent?

4. **The share-of-market approach.** This involves estimating the amount of future advertising spending for the market being served and relating a brand's share of this spending to its target share of the market. Here is an example:

Estimated total market advertising spending
in 1987:   £25 million
Target brand share for 1987:   10 per cent
Planned advertising budget for brand in 1987:   £2·5 million
(i.e. 10 per cent of £25 million)

This method is weak because all the figures being estimated are very speculative and there is no evidence to indicate the most profitable relationship between share of category advertising and share of market sales.

5. **The 'match-competition' approach.** This is the second worst method. It is both speculative and defensive.

6. **The 'residual' approach.** This is the worst method of all, but surprisingly it is used by some quite sophisticated companies. The system, if it can be called such, is to leave the advertising budget till last and put into it moneys left after costs and profit requirements have been calculated.

Advertising budgets set by this method are the most likely to be cut later, because there is no clear rationale for their levels.

Appendix 5:
Main Types of Acquisition

This table is subjective, and while it makes no claim at all to be authoritative, it does illustrate the approach to grouping acquisitions into the five types. It should spark off many arguments.

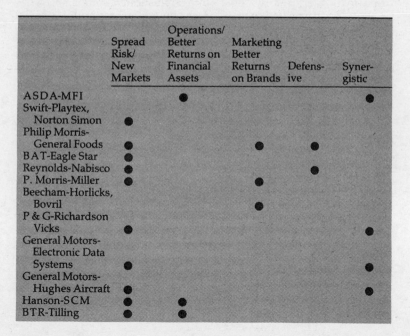

	Spread Risk/ New Markets	Operations/ Better Returns on Financial Assets	Marketing Better Returns on Brands	Defens- ive	Syner- gistic
ASDA-MFI		●			●
Swift-Playtex, Norton Simon	●				
Philip Morris- General Foods	●		●	●	
BAT-Eagle Star	●				
Reynolds-Nabisco	●			●	
P. Morris-Miller	●		●		
Beecham-Horlicks, Bovril			●		
P & G-Richardson Vicks	●				●
General Motors- Electronic Data Systems	●				●
General Motors- Hughes Aircraft	●				●
Hanson-SCM	●	●			
BTR-Tilling	●	●			

Table. *contd*.

	Spread Risk/ New Markets	Operations/ Better Returns on Financial Assets	Marketing Better Returns on Brands	Defensive	Synergistic
BTR-Dunlop		●	●		●
Avana-Robertsons		●	●		
Beatrice Foods-Esmark				●	
Dart-Kraft	●	●			
Habitat-Mothercare		●	●		●
Dee-International Stores		●			●
Nestlé-Carnation		●	●		
Allied-Lyons	●	●			
Standard Brands-Nabisco	●	●			●

Appendix 6:
Key Factors for Success in
Acquisition Programmes

1. Clear strategy, agreed by all levels of management.
2. Clear identification of authority and responsibility for each stage.
   (A formal structure for making an acquisition does not usually
   exist, since each is a 'one-off' situation and for most people is not a
   key part of their day-to-day job description.) It needs to be made
   clear who has authority to:
   - make the initial approach.
   - sign the letter of intent.
   - negotiate ballpark price.
   - negotiate the final price.
   - sign the contract.
   This may vary by size of acquisition.

   Management of the acquisition process would be the responsibility of one person. This person would pre-clear with other
   directors who in their departments are to be responsible for evaluating aspects of each acquisition (e.g. plant visit and evaluation,
   balance-sheet analysis, etc.). These are obviously part-time responsibilities for those involved, but intensive time commitment at
   short notice may be needed. It would be preferable if the same
   person in operations, finance or personnel could be used on all
   acquisitions, since a build-up of experience is valuable.
3. Good briefing and management of outside resources, e.g. merchant banks, consultants, if used, and other outside contacts used
   either as a source of leads, or as partners in evaluation.
4. Chief Executive availability is essential for the first approach, the
   final negotiation/contract, or for the informal solution of major
   snags involving the Chief Executive of the target company. Some
   things cannot be delegated.

391

5. Build up a widespread network of leads and data input on companies.
6. Skilful and speedy evaluation and a letter of intent.
7. Control of contact with the target company.
8. Others helping in evaluation process should be kept in the background as far as negotiations and contact are concerned.
9. Skill in identifying key-target individuals, building up trust and rapport with them and developing accurate understanding of the motivation and needs of the seller.
10. Flexibility in tailoring acquisition terms for the company and for key individuals (e.g. consultancies, directorships, tax treatment, etc.) within legal and ethical guidelines.
11. Skill in tax management and in identifying likely tax reduction opportunities at an early stage.

Appendix 7:
Acquisition Strategy:
Check-list of Possible Points
to be Covered (for U K-based
Acquisitions)

1. The Market

- minimum/maximum size.
- desired growth rate; unit and pricing trends.
- preferred distribution channels.
- degree of branding and trend.
- opportunity for product or service differentiation/ premium pricing.
- degree of government regulation/control.
- degree of reliance on commodity-based raw materials. Commodities liked/to be avoided.
- vulnerability to future duty/V A T rates or increases.
- life cycle of products. (Avoid short-life in/out of fashion products or services.)
- degree and type of seasonality which is acceptable.
- industry capacity utilization.

2. Competition

- desired competitive structure (e.g. many small companies or few dominant companies).
- desired competitive skills (e.g. prefer low skills and aggression, not a Citibank or IBM).

3. Company Under Review

- minimum/maximum size in terms of sales.
- past five years' growth rate.
- current profitability (profit before tax and return on assets).
- strength of market position/consumer franchise.
- quality/performance compared with the competition.
- industrial-relations profile.
- fit with the philosophy of acquiring company.
- quality of management.
- level of past media and capital investment.
- technical abilities (marketing, operations, finance).
- innovation/new product record.
- capacity utilization.

4. Financial Criteria

- PBT and ROA minimum targets after acquisition.
- attitude to minority positions, joint ventures, majority holdings less than 100 per cent, etc.
- method of payment (e.g. cash, stock, combination, etc.).
- attitude towards contested situations.

Recommended Reading List

The most widely used textbook on marketing and deservedly so is:
> Philip Kotler, *Marketing Management: Analysis, Planning and Control*, Prentice-Hall, 1984.

The following are classics on competitive analysis. They are not an easy read, but repay the effort handsomely. Both these books influenced the chapters on 'Strategic Groundwork' and 'Winning Strategies' in *Offensive Marketing*:
> Michael Porter, *Competitive Strategy*, Free Press, 1980.
> Michael Porter, *Competitive Advantage*, Free Press, 1985.

The best exposition yet on the reasons for Japanese marketing success and the lessons to be drawn from it is:
> Kotler, Fahey & Jatusripitak, *The New Competition*, Prentice-Hall, 1985.

The following two publications by the I P A comprise well-documented case histories on advertising:
> Simon Broadbent, *Twenty Advertising Case Histories*, Holt, Rinehart and Winston, 1984.
> Charles Channon, ed., *Advertising Works 3*, Holt, Rinehart and Winston, 1985.

An interesting account of the careers and experiences of thirteen successful British businessmen is:
> William Kay, *Tycoons*, Piatkus, 1985.

This annual publication is a 'must' for any marketer or student of marketing:
> *Social Trends*, Central Statistical Office, 1985.

Reading List

A fascinating compendium of marketing facts and figures, and the best of its kind, is:

> Ludwig Berlin, *Marketing Pocket Book, 1986*, The Advertising Association, 1986.

For a penetrating and original analysis of what makes major companies tick, including ICI, Habitat-Mothercare and Sinclair, see:

> Ronnie Lessem, *The Roots of Excellence*, Fontana, 1985.

An interesting account of best practice among UK companies is:

> Walter Goldsmith & David Clutterbuck, *The Winning Streak*, Penguin, 1985.

The following is stimulating and full of valuable lessons:

> Robert Heller, *The Supermanagers*, Sidgwick & Jackson, 1984.

The following is good for dipping into, especially on portfolio analysis:

> Barton, Weitz & Robin Wensley, *Strategic Marketing – Planning, Implementation and Control*, Kent, 1983.

See also:

> G. Foxall, *Corporate Innovation*, Croom Helm, 1984.

For a fuller understanding of the importance of design and the contribution it can make to product development, see:

> Christopher Lorenz, *The Design Dimension*, Basil Blackwell, 1986.

A comprehensive and authoritative review of marketing principles and basics by a British author is:

> Michael Baker, *Marketing – An Introductory Text*, Macmillan, 1985.

The best book on marketing planning is:

> Malcolm H. B. McDonald, *Marketing Plans: How to Prepare them and How to Use Them*, Heinemann, 1986.

Notes

Introduction: Offensive Marketing

1. Lee Iacocca, with William Novak, *Iacocca – An Autobiography*, Sidgwick & Jackson, 1985.
2. *The Marketing Mode*, McGraw-Hill, 1969.
3. Information derived from A. J. MacNeary, 'Strategy for Success: J. Sainsbury', in *International Trends in Retailing*, Spring 1985.

Chapter 1: Getting the Right Mix

1. Professor Peter Doyle, Professor of Marketing and Strategic Management, School of Industrial and Business Studies, University of Warwick, personal communication.

Chapter 2: Principles of Profitable Marketing in Action

1. See Arthur Koestler, *The Act of Creation*, Macmillan, New York, 1964, for this and many other fascinating examples.
2. Frozen foods were invented by Clarence Birdseye, and the first frozen foods were sold in Springfield, Massachusetts, on 6 March 1930. The Birds Eye name in the UK is owned by Unilever, not General Foods as in the USA.
3. Le Corbusier, *Towards a New Architecture*, Architectural Press, 1946.
4. A. C. Nielsen Co., *How to Strengthen your New-product Plan*, internal publication.

5. Michael Porter, *Competitive Advantage*, Free Press, 1985.
6. *Financial Times*, 11 December 1982.
7. Information partly derived from 'General Mills: Toys Just Aren't Us', in *Business Week*, 16 September 1985.
8. See Kotler & Rath, 'Design: A Powerful but Neglected Strategic Tool', in *Journal of Business Strategy*, Fall 1984.

Chapter 3: Offensive Attitudes

1. James Burke, Chairman of Johnson & Johnson.
2. Information derived from *Re-inventing the Corporation*, Megatrends Ltd, 1985.
3. *Daily Mail*, 26 April 1985.
4. Stratford Sharman, 'Eight Masters of Innovation' in *Fortune*, 16 October 1984.
5. 3M, *Annual Report*, 1983.
6. See Bennett & Cooper, 'The Misuse of Marketing', *McKinsey Quarterly*, Fall 1982.
7. See, for example, Kotler, Fahey & Jatusripitak, *The New Competition*, Prentice-Hall, 1985.
8. Procter & Gamble, *Annual Report*, 1983.

Chapter 4: Integrating for the Offensive

1. *Dun's Review*, December 1970.
2. Kotler, Fahey & Jatusripitak, *The New Competition*, Prentice-Hall, 1985.
3. Iacocca, *Iacocca – An Autobiography*, Sidgwick & Jackson, 1985.
4. Wendy Tansey, 'What Marketing Offers Banks', in the *Banker*, June 1985.
5. Sir Roy Griffiths (Managing Director of Sainsbury), *The NHS Management Inquiry*, HMSO, 1985.

Chapter 5: Organization for Integrated Marketing

1. Kotler, Fahey & Jatusripitak, *The New Competition*, Prentice-Hall, 1985.
2. For a fuller treatment of this issue, see Peter Krausher, *Practical Business Development*, Holt, Rinehart & Winston, 1985.

Chapter 6: Grinding Out the Strategic Base

1. Adapted from Philip Kotler, *Marketing Management: Analysis, Planning and Control*, Prentice-Hall, 1984.
2. H. Golombek, *The Game of Chess*, Penguin, 1986.
3. This section owes something to Michael Porter's books *Competitive Strategy* and *Competitive Advantage*, both published by Free Press, 1980 and 1985.
4. Porter, *Competitive Advantage*, 1985.
5. Michael G. Allen (Vice-President, General Electric), *Competitive Business Strategies*, McKinsey & Co. Inc., 1978.
6. Derived from Gordon Brunton, 'Implementing Corporate Strategy: The Story of International Thomson', in *Journal of Business Strategy*, Fall 1984.

Chapter 7: Developing Winning Strategies

1. Quoted by Robert Heller, 'The Making of Fortes', in *Management Today*, September 1969.
2. Professor Peter Doyle, Professor of Marketing and Strategic Management, School of Industrial and Business Studies, University of Warwick, personal communication.
3. These estimates are from the London office of Booz Allen & Hamilton, based on US data.
4. Adapted from Kotler, Fahey & Jatusripitak, *The New Competition*, Prentice-Hall, 1985.
5. *Economist*, 2 November 1985.
6. *Business Week*, 4 November 1985.
7. *Advertising Age*, 29 July and 26 September 1985.
8. *Business Week*, 26 August 1985.
9. Kotler, Fahey & Jatusripitak, op. cit.
10. *What Car?*, November 1985.
11. ibid., December 1985.
12. Che Guevara, *Guerrilla Warfare*, Penguin, 1969.
13. Peters & Waterman, *In Search of Excellence*, Harper & Row, 1982.
14. *Business Week*, 25 November 1985.
15. Wood Mackenzie & Co., Stockbrokers, 1985.
16. Gunnar Brock, Managing Director of Tetra-Pak, UK.

Chapter 8: Offensive Product and Packaging Development

1. Unpublished statement by R. H. Beeby (President, Pepsi-Cola International).
2. Heany & Vinson, 'A Fresh Look at New Product Development', in

Journal of Business Strategy, Fall 1984. The study was based on PIMS research data base.

3. Frederick Gluck, 'Big-bang Management', in *Journal of Business Strategy*, Summer 1985.

4. Adapted from A. Parasuraman & Linda Zeren, 'R & D's Relationship with Profits & Sales', in *Research Management*, January/February 1983.

5. ibid.

6. Freely adapted from Philip Roussel, 'Cutting Down the Guesswork in R & D', in *Harvard Business Review*, September/October 1983.

7. Rowland Schmitt (Senior Vice-President, Corporate R & D, General Electric), 'Successful Corporate R & D', in *Harvard Business Review*, May/June 1985.

8. Booz Allen & Hamilton, *New Product Management for the 1980s*, internal publication, 1982.

9. Concept adapted from Philip Roussel, op. cit.

10. Adapted from J. S. Bingham, ed., *British Cases in Marketing*, Business Books, 1969. The Andrews case was written by John Usher, now Marketing Director at Arthur Young, the accounting firm.

11. *Business Week*, 15 July 1985, and *Advertising Age*, 24 December 1984.

Chapter 9: Offensive Market Research

1. F. Goldstein, 'Practical Guide to Gathering US Marketing Information', *Journal of Market Research Society*, October 1985.

2. Goronwy Rees, *St Michael: A History of Marks & Spencer*, Pan, 1973.

3. Adapted from 'How Intrapreneurs Innovate', in *Management Today*, December 1985, and from 3M, *Annual Report*, 1983.

4. This apt phrase comes from George Scott, former Manager of R & D at Procter & Gamble.

5. Derived from Robert E. Hartley, *Marketing Successes*, John Wiley & Sons Inc., 1985; various articles in *Advertising Age*, April–December 1985; Jaclyn Fierman, 'How Coke Decided Taste Was It', in *Fortune*, 27 May 1985; and Anna Fisher, 'Coke's Brand Loyalty Lesson', in *Fortune*, 5 August 1985.

6. Research study conducted for *Advertising Age*, 1985.

Chapter 10: Offensive Pricing

1. *Fortune*, 24 December 1984.

2. Derived from several sources, including *Marketing*, *Advertising Age* and *Dataquest*.

3. Stephen L. Bogardo (Assistant to the President of *Esquire*) in G. Scott Hutchison, ed., *The Business of Acquisitions and Mergers*.

4. 'The Bloodbath in Chips', *Business Week,* 20 May 1985.
5. Peters & Waterman, *In Search of Excellence,* Harper & Row, 1985, and Kotler, Fahey & Jatusripitak, *The New Competition,* Prentice-Hall, 1985.

Chapter 11: Offensive Sales Promotion

1. *Marketing,* ISP Supplement, May 1985.
2. *Marketing,* ISP Supplement, March 1984.
3. Alan Wolfe, Director of Ogilvy & Mather, personal communication.

Chapter 12: Offensive Advertising

1. Malcolm McNiven, ed., *How Much to Spend for Advertising?,* AMA 1969.
2. James O. Peckham, *The Wheel of Marketing,* 1981.
3. I am indebted for this analogy to Ries & Trout, *Positioning,* 1981.
4. Stephen King, *Presentation to UK Price Commission,* December 1978. Expenditure converted to 1985 costs.
5. Most frequently attributed to the first Lord Leverhulme.
6. Charles Channon, ed., *Advertising Works 3,* Holt, Rinehart & Winston, 1985.
7. ibid., Chapter 1 by K. Green for Foote, Cone & Belding.
8. Quoted in Lee Adler, ed., *Plotting Marketing Strategy.*

Chapter 13. Offensive Branding

1. *Focus,* October 1983.
2. James O. Peckham, *The Wheel of Marketing,* 1981.
3. *Advertising Age,* 23 April 1984.
4. John Murphy, quoted in Angela Chatburn, 'Getting the Name Right', *Focus,* October 1985.

Chapter 14: Offensive Trade-channel Marketing

1. John Allen, formerly Marketing & Buying Director of Finefare, now a Director of BET.
2. James O. Packham, *The Wheel of Marketing,* 1981.
3. Peter Drucker, *Managing for Results,* Pan, 1970.
4. Derived from Alkarim Jivani, 'No Holding Coloroll', in *Marketing,* 25 April 1985.

5. Kotler, Fahey & Jatusripitak, *The New Competition*, Prentice-Hall, 1985.
6. Example derived from Robert F. Hartley, *Marketing Successes*, John Wiley & Sons Inc., 1985.
7. Derived from William Kay, *Tycoons*, Piatkus, 1985.

Chapter 15: New Products: Success and Failure

1. David J. Mahoney, quoted in J. T. Gerlach & C. A. Wainwright, *The Successful Management of New Products*, Pitman, 1970.
2. John Modell, *Where Do Successful New Brands Come From?*, unpublished paper, BMP 1980.
3. Peter Krausher, *Practical Business Development*, Holt, Rinehart & Winston, 1985.
4. ibid.
5. Bill Ramsey, *The New Product Dilemma*, Nielsen Marketing Trends, January 1982.
6. ibid., for study of failure rate in 1971–80 as compared with 1957–67.
7. Derived from J. H. Davidson, 'Why Most New Products Fail', in *Harvard Business Review*, March/April 1976.
8. Derived from a review of R. Gabrile, *Military Incompetence: Why the American Military Doesn't Win*, Hill & Wang, 1985, in *Business Week*, 14 October 1985.
9. Booz Allen & Hamilton, *New Product Management for the 1980s*, internal publication.

Chapter 16: New Products: Offensive Principles

1. *Industrial Performance Analysis*, ICC, 1985/86 edition.
2. Unpublished analysis by David Craton, Chairman of Craton, Lodge & Knight Ltd.
3. John Modell, *Where Do Successful New Brands Come From?*, unpublished paper, BMP, 1980.
4. Booz Allen & Hamilton, *New Product Management for the 1980s*, internal publication.
5. Robert Heller, *The Supermanagers*, Sidgwick & Jackson, 1984, and Seisi Kato, *My Years with Toyota*, Toyota Motor Sales Co. Ltd, 1981.
6. Ian Pavitt & Associates, *Where Do Ideas Come From?*, unpublished booklet.
7. William Rogers, *Think: A Biography of the Watsons and IBM*, Weidenfeld & Nicolson, 1970.
8. Derived largely from Ian Pavitt, op. cit.

Chapter 17: The Marketing Approach to Acquisitions

1. Leighton & Tod, 'After the Acquisition – Continuing Challenge', in *Harvard Business Review*, March to April 1969.
2. Hypothesis by Booz Allen & Hamilton, based on initial pilot work.
3. John Kitching, 'Why do Mergers Miscarry?', in *Harvard Business Review*, November/December 1967. Other studies since have drawn similar conclusions, e.g. Dr Burgman's analysis of 600 acquisitions in the USA.

Index

Page numbers in *italics* refer to Figures; those in **bold** type to Tables.

Index